DATE DUE

J. Robert Oppenheimer, the Cold War, and the Atomic West

THE OKLAHOMA WESTERN BIOGRAPHIES
RICHARD W. ETULAIN, GENERAL EDITOR

J. Robert Oppenheimer at Los Alamos National Laboratory, April 18, 1964. *(Courtesy of J. Robert Oppenheimer Memorial Committee)*

J. Robert Oppenheimer, the Cold War, and the Atomic West

Jon Hunner

UNIVERSITY OF OKLAHOMA PRESS : NORMAN

Also by Jon Hunner

Inventing Los Alamos: The Growth of an Atomic Community (Norman, 2004)

Library of Congress Cataloging-in-Publication Data

Hunner, Jon.
J. Robert Oppenheimer, the cold war, and the atomic West / by Jon Hunner.
p. cm. — (Oklahoma western biographies ; v. 24)
Includes bibliographical references and index.
ISBN 978-0-8061-4046-9 (hardcover : alk. paper) 1. Oppenheimer,
J. Robert, 1904–1967. 2. Physicists — United States — Biography.
3. Nuclear physicists — United States — Biography. 4. Atomic bomb —
United States — History. 5. Los Alamos National Laboratory. I. Title.
QC16.O62H86 2009
530.092 — dc22
[B]   2008047909

J. Robert Oppenheimer, the Cold War, and the Atomic West is Volume 24 in The Oklahoma Western Biographies.

The paper in this book meets the guidelines for permanence and durability of the Committee on Production Guidelines for Book Longevity of the Council on Library Resources, Inc. ∞

1 2 3 4 5 6 7 8 9 10

For my parents, Col. Paul C. Hunner and Anna Jane Fair

Contents

Illustrations

Series Editor's Preface

STORIES of heroes and heroines have intrigued many generations of listeners and readers. Americans, like people everywhere, have been captivated by the lives of military, political, and religious figures and intrepid explorers, pioneers, and rebels. The Oklahoma Western Biographies endeavor to build on this fascination with biography and to link it with two other abiding interests of Americans: the frontier and American West. Although volumes in the series carry no notes, they are prepared by leading scholars, are soundly researched, and include a discussion of sources used. Each volume is a lively synthesis based on thorough examination of pertinent primary and secondary sources.

Above all, the Oklahoma Western Biographies aim at two goals: to provide readable life stories of significant westerners and to show how their lives illuminate a notable topic, an influential movement, or a series of important events in the history and cultures of the American West.

Jon Hunner accomplishes these goals in this lively and appealing biography of a giant among recent American scientists, J. Robert Oppenheimer. Hunner's smoothly written story of "Oppie" emphasizes his subject's central role in the planning and production of the atomic bomb. The author also demonstrates how Oppie played a major part in a developing scientific West—in his helping establish the University of California, Caltech, and Los Alamos as premier sites for scientific and atomic research.

Hunner's biography reveals his comprehensive understanding of Oppenheimer and the Atomic West. The author's discussions of the "complexity" of Oppenheimer's formative years; his dealings with other scientists, friends, and family members; and his controversial post–World War II days are particularly illuminating. Alongside these glimpses into Oppie's humanity, Hunner shows how much Oppenheimer helped reshape science and scientific research in the American West—in short the westward tilt of science—from the early 1930s into the Cold War era. Oppenheimer was obviously a key figure in what historian Gerald Nash called the "transformation of the American West" in these decades.

Readers will also profit from Hunner's illuminating discussions of the scientific communities that surrounded Oppenheimer. The author not only explains the making of the atomic and hydrogen bombs and new directions in twentieth-century scientific research in western Europe and the United States, he clarifies the differences, even civil wars, between Oppenheimer and leading scientific and bureaucratic figures such as Edward Teller, Leslie Groves, and Lewis Strauss. All these discussions are presented in sparkling prose, understandable to lay and specialist audiences.

Other strengths of Hunner's book will attract additional readers. He smoothly stitches together larger events (the New Deal, World War II, and the Cold War), biographical details of Oppenheimer's life, and major shifts in scientific thinking in the twentieth century. Hunner even spices his story with bits of mystery and intrigue. Particularly well done are the sections treating Los Alamos, the Trinity explosion in 1945, and the controversies involved in security clearances.

Overall, Jon Hunner's *J. Robert Oppenheimer, the Cold War, and the Atomic West* is a worthy sequel to his prize-winning *Inventing Los Alamos: The Growth of an Atomic Community* (2004). This book clearly achieves the aims of volumes in the Oklahoma Western Biographies series, dealing with a notable westerner whose life illustrates larger happenings in western history.

Richard W. Etulain
Professor Emeritus of History
University of New Mexico

Preface

LIKE many historians, I write the type of history that I do for autobiographical reasons. I grew up in a household whose main breadwinner worked with atomic bombs. My father, Paul Hunner, administered nuclear weapons for the U.S. Air Force. Several family stories illustrate how these weapons pervaded the Hunner household. My father hung large photographs of aboveground nuclear explosions on our family-room walls. From a black-and-white picture of the Trinity detonation in New Mexico in 1945 to the color photos of bigger explosions in the Nevada desert, the awesome beauty of the towering mushroom clouds surrounded us as we watched television in our house in the 1960s. Late in his life, my father admitted that over the course of his career, he had witnessed a dozen aboveground nuclear test shots.

I also remember one autumn afternoon, possibly on Veterans Day in November 1959, when my father and mother, Anna Fair, unloaded Chuck and Pete (my two brothers) and me out of our station wagon at the parade grounds at Sandia Base in Albuquerque, New Mexico. Flanking the flagpole (where most military bases display artillery pieces) were replicas of Fat Man and Little Boy, the atomic bombs dropped on Japan. As a young boy of six or seven, these structures looked to me like playground equipment, and with my brothers, I jumped on Fat Man and started climbing. Our father grabbed us off of the replica and quickly put us back into our station wagon. As a historian, I still clamber over nuclear weapons.

Like FBI agents in the past, I have chased Robert Oppenheimer over the past decade. I have chased him through archives, have visited places where he lived, and have studied what he said in his lectures and writings and what other historians have said about him. Of course, I am interested in Oppie for reasons different from those of the FBI, but on one level, our purposes coincide: like the federal agents, I want to know all I can about J. Robert Oppenheimer. For a historian of someone like Oppenheimer, this search can go on for decades and in many places around the country and the world. The thousands of documents in hundreds of boxes and many rolls of microfilm reveal a man who remains an enigma. Nonetheless, this complex man helped create a massive weapon and a new and dangerous age. He then played a key role as a leader in the early Cold War era in deciding what to do with the newly unchained power of the atom. Despite all this, we will perhaps never know the complete Oppenheimer.

Acknowledgments

DURING the years that I have wandered through the field of nuclear history, I have accumulated many debts. First and foremost, Richard W. Etulain has provided insight and support for my forays into the Atomic West as well as into the halls of academia. He also serves as the series editor for The Oklahoma Western Biographies and suggested that I write *J. Robert Oppenheimer, the Cold War, and the Atomic West* for this series. My editor at the University of Oklahoma Press, Charles Rankin, took a chance on my first book on the Atomic West, *Inventing Los Alamos*, and has enthusiastically embraced *J. Robert Oppenheimer, the Cold War, and the Atomic West*. Emily Jerman, my manuscript and copy editor at the Press, halted the proliferation of errors big and small in the manuscript. Emily, Richard W. Etulain, and three anonymous peer reviewers greatly assisted in making this a better book. I am forever in their debt.

One could not dream of better colleagues than those in the History Department at New Mexico State University. The support and encouragement of Jamie Bronstein, Nathan Brooks, Jeffrey Brown, William Eamon, Iñigo Garcia-Bryce, Elvira and Ken Hammond, Elizabeth Horodowich, Dulcinea Lara, Margaret Malamud, Andrea Orzoff, Dwight Pitcaithley, and Marsha Weisiger make it a joy to work there.

The cohort of atomic historians — in particular those who focus on Oppenheimer — has also contributed to my research over the years. In particular, Ferenc Szasz, Kai Bird, Spencer Weart, Cindy Kelly, Michael Amundsen, John Findlay, Joseph Kanon, Stanley Goldberg, and Barton Hacker have in their own ways contributed to my expanding understanding of Oppie and the Atomic West. I am indebted to the Faculty Research Committee at New Mexico State University for awarding me a grant to conduct research into Oppenheimer's papers at the Library of Congress. The American Institute of Physics also generously provided a travel grant for me to use their facilities in researching *J. Robert Oppenheimer, the Cold War, and the Atomic West.* Randy Sowell at the Truman Library and Jim Leyerzapf at the Eisenhower Library provided professional assistance to my entreaties. I am likewise indebted to Roger Meade and Alan Carr at the Los Alamos National Laboratory archives for their help in chasing Oppie. Nancy Brown at the Center for Southwest Research at the University of New Mexico also ably assisted me with my research.

Although a historian's work often entails solitary toil in front of the glow of a computer screen, we do not work alone. My family has joined with me in writing this book. Mary Ellen, my wife, has vetted many of my ideas and is my best non-historian critic. Our son, Harley, grew up in a generation that did not duck and cover or fear the mutually assured destruction of our world. I hope future generations are able to continue in this ignorance of nuclear deterrence and civil defense. As I mention in the preface, my parents, Paul Hunner and Anna Fair, did worry about an atomic Armageddon, and worked to make us safe.

J. Robert Oppenheimer, the Cold War, and the Atomic West

Introduction
Chasing Oppenheimer

WITH a flash of blinding light and a noise like doomsday, the Atomic Age cracked open in the desert darkness of the American West on July 16, 1945. Three weeks later, atomic bombs devastated two cities in Japan. The creation of atomic weapons culminated not just two years of feverish work but also centuries of scientific research and discovery. As an artificial sun rose in the predawn sky at the Trinity site on that July day, the atomic pioneers knew they had manipulated time and space and split the indivisible atom. They had made an awesome weapon of mythical magnitude.

The men and women who invented the bomb hailed from around the world and had created it at the project's central civilian laboratory at Los Alamos, two hundred miles north of Trinity. Directing the laboratory since 1943 was an unlikely theoretical nuclear physicist, Dr. J. Robert Oppenheimer. Oppenheimer was one of the keys to the success at Trinity, and without his direction and leadership, the atomic bomb—the world's first nuclear weapon—might not have detonated in 1945.

On August 6, 1945, such a weapon devastated the Japanese city of Hiroshima, and three days later, another one incinerated Nagasaki. After the atomic bombings of Japan, World War II came to an abrupt end. With the victory over Japan, Oppenheimer and the other atomic scientists became national and even international heroes. Politicians sought their counsel. Newspapers featured their stories. As an architect of the Atomic Age, Oppenheimer's face graced the cover of *Life* and *Time* magazines. He maneuvered through the whirlwind of policy debate and controversy about the future of atomic energy as powerful governmental officials consulted him. He helped draft legislation about atomic energy for the U.S. Congress and the United Nations. Oppenheimer lectured around the world on the meaning of modern science for human affairs, and those lectures quickly became books that sold well.

In fact, Oppenheimer's life illuminates the twentieth century, often called the American Century. Born in New York City into a wealthy immigrant's family in 1904, he showed brilliance at an early age, went to prestigious universities in the United States and Europe, tackled atomic physics as a theoretical physicist, and helped fuel a wave of discoveries that revolutionized not just science but our world. He utilized his scientific knowledge to help create a horrendous weapon that ended a horrific war. After having released the enormous energy of the atom, he grappled with the consequences of his actions and sought ways to prevent future atomic wars. Then, at the height of his power and influence, Oppenheimer's own government attacked him, stripped him of his security clearance, and publicly disgraced him.

Oppenheimer, using the invisible atom as a mighty fulcrum, levered history and shook the world to its core. World leaders sought to protect their citizens from the threat of atomic weapons, religious elders debated the morality of the bombs, media outlets featured Oppenheimer's opinions, and ordinary people listened to his radio lectures and flocked to his public presentations. Desperate for information, everyone wanted his insights into the weapon of Armageddon. He had manipulated the atom to warp time, space, and history, and he opened up a new age that transformed our hopes for ourselves, our world, and our future.

Robert Oppenheimer had an enigmatic presence. Slight of build, he developed a nervous temperament, offset by his startling blue eyes. One associate described his face as that of an "overgrown choirboy . . . both subtly wise and terribly innocent." Some photographs of him show a person who looked shy and even somewhat lost, while others captured a keen, piercing stare. Thin, intense, urbane, Oppenheimer was different things to different people.

Oppenheimer was a complex person. Physicist Victor Weisskopf, who worked with him at Los Alamos, said as much: "We all know he was tremendously quick. . . . But he was one of the most complicated, if not the most complicated, character I ever met in my life. . . . He was sometimes very disagreeable . . . he could hurt people by remarks terrifically. On the other hand, he can be extremely pleasant and extremely unselfish and helping people. He changed from one to the other." Another close associate, Robert Serber, commented: "Many facets of Oppenheimer's character contributed to his greatness as a teacher: his great capacity as a physicist, his wide intellectual interest, his astonishing quickness of mind, his great gift for expression, his sensitive perception, his social presence, which made him the center of every gathering." I. I. Rabi, one of the scientist's closest colleagues, ventured this view: "Oppenheimer, after Einstein, emerged as the great charismatic figure of the scientific world." Priscilla Greene Duffield, who was his secretary at Los Alamos, recalled: "I found Dr. Oppenheimer unbelievably charming and gracious. He has a marvelous voice. . . . His voice was one of the most appealing things about him. In addition, he was a person of enormous culture."

Duffield commented on the complexity of Oppenheimer's personality: "Certainly in reading about things since, I have found many puzzles at which I don't think anyone is ever going to answer. I don't know why he did some things he did. He must have been very confused in his personal relations to security problems." To this day, some of the aspects of Oppenheimer's conflicted personality continue to puzzle historians.

Parts of his complex personality attracted the attention of the authorities. The FBI had chased Oppenheimer since 1940, even before he became the director of the atomic bomb laboratory in New Mexico. At the root of the FBI's interest was his attendance at meetings organized by the Communist Party in the late 1930s. In 1943, both the FBI and Army Intelligence argued against giving Oppenheimer the security clearance he needed to direct the lab at Los Alamos. After the war, because of his success with the bomb and his popularity with the public, he remained untouchable for a while by those who distrusted him, but they waited for an opportunity to strike.

Oppenheimer's prewar left-wing activities led the FBI to put him under surveillance for almost fifteen years. The FBI worried about his "security problems" so much that at times it had agents follow him around the United States and Europe, recruited his secretaries and colleagues to spy on him, interviewed past associates and friends, and tapped his phone calls. The FBI even listened in on privileged conversations between him and his lawyers. Less than a decade after Trinity and Hiroshima, Oppenheimer fell from grace as the FBI, the military, and even President Eisenhower feared he was a Soviet spy.

Oppenheimer cut a distinctive figure. His slight frame usually sported a custom-tailored, if somewhat wrinkled, suit. The thick shock of black hair he had early in life gave way to a closely cropped head of gray later on. He smoked constantly, often lighting his next cigarette from the butt of the last, and his little finger developed a callus from flicking the glowing ash off of his cigarettes. Some said he smoked a pipe during those moments when he took a break from cigarettes. Oppenheimer loved eating spicy foods, and his trademark martinis packed a wallop. He walked with a quick, duck-footed gait. His somewhat nasal voice held people's attention with its precise diction and expression of engaging ideas. Oppenheimer had refined tastes and cultivated manners, but he also galloped on horses with wild abandon through the western wilderness. Though generous to his friends and students, he also sacrificed one of his best friends to Army Intelligence and the FBI. He maintained a powerful presence, a charisma that made people around him feel special. He continues to be an enigma.

There are few easy answers to questions raised by the life of Robert Oppenheimer. He served his country admirably, but he also caused top officials to question his loyalty. He could be charming and cultured, but also quick to strike with verbal assault. He was brilliant, even a genius, but also committed basic mistakes in dealing with friends, authority, and even presidents. *J. Robert Oppenheimer, the Cold War, and the Atomic West* will pursue this enigmatic character who helped create the Atomic Age.

J. Robert Oppenheimer also explores how the scientist's life changed the course of history. Until 1945, Oppenheimer was an obscure physicist working in California. Although a prominent professor in the world of atomic science, he was unknown to most people outside this exclusive field. After 1945 he became a spokesperson—sometimes for official governmental policy, but at other times for alternative ways to deal with atomic power and nuclear weapons. A popular voice in the national media, Oppenheimer influenced the direction of policy as the federal government struggled to oversee the enormous impact of atomic energy.

When Oppenheimer first arrived in the West as an eighteen-year-old, activity in the wide open spaces and interaction with the region's diverse peoples helped him regain his health and strengthened his frail body. For the next twenty years, he returned time and again to the mountains and valleys of the West, first as a tourist, then as a professor, and finally as an atomic pioneer. The West succored him, and in return, he helped create respected programs in two universities in California in what had previously been a desert for theoretical physics. Then, during a national emergency, he located the most advanced nuclear laboratory of its time at Los Alamos. First from his universities in California and then from the mountains of New Mexico, he led some of the brightest scientific minds through the frontier of physics in the West.

Choosing Los Alamos as the location of the primary atomic weapons laboratory during World War II created a nucleus of atomic research that impacted not just New Mexico but the whole western region of the United States. World War II transformed the West in the twentieth century as much as the Gold Rush did in the nineteenth. As the significance of the West shifted from the periphery of the nation's affairs to the center of technological advances and the front line of the Cold War, Oppenheimer aided that transformation. With the installation of atomic outposts at Los Alamos, New Mexico; Hanford, Washington; Livermore, California; the Nevada Test Site; and other places in the West, the region attracted talented people who flocked to the jobs and opportunities at such facilities. These atomic immigrants transformed these places by bringing high-paying jobs to previously underdeveloped regions and creating an infrastructure of talent and governmental support that made the West an advanced technological center. The atomic centers helped shift the region's economy from agriculture and extractive industries to Big Science, multinational corporations, and international attention. The atomic bomb burst over the New Mexican desert in 1945, adding a new dimension to the American myth of the Wild West—that of atomic sheriffs riding off into the sunset to save the world for democracy.

The atomic pioneers journeyed into the unknown during World War II. They experimented on something they could not see, theorized about an explosive force that some feared could burn up the earth's atmosphere, and, while anticipating a swift end to the war, also worried about the moral, political, and scientific consequences of their creation. These scientists worked with radioactive elements, some of which had just been created by humans, and many of which could endanger one's health. They talked in code about what they were doing, mainly to ensure secrecy of the bombs, but also at times to avoid a personal exploration of the ethics of their work. Some thought they were witnessing the birth of a new age; others, the end of humanity. These scientists destroyed an elemental unit of matter and focused the resultant energy into an explosion whose detonation they measured in milliseconds and destruction in tens of thousands of tons of TNT. After the success of the atomic bomb project, Oppenheimer left for the East Coast, where, like many before him, he built on his achievements in the West.

Oppenheimer at first led a compact group of scientists and

military personnel, then other governmental officials, and finally the nation along the rocky path of atomic affairs. People followed him as if he were an atomic pied piper. They followed his logic and reasoning. They followed his cultured voice and charisma. And they listened to his growing opposition to governmental policies. His marriage of atomic physics and warfare had ended the war, and people listened to what he had to say.

The success of the scientists at Los Alamos ushered in a new age. They created new weapons, new sources of electricity, new diagnostic tools for medicine, new treatments for cancer, new machines to compute and process information, new relationships between science and government, and new fears about living in the twentieth century. Fears of doomsday have figured in the beliefs and literature of humans for millennia. But with the success of the Manhattan Project, Armageddon could now be caused not by a vengeful and immortal God but by fallible and mortal human beings. Consequently, physicist Victor Weisskopf worried about this atomic future: "It has developed into the greatest danger that humankind has ever faced. . . . Future generations, if there are any, will regard this as a virulent case of collective mental disease." Oppenheimer himself admitted that the dawn of the Atomic Age brought both promise and peril. Hopes for a safer and abundant future fueled by nuclear energy were tempered by concerns over the destructive potential of atomic weapons.

In a lecture broadcast over BBC Television in Britain in January 1960, Oppenheimer looked to the coming decade: "I hope that these ten years, especially in the West, perhaps most especially where we need it so much, in America, in my country, that we will begin to re-knit human culture, and by the insight and the wonder of the world of nature, as science has revealed it, into relevance and meaning for the intellectual life, the spiritual life of man." Having helped unleash atomic weapons that threatened all life, Oppenheimer held the hope that nature and science would bring new life to the battered intellectual and spiritual pursuits of humankind.

CHAPTER ONE

A Strange Childhood

This has been a great century in physics, a century of
unexpected, profound, and moving discoveries, and of
applications that have changed a great deal in the condition of
human life. . . . I am confident that the years ahead will teach us
more than all preceding history of man about how living
organisms perform their miraculous functions and about man
as a part of nature.

J. Robert Oppenheimer, *Atom and Void*

IN 1904, the year of Robert Oppenheimer's birth, the United
States had just entered onto the world stage as a young international power. Six years earlier, the Spanish-American War had
made the United States an imperial power with a modern navy
that steamed around the globe to its new territories in the Pacific
and the Caribbean. At the turn of the twentieth century, the U.S.
population topped 76 million, and New York City, Oppenheimer's birthplace, held almost 3.5 million people. Only the rich
motored around in automobiles, and most homes had no electricity. At the dawn of the new century, the United States and the
rest of the world looked vastly different than they do today. As
one of the people born at the century's beginning, Oppenheimer
would play a dramatic role in transforming the period through
the creation of the atomic bomb. From an early age, Robert held
promise as someone who might have great impact later in life. A
gifted child, he showed signs of genius. As with other potential
geniuses, Robert had to grow in his own way.

A FAMILY OF ORIGIN

Oppenheimer led a privileged childhood. His parents, Ella and Julius Oppenheimer, lived at 155 Riverside Drive in an elegant apartment building on the Upper West Side. Ella's family, the Friedmans, were of German descent and had lived in the United States for several generations. As a painter, she had studied in Paris and had returned to New York to teach art. Ella always wore a mysterious glove on her right hand—mysterious because no one in the family talked about it with his or her friends. This glove covered a disabled hand and contained an early prosthetic device that allowed movement of an artificial thumb and forefinger. Paul Horgan, a southwestern author and friend of Robert, remembered Mrs. Oppenheimer as "a very delicate person . . . highly attenuated emotionally, and she always presided with a great delicacy and grace at the table and other events, but a mournful person."

Robert Oppenheimer's father, Julius, had come to the United States more recently than Ella's family, having arrived in 1888 when he was only seventeen. Julius had left Hanau, Germany, where his father was a farmer and grain merchant. As soon as Julius got off the passenger ship in New York City, he started working at the Rothfeldt-Stern Company, a textile import business run by two of his uncles. By the late nineteenth century, individually tailored suits had given way to mass-produced ready-to-wear clothing. The firm specialized in importing the linings for men's suits, and Julius quickly worked his way up through the ranks, partly because he had a talent for identifying and matching colors. Robert's brother, Frank, later commented: "My father was always proud of his color memory. We'd ask him to match a color, get the right color for a suit or yarn, and he'd find just the right thing." Julius dedicated himself over the next fifteen years to both the family business and self-improvement. In addition to arranging for the latest fashions in men's clothing to hit New York stores, he perfected his English, collected paintings by European artists, and read widely. He became a sophisticated gentleman with cultured tastes. When

Horgan visited the Oppenheimer family in the 1920s, he noted that "Mr. Oppenheimer was . . . desperately amiable, anxious to be agreeable, and I think essentially a very kind man."

Ella and Julius might have met at an art exhibition in New York. Together, they eventually collected works by famous artists, so that paintings by Van Gogh, Renoir, and Picasso hung alongside an etching by Rembrandt and enlivened the walls of their Upper West Side apartment. They married in 1903, and on April 22, 1904, Robert Oppenheimer was born to the couple after a long labor. Originally, Robert's name did not have the *J.* at the beginning. His father added it later to give his son distinction.

Looking back, Oppenheimer remembered that when he was ten or twelve, his main interests were "minerals, writing poetry and reading, and building with blocks." On one of the family's trips to Germany when Robert was around six years old, a grandfather, Ben, gave him a small collection of rocks with labels written in German. The rocks fueled the boy's scientific interest as he tried to understand what he saw in them — things like crystal structure, polarized light, and the rocks' origin. Oppenheimer corresponded with members of the New York Mineralogy Society and eventually was invited to join and then present a paper at one of their meetings. Accompanied by his father, Robert showed up for his lecture and met for the first time those with whom he had corresponded. The rest of the members were surprised to find out that the Robert Oppenheimer they had expected to appear was only a boy of eleven. The next youngest member of the Mineralogy Society was in his seventies.

Oppenheimer's parents fostered his brilliance. Later in life, Robert recalled: "I think that both [my father] and my mother were pleased that I was a good student, were pleased that I was highbrow, were perhaps somewhat mockingly proud of my vigor in collecting and learning about minerals." However, his intellectual intensity did worry his mother. "I think my mother especially was dissatisfied with the limited interest I had in play and in people of my own age," he said. "I know she kept trying to get me to be more like other boys, but with indifferent success." Perhaps the lack of success in playing with boys his own age came from Robert's own personality. As he later recalled, "I repaid my parents' confidence in me by developing an unpleasant ego . . . which I am sure must have affronted both children and adults who were unfortunate enough to come into contact with me." Oppenheimer's ego would create difficulties for him off and on throughout his life.

In August 1912, Robert gained a brother when Frank Oppenheimer was born. Another brother had died in infancy earlier. Eight years Frank's elder, Robert was both a big brother and, as they became adults, a mentor to his sibling. Perhaps not as gifted as Robert, Frank also distinguished himself as a scientist, eventually creating the Exploratorium, an experiential science museum in San Francisco. Throughout most of their lives, the brothers stayed close. They shared many common interests, from their passion for the American West to their pursuit of physics to their involvement in left-wing causes. This support of liberal organizations in the 1930s came back first to trouble and then to destroy both brothers' lives in the 1950s.

THE ETHICAL CULTURE SCHOOL

Although both of Robert's parents were of Jewish descent, they did not strictly practice their religion. Instead, the Ethical Culture movement, a secular offshoot of Judaism, attracted both parents. Founded in 1876 by Felix Adler, the Ethical Culture movement sought to create a "Judaism of the future." Adherents undertook beneficial social activities, in particular the moral and intellectual education of the working classes. At first, the movement's Workingman's School in New York City attracted nondenominational working-class students, but it provided such a good education that upper-class Jews like the Oppenheimers (whose children were barred admittance to many private schools because of anti-Semitism), sought to have the school open its doors to their children. By the time Julius joined its Board of Trustees in 1907, the renamed Ethical Culture

School had expanded to accept non–working-class children. In 1911 Robert entered the school.

At an institution where students' education often accelerated, Robert excelled. His Greek and Latin instructor, Alberta Newton, recalled that "he received every new idea as perfectly beautiful." Even at an early age, Robert quickly grasped complex concepts and ideas and impatiently waited for his peers to catch up. As a result, he often went to the library to do advanced work in math, and when he returned, explained his solutions to the other students.

At the Ethical Culture School, students from rich and poor backgrounds learned not just reading, writing, and arithmetic but how to improve the world. As Adler told the students two years before his 1931 death: "What the school is for is to make a better world. . . . In order to do that, to make yourself fit for such an undertaking, it is necessary that you should make something of yourself. You must cultivate your best talents in relation to those of others." To accomplish this lofty goal, students at the school intellectually mastered many topics, with an emphasis on the study of nature and art. They also focused on ethics in an Education in Life Problems seminar in which they confronted such issues as the ethics of wealth and poverty, racism, gender relations, and authority. Through such courses, students at the school developed their intellectual knowledge, their ethical abilities, and their cultural sensitivity. Ideally, they developed a well-rounded personality, tempered with the heat of moral convictions. In practice, however, problems arose. One of Oppenheimer's favorite teachers, Herbert Smith, later complained: "They were trying to develop a nation of quiz kids. They strained too much to train leaders. The result was that many students had a hard time adjusting to run-of-the-mill students at Columbia, Harvard and so forth."

Central to the mission of the Ethical Culture movement was the belief that man must assume responsibility for the direction of his life and destiny. Humans must answer to themselves, not to God, for their actions. Oppenheimer worked throughout his life to take responsibility for himself, but some of his actions would remain harder to justify than others.

As a teenager at the Ethical Culture School, Robert was thin and gangly, with a mass of brown hair and vivid blue eyes. Two teachers had a great impact on Oppenheimer — Augustus Klock and Herbert Smith. Klock taught high school chemistry and physics. Building upon Robert's childhood interest in mineralogy, Klock sparked a deeper fascination in science and in trying to understand the mechanics of the physical world. Chemistry was key, Oppenheimer later noted: "Compared to physics, [chemistry] starts right in the heart of things and very soon you have that connection between what you see and a really very sweeping set of ideas which could exist in physics but is very much less likely to be accessible." Klock introduced Robert to the mysteries of the universe at the classroom lab tables. For a young person with an inquiring mind and an active imagination, the connection between what was visible in experiments and how that answered questions both practical and profound satisfied a hunger for knowledge.

The other teacher who greatly influenced Oppenheimer was Herbert Smith. A 1948 FBI report on Smith described him as "a big man (six feet one and 195 pounds) with a pinkish, un-lined, mobile face. . . . He is a courtly, amusing, brainy and delightful guy." Smith had received his bachelor's degree from Harvard in 1911 and had taught at both Harvard and the Massachusetts Institute of Technology before he secured a position as the English instructor at the Ethical Culture School in 1917. Beginning in Robert's freshman year, Smith served as his homeroom teacher. Smith also taught English to Robert in his junior year. Smith recalled: "Robert simply towered above all his brilliant contemporaries. He is certainly the most brilliant man I have ever met and I know such men as [Harold Joseph] Laski and [James Bryant] Conant. It was immediately obvious that he was a genius." In Smith's English class, which was a college-preparatory course, Robert honed his already lively interest in literature and poetry. Even though Robert usually only sat and listened, Smith remembered him as "a flawless student." Outside of class, Smith continued to hold lively discussions with his students, sometimes inviting them to his home in West Orange, New Jersey. A fellow student of Robert's, Francis Fergusson, remembered Smith as "very, very kind to his students. . . . He took on Robert and me and various other people . . . saw them through their troubles and advised them what to do next." Many years after Oppenheimer had left the Ethical Culture School, he still exchanged letters and poetry with Smith.

Part of the "troubles" Robert confronted was his awkwardness in social settings. One of the causes of this awkwardness was a sense of embarrassment about his parents. Smith later recalled: "The most important element I think in Robert's life was his feeling that his own parents, particularly his father's maladroitness, had resulted in all sorts of humiliation to him." When he was fourteen, Robert attended a summer camp. In the midst of an energetic outdoor setting, his brainy nature and arrogant attitude set him up for harassment by the other boys. A letter he wrote home announcing that he was hearing all about sex brought his parents running to see the den of iniquity to which they had sent their son. The resultant crackdown at the camp against telling sexual jokes and stories made him a further target. The other boys locked Robert in an icehouse overnight without any clothes.

A different view of the young Oppenheimer emerged from a high school classmate. Jane Didisheim still held vivid memories of Robert fifty years after she went to the Ethical Culture School with him: "He was very frail, very pink-cheeked, very shy, and very brilliant of course. Very quickly everybody admitted he was different from all the others and very superior. . . . Aside from that he was physically . . . rather undeveloped, not in the way he behaved but the way he went about, the way he walked, the way he sat. There was something strangely childish about him."

All students at the Ethical Culture School had to play basketball or run track. Robert, favoring intellectual pursuits over physical ones, was not very good at those sports, but, unlike some of his fellow students, he did not complain about the requirement. He did like to ride horses, an activity he continued as an adult in the mountains of the West. Additionally, Oppenheimer was passionate about sailing. He had his own sailboat, which he piloted through the waters off Long Island. In conjunction with his easy mastery of math, science, and literature, Robert also learned languages quickly. He wrote sonnets in French, spoke German, and knew some Chinese. His absorption of new languages continued after he left school. In the 1930s, he taught himself Sanskrit so he could read the sacred texts of Hinduism. Once when he was a visiting professor at the University of Leiden in the Netherlands, he learned Dutch in six weeks so he could present a lecture in that language. Reflecting on Oppenheimer's daunting intellect, English instructor Herbert Smith said, "His mind [is] so tremendous that it makes you really uneasy." Throughout his life, some people would continue to react to Robert's genius with uneasiness.

Others, however, such as Francis Fergusson, a westerner who came to New York from the desert Southwest, felt at ease with Robert. With his parents living in Washington, D.C., most of the year (Fergusson's father was a U.S. representative from New Mexico), Francis attended the Ethical Culture School. There, he met and became good friends with Robert. Francis went on to write plays, essays, and histories of the arts and to produce theatrical pieces. For Robert, Francis not only held a similarly keen intellect and intensity but also offered a window into a different way of life—a western sensibility of vast panoramas, ancient cultures, and wide-open opportunities. From their senior year at the Ethical Culture School through their undergraduate and graduate years, the New Yorker and the westerner were close friends.

Robert graduated from the Ethical Culture School in February 1921 at the age of seventeen. He planned on entering Harvard University in the fall, but kept active by conducting a science project at the high school throughout the spring. That summer, he traveled to Europe with his parents and brother. He and Frank went on a prospecting trip in the mountains of southern Germany, where Robert contracted a severe case of dysentery. Already frail, the sickness forced him to postpone his entrance into Harvard while he recovered, first in Europe and then back in the States. Along with the dysentery, he also was struck with colitis. The extended convalescence began at his parents' apartment in New York and, when he was healthy enough, continued with several long trips. These trips allowed Robert not only to recover but also to experience new parts of the country. In the spring of 1922 he traveled to the South. That summer, Robert headed west. To cap off the year of recuperation with a vigorous trip west, Robert's parents asked the genial Herbert Smith to accompany their son on his travels.

GOING WEST

Over the decades, health seekers in the United States had ventured west to "take the cure" and regain their strength. The journey not only restored health to many travelers but also introduced them to a world different from the rest of the country. Theodore Roosevelt, who was president when Robert was born, spent several years on a ranch in the Badlands of the Dakotas as a young man. His time in the saddle changed him from a sickly person to the historic persona, full of vigor and charisma.

The Southwest offered dramatic landscapes with high mountains and distant vistas, American Indians and Hispanics with unique cultures, and a worldview distinctly different from anything even the travel-savvy Robert had experienced in Europe. Going west offered an escape not only from bodily ills but also from industrial America. At about the same time that Robert and Herbert disembarked from the train in New Mexico, other people from the East—intellectuals, writers, and artists—sought refuge from the disappointments of the failed peace after World War I and from the rampant consumerism and hustling industrialism of the Roaring Twenties. These internal expatriates escaped the United States but stayed in the country. People like patron Mabel Dodge, activist John Collier, and artist Georgia O'Keeffe encountered a world strange and enticing in the Southwest, one of the most isolated parts of the nation. The American Indians and Hispanics of New Mexico lived a different life, full of ritual, with roots that tapped the centuries. For the disillusioned, the West offered a tonic to the industrialized soul.

Like other refugees to the West, Robert and Herbert found a cure in the mountains and villages of New Mexico. For weeks, they hiked and rode horses over steep mountains, camped in the great outdoors, and bunked at guest ranches. Their headquarters was Los Pinos, a guest ranch at Cowles, high in the Sangre de Cristo Mountains east of Santa Fe. Los Pinos was run by Katherine Chaves Page and her new husband, Winthrop. Katherine came from an established Hispanic family headed by Don Amado Chaves, and they accepted Oppenheimer and Smith into their circle of family and friends. Smith later commented that because of Robert's acceptance by the patriarch Don Amado and the aristocratic Chaves clan, "for the first time in his life, [Robert] found himself loved, admired, sought after." For an insecure and sheltered young man, this acceptance did as much as the crisp desert air to cure him of his ailments.

Another family that embraced Robert in New Mexico was the Fergussons, who were back at their Albuquerque home during a summer recess from Congress. Robert and Herbert visited them and met Francis's brother Harvey and sister Erna. Both Harvey and Erna would distinguish themselves as southwestern writers in coming years. In one of Harvey's later novels, *Grant of Kingdom*, he wrote of northern New Mexico in a way that helps explain the attraction of the landscape: "To the west, the country tumbled steeply to purple depths where the Rio Grande crawled through lava gorges, then rose again to a pale blue horizon of distant ranges." This could have described the view from the mountaintops that Robert and Herbert ascended that summer.

Robert, Herbert, and their companions traveled over a wide area of the Southwest during their month in the region. They climbed the lofty Sangre de Cristo and Jemez Mountains, and they drove northwest to Telluride and Ouray, Colorado. They rode horses through landscapes where American Indian ruins from the 1300s hid among the stunted piñon and towering ponderosa pines. They met Hispanic sheepherders tending their flocks, and they were welcomed by the Chaves family, which had lived in the Land of Enchantment for hundreds of years. Riding into the deeply crevassed plateaus and along high mountainsides, they interacted with both the landscape and the peoples of New Mexico. Their trip to the Southwest also introduced Robert to a place that would dramatically alter his future. Twenty-one years later, he would pick this part of the country as the place to create an atomic bomb.

Vigorous physical activity in the fresh air challenged Robert's frail body, and he revived and even thrived. The trip to the Southwest was the final touch of his recovery, and he impressed Herbert with his stamina and natural ability with horses. In fact, Herbert commented that when riding, Robert displayed a carefree attitude that bordered on recklessness. He galloped down mountains at breakneck speed, rode for hours even long after the sun went down, and sometimes stopped for lunch on top of a peak during lightning storms.

For Robert, in addition to recovering his health in the rarefied air of the arid Southwest, he also found refuge—from his eastern life, from his family of wealth, and from his Jewish heritage. During one stop on their trip, a harried Herbert asked Robert to help him pack by folding a jacket. Robert looked sharply at Smith and snapped: "Oh, yes. The tailor's son would know how to do that, wouldn't he?" Robert was self-conscious of his Jewish roots. In fact, he had suggested to Herbert that they travel as brothers, which Smith thought was a ploy on Robert's part to hide that he was Jewish. Perhaps the prejudice he experienced in the United States and in his travels in Germany made him want to hide this part of his identity.

During Robert's visit to Albuquerque, the Fergussons introduced him to Paul Horgan, a dashing young New Mexican who became an even more famous writer than Harvey, Erna, or

Francis. Once Robert left New Mexico and went back to the East, he stayed connected to the desert Southwest and to many of his new friends through correspondence and rendezvous with them on the East Coast. Paul visited the Oppenheimers and even stayed with them at their Long Island estate. The people Robert met in provincial New Mexico that summer of 1922 remained his friends for years. Their companionship, liveliness, and alternative lifestyles counteracted Robert's conventional East Coast upbringing and expanded his sheltered, privileged worldview.

Even though the search for personal identity separate from parents and family consumes many teens and young adults, people continue to assume new identities throughout their lives. On his trip west, Robert found an attractive addition to his urbane and cosmopolitan persona through his contact with westerners and, in his unique way, incorporated a western component into his personality. He started cooking food with hot chile spices, wore a silver belt buckle with an American Indian design, and longed for the wide-open spaces of the West when he was in the East. Robert did not forsake his New Yorker identity, but added a layer of western identity over it like the dust that covered him at the end of one his trail rides through the Rocky Mountains.

Robert would return to the high mountains of New Mexico time and time again over the next two decades to recover from his hectic life. He would visit the West, praise it in letters to friends, and eventually buy land there even before he bought a home of his own. The West changed him over those twenty years.

BACK EAST

After a month in the Southwest, Robert and Herbert went back to the East Coast. From the dusty trails along steep canyon walls to the bustling streets between the skyscrapers of New York City, Robert returned to his family's wealth and privilege and a future at Harvard University. Over the years, one of the

places where the Oppenheimer family entertained their friends
was at Bay Shore, a town on the Atlantic side of Long Island
about fifty miles from Manhattan. On an estate of six acres, the
family spent many summers away from the heat of the city.
Robert described his Bay Shore activities in one letter to Francis Fergusson: "We have been spending a most civilized and
unexciting time down here, writing, reading enormously, traveling to town [Manhattan] from time to time for books and
exhibits and plays, and sallying every evening in tuxedoes,
pathetically to ransack Bayshore [sic] or Islip for a vestige
of adventure."

Sailing one of their two boats also occupied the Oppenheimers' time at their summer house. The forty-foot yacht, *Lorelei*,
and a twenty-eight-foot sloop were tied up at the pier on the
property. Robert and Frank named the sloop *Trimethy* after the
colorless liquid trimethylamine, which they thought smelled
like pickled herring. The brothers often took *Trimethy* and any
visiting friends out on the bay between their house and the
outer banks of the island. Not known for his physical prowess,
Robert nonetheless was an aggressive, even at times reckless,
sailor. Once, Robert and Paul Horgan sailed too close to the
Fire Island inlet and were carried out on the tide into the storm-
tossed Atlantic breakers. For several hours, they struggled to
tack back into the more tranquil bay. Once in the bay, their
progress home was slow. Robert's worried father sent a revenue
cutter out to search for them, and around 11 P.M., it finally
rescued the young men. When they returned, however, Robert's parents did not admonish them, and the mad dashes across
the bay in *Trimethy* continued. Looking back at his experiences
with Robert, Paul recalled: "There were high spirited goings
on all the time. I think it is perfectly right to say that even then
and all my life I've felt this: he was the most intelligent man I've
ever known, the most brilliantly endowed intellectually. And
with this, in that period of his life, he combined incredibly
good wit and gaiety and high spirits."

Another aspect of Oppenheimer's personality emerged as he
grew: at times, he suffered from depression. Horgan later said:

"Robert had bouts of melancholy, deep, deep, depressions as a youngster. . . . He would seem to be incommunicado emotionally for a day or two at a time." Other friends also observed in the young man a moodiness, which, combined with Robert's social fumbling and lack of patience with those he considered fools, suggests that he struggled with some personality conflicts. Whether Robert had what is now called manic-depressive illness or some other psychological affliction, he was never adequately diagnosed and treated. He continued to struggle with himself for years. In 1923 he wrote to Francis Fergusson, "I find these awful people in me from time to time, and their expulsion is the sole excuse for my writing." Driven by his genius and his emotional turmoil, Robert headed to Harvard.

HARVARD UNIVERSITY

After taking a year off to regain his physical and mental health, Robert entered Harvard University in the fall of 1922. He planned on majoring in chemistry, but only after deciding against the fields of architecture, the classics, poetry, and art. He also planned on completing the four-year bachelor's degree in only three. To do this, he pushed himself hard. He arrived at the laboratories early, took heavy loads of classes, and still had time to audit courses in subjects not required for his degree. For most Harvard students, a normal load of courses per semester was five, but Robert took six for credit and often audited more. In one year, he took for credit four chemistry classes, two in French literature, two in mathematics, one in philosophy, and three more in physics. A Harvard classmate noted that Robert "intellectually looted the place."

One of Robert's friends at Harvard, William Boyd, recalled that even though Robert wanted to graduate in three years, he never seemed to hurry and never seemed to study. During that first year, Robert sent a letter to Herbert Smith about a short story he had written for an English composition course. In the story, a young mining engineer who has just graduated from an eastern college arrives at his first job with lofty goals but condescending ideals. This character quickly realizes that in the future he may become like the residing superintendent, who also came from an elite college but is now a "disgusting and doddering syphilitic," and that "he too is rather likely to disintegrate." Despite his creative way with words, Robert feared he would only get a C in the course because he had skipped the last three classes of the semester.

Pushing himself hard at Harvard took its toll on Oppenheimer. In a letter to Smith in January 1923, he complained: "The outlook is so dismal that I can't be at all successfully flip. Imbecile examinations, weeks of slush, tantalizing courses in chemistry that it will take me years to reach." The next fall, he told Smith: "My labors this year promise to be positively overwhelming. There is an imposing little thing in Epistemology; and Physics grows daily grimmer. So I have done only one story, a fair one. I am very glad for I suspect that my work, together with such sailing and riding as is necessary to keep me from positive physical decrepitude, will leave me little energy." Several weeks later, Robert wrote Herbert again: "The infiltration of thermodynamics continues undisputed. I am working very hard now, so hard that I fear your epithet of grind. But if you could see the careless way in which I neglect French 6 or Chem to complete a theory about identity in Tensor Calculus, or how I flee the entire melange for a weekend in a sailboat off Gloucester, you might forgive me. But then you would see my grades, and your accusing finger would return." Work, weather, and worry dogged Robert as he forced himself to rush through Harvard and as he juggled his nascent identities as a chemist, a writer, and a physicist.

In another letter to Smith that winter, Robert pined for the open spaces of the West. Replying to Smith's plans to spend the summer in New Mexico, Robert wrote: "Of course, I am insanely jealous. I see you riding down from the mountains to the desert at that hour when thunderstorms and sunsets caparison the sky; I see you in the Pecos . . . spending the moonlight on Grass Mountain; I see you vending the marvels of the upper Loch, of the upper amphitheater at Ouray, of the waterfall at

Telluride, the Punch Bowl at San Ysidro — even the prairies around Antonito to philistine eyes." For many people, a summer spent sailing on Long Island Sound and lounging at the family estate while being waited on by servants would be ideal. But Robert longed for the rugged landscape, the people, and the freedom of the West. Despite several attempts to avoid spending the summer on his family's Long Island estate — first through a feigned recurrence of illness and then by trying to persuade his parents to accompany him to New Mexico — Robert remained on the East Coast over the summer of 1923. He admitted to Smith in a letter, "I fear that if I transported father and mother to the midst of the desert and dropped them, I should jeopardize my puny inheritance and to chaperone them to Los Pinos would insure a new nervous breakdown."

A year later, after missing another summer in the rarified air of the Southwest, Robert asked Herbert about his latest trip west: "I should like to hear about your adventures, and Los Pinos and the desert and Mrs. Page, about all those things that gripe and make me notice how blue and sunny the sky is, and what an exquisite filigree the chrome and coral leaves make against it." Although family and studies kept Robert in the East once he entered Harvard, he often thought about New Mexico and corresponded with his acquaintances about their lives and adventures there. Those letters often ended with *"Adios"* or *"Vaya con dios"* (Go with God).

Because of his heavy load of courses, his extracurricular reading, and his self-imposed mandate to graduate in three years, Robert had limited time for a social life. His roommate, William Boyd, mentioned that he never saw Robert go out on a date. Another friend, Jeffries Wyman, admitted that none of the friends had much time for dating: "We were all too much in love with the problems of philosophy and science and the arts and general intellectual life to be thinking about girls." According to Wyman, Robert's unease with people was also a hindrance: "He found social adjustment very difficult, and I think he was often very unhappy. . . . I suppose he was lonely and felt he didn't fit in well with the human environment. . . . We were young people falling in love with ideas right and left and interested in people who gave us ideas, but there wasn't the warmth of human companionship perhaps." For Robert and his cohort of friends at Harvard, ideas and intellectual challenges were what excited them.

A SWITCH TO PHYSICS

Percy Bridgman, the professor who taught the thermodynamics course at Harvard, was a distinguished experimental physicist who changed Robert's life. Robert later said: "I can't recall how it came over me that what I liked in chemistry was very close to physics." For him, physics went to the heart of matter, even more than chemistry: "It was the study of order, of regularity, of what makes matter harmonious and what makes it work." Physics appealed to the philosopher in Oppenheimer, and even though he did not take any courses in physics his freshman year, he asked the physics department to allow him to start taking graduate-level courses. He was permitted to jump over the more basic classes, with one of the professors commenting, "Obviously, if he says he's read these books he's a liar, but he should get a Ph.D. for knowing their titles." In his shift to physics, he began to master the mathematics basic to any exploration of the subject. By his last year at Harvard, Robert conducted experiments under Bridgman's guidance. Nevertheless, despite his attraction to physics, Oppenheimer finished his work in chemistry and in June 1925 graduated summa cum laude with a major in it. Under his yearbook picture, where a less modest person might have bragged about his or her achievements at one of the most prestigious universities in the country, Robert simply wrote, "In college three years as an undergraduate." Perhaps this did not so much reflect Robert's modesty as it did his dislike of his time at Harvard, as indicated in his letters to Herbert.

Even though he plowed "through about five or ten big scientific books a week, and pretend[ed] to research," Oppenheimer did not focus totally on science. He took a course with the renowned philosopher Alfred Whitehead, which prompted this comment in a letter to Smith: "The work goes much as before: frantic, bad and good. I have got to debate with Whitehead at the Seminar next week, and am already trembling, of course. There are [some] books I have read, and some I hope you like. . . . *A Miller's Tale, Anna Karenina, The Brothers Kara[mazov], The Mysterious Stranger, Daisy Miller.*" In the same letter, Robert wrote of his postgraduate plans: "I have, by the intervention of strangely kindly Gods, been unbeknownst admitted to Christ's at Cambridge; but I cannot decide to leave this Puritanical hole, even for all the vacuity of my life here, if I can do research next year with Bridgman." Although accepted into the graduate program at the most prestigious university in England, Robert initially hoped to remain at Harvard to work with his mentor in physics, Percy Bridgman.

"NEAR THE CENTER"

Oppenheimer did not have a strong foundation in experimental physics, in the actual manipulation of the basic elements of our world. His rush to graduate in three years, his skipping over of some of the basic physics courses, and his sometimes competitive style of showing off his knowledge contributed to an underlying insecurity about his mastery of physics. Despite his insecurity and initial preference to remain with Bridgman, he nonetheless chose to attend the Cavendish Laboratory at Cambridge University in England. He later admitted: "I don't even know why I left Harvard, but I somehow felt that [Cambridge] was more near the center." With Nobel Prize–winner Sir Ernest Rutherford directing Cavendish, this Physics Department was indeed near the center of the world of experimental physics. Professor Bridgman wrote a letter of recommendation to Rutherford highlighting Oppenheimer's "perfectly prodigious power of assimilation." "His weakness is on the experimental side," Bridgman noted. "His type of mind is analytical, rather than physical. . . . It appears to me that it is a bit of a gamble as to whether Oppenheimer will ever make any real contributions of an important character, but if he does make good at all, I believe he will be a very unusual success." Reflecting the prejudices of the time, Bridgman also addressed Robert's ethnicity: "As appears from his name, Oppenheimer is a Jew, but entirely without the usual qualifications of his race. He is a tall, well set-up young man, with a rather engaging diffidence of manner, and I think you need have no hesitation whatever for any reason of this sort in considering his application." Rutherford was not impressed either with Bridgman's qualified endorsement or Oppenheimer's "prodigious" credentials (despite graduating summa cum laude) and did not accept him as one of his students. Rutherford did arrange for Oppenheimer to work with a different experimental physicist and Nobel Prize winner in his laboratory, J. J. Thomson.

With his entrance to Cambridge finalized, Robert went to the mountains of New Mexico before leaving for England to pursue a Ph.D. in physics. This was his first time back west since he had roamed the forested high-desert plateaus with Herbert Smith in 1922. Although he had not visited for three years, he had kept in touch with the friends he had made around Cowles. One time, he sent at considerable expense a cake made in New York City for the seventieth birthday celebration of Amado Chaves, the patriarch of the family that had provided shelter and good cheer to Oppenheimer and Smith in 1922. On the cake was the Chaves family crest.

For the visit in 1925, Robert had the rest of his family with him. Frank stayed with him at the ranch near Cowles, and their parents resided in the more luxurious Bishop's Lodge in Santa Fe, with side trips up to the mountain retreat. The Oppenheimer family and their friends enjoyed a wide range of activities — trips to American Indian dances, carousing at the annual Santa Fe Fiesta, and most of all, riding horses up to the high peaks that towered over the cabin at Cowles. Paul Horgan visited the group and described one of their jaunts. They hired horses in Santa Fe, which lies at seven thousand feet above sea level, with the plan to ride up over the Sangre de Cristo Mountains and down into Cowles. As the crow flies, the distance is ten to fifteen miles, but the peaks they ascended rose well over ten thousand feet. As Horgan recalled: "It turned out to be a day-long venture, full of merriment and nonsense as we rode. . . . We hit the divide at the very top of the mountain in a tremendous thunderstorm . . . immense, huge, pounding rain. We sat under our horses for lunch and ate oranges, [and] were drenched. . . . I was looking at Robert . . . and all of a sudden I noticed his hair was standing straight up . . . responding to the static." Surviving the storm, they arrived at Cowles at 7 P.M., fortunate not to have been struck by lightning on the mountain. From this idyllic romp in the Southwest, Oppenheimer boarded an ocean liner in New York City to head across the Atlantic and devote himself to experimental physics. His brother rode with the captain of the family's yacht out beyond Long Island to wave a final good-bye to Robert and his ship. Full of hope, Robert soon ran into difficulties at Cambridge.

A CRISIS AT CAMBRIDGE

In his formal application to Christ's College at Cambridge, Oppenheimer wrote that he was particularly interested in the theory of electronic conduction as a means of better understanding the motion of electrons. He also mentioned that he wanted to start working on a research problem in physics, but was informed that he needed to take a course in laboratory skills and techniques during the first semester. By November, Robert complained in a letter to Francis Fergusson: "I am having a pretty bad time. The lab work is a terrible bore, and I am so bad at it that it is impossible to feel that I am learning anything. . . . The lectures are vile." Robert admitted that he held little talent for the physical preparation of slides and the setting up of equipment—tasks that graduate students did for their professors. At one point, he had to cover glass slides with a thin coating for an experiment. Whether he could not get the coating to the appropriate thinness or the activity quickly bored him, he was dissatisfied with the work. He did enjoy the fresh ideas and theories that flew around the labs and classrooms at

Cambridge, but his mental state deteriorated throughout the fall semester.

Over Christmas break, Robert and Francis — who was in England on a Rhodes scholarship — traveled to Paris. They continued the practice they had begun at the Ethical Culture School — they argued about ideas and personal beliefs. This time, though, Robert snapped. He jumped on Fergusson, grabbed him by the throat, and tried to strangle him. Francis quickly pushed Robert away, but the bizarre attack revealed the stress that Robert struggled with at Cambridge. Several factors contributed to Robert's actions. Besides his frustration with the elementary level of his lab work and his impatience at being a beginning graduate student when so many exciting developments were taking place in the field of nuclear physics, there was his ineptness in his relations with women. In an apologetic letter to Fergusson several weeks after the blowup, Robert wrote that he should come to Francis in "a hair shirt, with much fasting and show and prayer" to make up for the attack. Toward the end of the letter, Robert alluded to his "inability to solder two copper wires together, which is probably succeeding in getting me crazy."

Others noticed that Oppenheimer was in trouble. John Edsall, a classmate from Harvard who was also doing graduate work at Cambridge, observed, "There was a tremendous amount of inner turmoil, in spite of which . . . he kept doing a tremendous amount of work, thinking, reading, discussing things, but obviously with a sense of great inner anxiety and alarm." Robert confided to John that he was seeing a psychiatrist.

During spring vacation, Oppenheimer joined Edsall and Jeffries Wyman in a tour of the islands of Corsica and Sardinia in the Mediterranean Sea. Although Robert at times complained of feeling depressed, the three friends had a good time exploring Corsica on foot, and Robert's mood improved. However, on their last night on Corsica before going to Sardinia, Robert abruptly announced that he had to return to Cambridge. When pressed for an explanation, he said he had left a poisoned apple on the desk of one of his professors in England and had to return to make sure the man was all right. Oppenheimer went back to England alone, to the great puzzlement of his friends, who chalked it up to Robert's inner turmoil. No professors died from poisoning that spring, and perhaps Robert merely needed to correct a mistake in some research he had conducted for a professor.

The holiday on Corsica did alleviate one source of Oppenheimer's feelings of inadequacy: he met a woman on the island. Little is known of this mysterious encounter, but he wrote years later: "The psychiatrist was a prelude to what began for me in Corsica. . . . What you need to know is that it was not a mere love affair, not a love affair at all, but love." For a socially immature twenty-two-year-old who had few if any prior intimate experiences with women, the love affair on Corsica was possibly his first romantic encounter.

Back at Cambridge, officials at the university became so alarmed with Oppenheimer's erratic behavior that they notified his parents, who rushed across the Atlantic to check on their son. They arranged for him to get treatment from a different psychiatrist, but his mental state showed little improvement. Oppenheimer confided to Edsall that he had been diagnosed with dementia praecox, now known as schizophrenia. Before Fergusson returned to the States that summer, he met Oppenheimer in front of the psychiatrist's office. Fergusson remembered the meeting as a turning point in Robert's difficulties: "I [saw him] standing on the corner, waiting for me, with his hat on one side of his head, looking absolutely weird. I joined him . . . and he walked at a terrific speed; when he walked his feet turned out . . . and he sort of leaned forward, traveled at a terrific clip. I asked him how it had been. He said . . . that the guy was too stupid to follow him and that he knew more about his troubles than the [doctor] did, which was probably true." A sign of Oppenheimer's intense intellect was that he now seemed to cure himself of his emotional turmoil. "There's no doubt about it," Fergusson recalled. "Robert had this ability to bring himself up, to figure out what his trouble was, and to deal with it."

A SHIFT TO THEORETICAL PHYSICS

Robert solved another difficulty that summer. During his professional and personal struggles at Cambridge in the spring of 1926, he heard of Erwin Schrödinger, a University of Göttingen physicist, who had offered a revolutionary theory about the way atoms behave. Schrödinger speculated that electrons were not distinct particles but more like a wave that curved around the nucleus of an atom. Schrödinger's theory of "quantum mechanics" swept the scientific world and kept the physicists at Göttingen and elsewhere abuzz with the implications of the theory. This theory sparked Robert's scientific curiosity, and he began reading all he could find about quantum mechanics. That spring, he also met the great Danish physicist Niels Bohr. Later, Robert wrote: "At that point I forgot about beryllium and films and decided to try to learn the trade of being a theoretical physicist. By that time I was fully aware that it was an unusual time, that great things were afoot." To get in step with the times, Robert headed to the center of such theoretical fervor: Göttingen.

The illustrious theoretical physicist Max Born had invited Oppenheimer to join him at the German university. Just as Cambridge held a prestigious position in experimental physics, Göttingen was a world famous center for theoretical physics. The shift suited Robert's intellectual strengths, and he began to recast himself as a theoretical physicist. He recalled: "By the time I decided to go to Göttingen, I had very great misgivings about myself on all fronts, but I clearly was going to do theoretical physics if I could. . . . I felt completely relieved of the responsibility to go back into a laboratory. I hadn't been good; I hadn't done anybody any good, and I hadn't had any fun whatever, and here was something I felt just driven to try." The year since he left Harvard had taken its toll on Oppenheimer. He had changed from a chemist to an experimental physicist, and had abandoned that for theoretical physics. For a brilliant person trying to find his way, the time at Cambridge had severely tested him, but he had high hopes for Göttingen.

The physicists there had high hopes for Oppenheimer, as well. Robert arrived in the midst of a heady time. Some of the best minds in physics were at Göttingen revolutionizing the field with their theories on the inner workings of the atom. Nobel Prize–winning scientists contemplated the latest theories amidst an exciting international mix of senior and junior physicists. The fervent rush toward unlocking the secrets of atomic structure grabbed the young and old alike as they discussed their speculations.

This search had originated in ancient Greece, where atomic theory began with Democritus and his concept of an indivisible particle that comprised the primary matter of the physical universe; however, the Greeks did not have the technology to pursue and experiment on the atom. A Roman philosopher, Lucretius, preserved the atomic theory, but it remained purely a theory. Experimental atomic science, lacking the sophisticated tools and equipment to search for minute particles, did not catch up with theory until the Enlightenment. Sir Isaac Newton, the father of modern science, resurrected the idea of the atom to help explain some of the results in his investigations of the physical world.

For two hundred years after Newton, physics developed unevenly with an emphasis on mechanics while neglecting optics, electricity, and magnetism. Scientists continued to be hampered by the lack of equipment necessary to make peering into the inner spaces of molecules and atoms possible, and most were preoccupied with accounting for the behavior of seen objects. James Clerk Maxwell changed the nature of physics in 1864. Prior to Maxwell, physicists considered space to be empty. Maxwell challenged that notion by suggesting that unseen atoms absorbed and radiated energy, and thus emitted light. Without this theory, atomic physics would have been unable to open the atom to minute examination.

The evolution of atomic theory illustrates the process of scientific exploration and interpretation first proposed by twentieth-century American historian of science Thomas Kuhn. Scientists develop a theory that attempts to account for certain behaviors or properties of nature. This theory advances through the ranks of experimental scientists who try to prove or disprove it. Scientific investigation demands that theories be subjected to rigorous experimental trials where the same result is repeated in different laboratories to verify that a result is not just the product of one person's work. Based on the experiments, theorists then come up with more refined explanations for the results. The resultant theory or paradigm has to account for all of the behaviors and properties that occur during the experiment, but anomalies often exist that are not explained by the theory. Anomalies are often ignored by scientists — at least until the anomaly becomes too obvious to avoid any longer. Then, a new theory arises that incorporates some of those discrepancies and better explains the physical observations. If a radically new theory emerges, a paradigm shift occurs that can drastically alter understanding of the natural world.

In nuclear physics, the theory of small, indivisible particles making up matter hailed from antiquity, but the actual ability to experiment on the particles came with advances in the technical capability of the laboratory. Through experimentation and refinement of atomic theories, new paradigms emerged that explained the gaps in the old theories. However, experimenters through Oppenheimer's time were hampered by their inability to actually see the atom. Even today, scientists have not seen an atom. In fact, at first, atomic theory was used more by chemists to explain the reactions they witnessed in their test tubes than by physicists trying to understand the mechanics of the physical universe.

To complicate matters, some scientific theories contradict each other. For example, Schrödinger speculated that light travels in waves, but it also travels in particles. Can light be both a wave and a particle? Can two contradictory axioms both be true? Schrödinger said yes, that even though the axioms contradict each other, this paradox explains how light works. Named the "complementarity of light" theory, the paradox shows that two contradictory ideas can explain phenomena. Later in his life, Oppenheimer wrote that this "complementarity . . . recognizes that various ways of talking about physical experience may each have validity, and may each be necessary for the adequate description of the physical world, and may yet stand in a mutually exclusive relationship to each other, so that to a situation to which one applies, there may be no consistent possibility of applying the other." The paradox of complementarity — that contradictory explanations can both be true—helps explain light and other physical phenomena. But it also can help account for some of Oppenheimer's later personal decisions, both in relation to atomic weapons and his friends.

A REVOLUTION IN ATOMIC THEORY

Three key discoveries energized the physics world at the turn of the twentieth century and helped physicists understand what was under the hood of the atom. In November 1895, German scientist Wilhelm Conrad Röntgen announced the existence of x-rays. Invisible to the eye, x-rays resembled light waves, but with very short wavelengths. Medical uses of x-rays for peering under the skin and detailing the body's structure were immediately recognized. Working from Röntgen's discovery, Frenchman Antoine-Henri Becquerel determined that minerals containing uranium and thorium produced spontaneous radiations (or energies) that blackened photographic plates. A new property of matter, this "radioactivity" raised further questions about what was active in the radio waves and from where the waves came. The final revolutionary finding around the turn of the twentieth century pinpointed a specific part of the atom. In 1897, English physicist J. J. Thomson, also building upon Röntgen's discovery of x-rays, found electrons in the atomic structure. Contrary to the beliefs of the ancient Greeks, Thomson realized that the atom did have parts. Thomson's view of the electron created a paradigm shift as it completely revised the physical idea of matter by introducing charged particles into the atomic equation. Whether the atom was still indivisible came under increasing attack as experiments shook it up to see what fell out. Using this revolutionary development, Ernest Rutherford, a New Zealand physicist working in Canada, announced in 1911 that in addition to electrons, the atomic structure held a nucleus — a central core of positively charged particles. Combining these theories, the Danish physicist Niels Bohr proposed that atoms contained a solar system–like structure, in which groups of electrons revolved in expanding orbits around the nucleus like planets around the sun. In 1922, Bohr won the Nobel Prize in Physics for his theory. Bohr's atomic model explained many of the anomalies that the intense examination of and experimentation on the atom had uncovered. Most physicists accepted his theory and, in collaborative efforts that often crossed national boundaries, refined their ideas and concepts into more complex theories.

QUANTUM MECHANICS

The fevered pitch of the work at Göttingen matched Oppenheimer's own inner fire, and his work there helped advance quantum mechanics. Expanding on the two papers ("On the Quantum Theory of Vibration-rotation Bands" and "On the Quantum Theory of the Problem of the Two Bodies") that he had written at Cambridge, Robert forgot the difficulties of the laboratory in England and attacked the theories of quantum mechanics. Having languished at Cambridge for a year, Oppenheimer wasted little time at Göttingen. During such revolutionary times in science, professors and students are almost on equal footing as traditional ideas are replaced by whoever can come up with the paradigm shift to address anomalies and new problems. At first, Robert dazzled his colleagues, but some of them grew annoyed with his quick mind and cutting remarks. Another American in Göttingen, Edward Condon, remembered: "The trouble is that Oppie is so quick on the trigger intellectually that he puts the other guy at a disadvantage. And dammit, he is always right, or at least right enough." Oppenheimer's expensive clothes and obvious wealth also rubbed some of his fellow students the wrong way as they struggled to buy books and food in the difficult economic times of Germany in the 1920s.

Robert's dissertation, "On the Quantum Theory of Continuous Spectra," was accepted by his professors "with distinction" and was quickly published in the prestigious physics journal *Zeitschrift für Physik*. As Oppenheimer made his mark among the professors and graduate students at Göttingen and began to be noticed by others in the field of physics, he almost did not receive his doctorate there. He had failed to register at the university officially when he first arrived so he hurriedly did so in the spring of 1927. Oppenheimer received his Ph.D. in physics three weeks later. Following the tradition for graduates at Göttingen, he waded through the fountain in the city's center and kissed the "Goose Girl," a life-size bronze statue in front of the medieval town hall.

The theory of quantum mechanics Oppenheimer explored in his dissertation is one the most important new concepts in the twentieth century concerning how nature is understood. Similar to the atom, which is the basic particle making up the physical world, a quantum is the smallest quantity of radiant energy that moves an atom. Quantum mechanics defines and measures the interaction of these units of energy. To do this, one entertains a curious paradox called the uncertainty principle. When one looks at an electron — which might be a particle or part of a wave — one can measure its movement but cannot establish its position at the same time. Conversely, when one pinpoints an electron's position, its movement can no longer be measured. In short, the uncertainty principle, formulated by the German physicist Werner Heisenberg, states that the accurate measurement of an observable quantity, such as position or momentum, produces uncertainties in the measurement of the other. Just in the process of observing, one affects the thing one observes.

OPPENHEIMER, THE THEORETICAL PHYSICIST

The Physics Department at Göttingen inspired Robert to establish himself as a theoretical physicist. He went from an inept graduate student fumbling his way through the labs at Cambridge to an original thinker on atomic theory. Robert took the nascent theory of quantum mechanics and, by using mathematical equations and formulas, explained how the experimental results proved the emerging paradigms. As he later recalled, "It was a time of earnest correspondence and hurried conferences, of debate, criticism, and brilliant mathematical improvisation." At Göttingen, Oppenheimer also collaborated with German physicist Max Born on applying quantum mechanics to molecules, and even though many of the ideas from that time are now obsolete, the Born-Oppenheimer approximation continues to be used today. From 1926 to 1929, Robert published sixteen papers that came from his work in Germany. He gained an international identity as a brilliant young theoretical physicist.

Social life in Göttingen offered visiting students and professors a welcome relief from the intense work at the university. For people who had money, the town of Göttingen held many charms, like walled mansions, places to drink locally brewed beer, and centuries-old restaurants that served wiener Schnitzel. Robert stayed at the mansion of Dr. Cario, a bankrupt medical doctor who took in boarders to help make ends meet. At this house, Robert met some of the scientists who later would champion him, especially during World War II. For part of the time that Oppenheimer lived there, Princeton University physicist Karl T. Compton, who later played a key role in the United States' atomic bomb project, stayed at the mansion with his wife and daughter. At one point, Robert came upon the two-year-old Jean Compton pretending to read a book. When he saw that the book was about birth control, he looked at Mrs. Compton, who was visibly pregnant, and commented, "A little late."

The visiting professors and graduate students who descended on Göttingen from around the world changed the field of atomic physics in several ways. They helped solidify the quantum theory that revolutionized the field, but they also established friendships and trust with each other that enabled them to work together and build an atomic bomb more than a decade later during World War II.

During his time at Göttingen, Robert also began a romance. He met Charlotte Riefenstahl, another graduate student in physics, on the train returning from a seminar in Hamburg. On the platform before boarding, she noticed his expensive pigskin luggage. Later, she sat next to him and complimented him on the traveling bag. Afterward, another student who heard about this exchange wagered that Robert would try to give her the piece of luggage. It was well known at the university that when anyone liked something of his, Robert would find some way to give it to the admirer. Just before Charlotte left Göttingen, Robert gave her the bag. In the meantime, he courted Charlotte, and they became close enough that when they returned to the United States, they spent several weeks together in New York City. Robert ushered her around to expensive restaurants, and when Charlotte met his parents at their Upper West Side apartment overlooking the Hudson River, she was surprised at how much they fussed over him. Even though the young couple had grown close, Robert resisted talking about himself and his family. When Charlotte asked about his mother's gloved right hand, she was met with a stony silence. She decided Robert was not ready to commit to a mature relationship.

During the exciting work of the physicists and their shared companionship at Göttingen, storm clouds gathered over Germany. The prolonged economic crisis of the 1920s, the growing demands for radical solutions, and the search for scapegoats for the decline of the once proud nation contributed to a worsening social and political climate. Later, Oppenheimer noted: "Although this society [at the university] was extremely rich and warm and helpful to me, it was parked there in a very miserable German mood . . . bitter, sullen, and, I would say, discontent and angry and with all those ingredients which were later to provide a major disaster. And I felt this very much." The seeds of Nazism and anti-Semitism began to sprout and grow in Germany while Robert lived in the midst of the country.

With his Ph.D. in physics in hand, Oppenheimer sailed to the United States from Liverpool in July 1927. He returned to New

York, having made a name for himself at Göttingen. Several universities sought him, including Harvard and the California Institute of Technology in Pasadena. Additionally, Robert had applied for a postdoctoral fellowship to continue his work in atomic physics and quantum mechanics. The twenty-three-year-old had weathered crises in England, found his calling in Germany, and come home with expertise, self-confidence, and an identity as a brilliant young scientist. Physicists around the world began to read articles by Dr. J. Robert Oppenheimer with interest, and schools courted him to join their physics department. Once back in the States, the West beckoned, and Robert heeded its call.

CHAPTER TWO

Physics Goes West

Science has changed the conditions of man's life. It has
changed its material conditions; by changing them it has
altered our labor and our rest, our power, and the limits of that
power. . . . It has altered the communities in which we live and
cherish, learn and act.

J. Robert Oppenheimer, *Atom and Void*

IN the 1920s, Oppenheimer had found his calling with theoretical physics at the University of Göttingen in Germany. As a
young physicist, he faced many challenges in the coming decade. He would find his teaching style, tackle some of the most
perplexing problems concerning the universe, and help establish theoretical physics as a premier discipline in several universities in California. In the same decade, Oppenheimer grew
into a top-notch physicist who, according to his physicist colleagues, "established the style and pattern of American theoretical physics." He not only advanced humankind's understanding of atomic structure but also trained numerous students
who would help win a future war and alter the course of history.
With his love of the West, Oppenheimer also tilted the balance
of scientific activities westward. This shift continues to the present, as universities and scientific facilities in the western United
States both contribute and, at times, set the pace for the country and the world in their teaching and research concerning
physics. Oppenheimer assisted in creating this paradigm shift.

"I PREFER TO LIVE WHILE I AM ALIVE"

After leaving Germany in 1927 with his Ph.D. in hand, Oppenheimer went to teach and conduct research as a National Re-

search Fellow at Harvard University and the California Institute of Technology. During his time as a postdoctoral fellow in the late 1920s, he began receiving offers of employment from universities — ten in the United States and two in Europe. He eventually chose the University of California at Berkeley, partially because, as he later recalled, it was "a desert. There was no theoretical physics and I thought it would be nice to try and start something." Along with the appointment at Berkeley, Oppenheimer also secured a position at the California Institute of Technology (Caltech) in Pasadena, where he would teach courses in late spring. However, because Oppenheimer had rushed through Harvard, he lacked a solid foundation in mathematical computations necessary for complex physics. Consequently, he asked for a leave even before he began teaching at the California universities to focus on his deficits. The universities granted his request, but then Robert, who had developed a persistent and nagging cough, was diagnosed with tubercolosis. Like millions of tubercular patients before him, Oppenheimer retreated to the healthier air of the desert Southwest, back to the mountains of northern New Mexico, to be cured.

While there, Oppenheimer's friend from the Chaves family, Katherine Page, showed him a cabin for rent high in the mountains. Set at the end of an alpine meadow and surrounded by towering evergreen trees, the rough-hewn cabin had a spectacular view of the surrounding twelve-thousand-foot mountain peaks and distant valleys. The cabin lacked running water and toilets. For roughing it, Robert had found an ideal retreat, and when he heard that he had rented it, he exclaimed, "Hot dog!" He translated that phrase into Spanish and Perro Caliente became the permanent name of the mountain hideaway. Oppenheimer and his brother, Frank, and later their wives, children, and assorted friends and colleagues spent summers at Perro Caliente riding the high country, talking physics, and recovering from their hectic lives at the university. The Oppenheimer family owns the cabin today.

At the end of the summer, an exam of Robert's lungs showed

that even though he had a persistent cough, he did not have tuberculosis. Perhaps he had been misdiagnosed. With a clean bill of health and to make up for lost time, Oppenheimer rushed to Europe. As a Fellow of the International Education Board (IEB), he first went to the University of Leiden in the Netherlands to study with Paul Ehrenfest, a colleague of Albert Einstein. At Leiden, Robert received his nickname: Oppie. The Dutch contracted Oppenheimer to "Opje," with the *j* pronounced like a soft *h*. For the rest of his life, friends and students called him Opje, Oppie, or Oppy, and in surviving letters to him even close friends inquired how to spell his nickname correctly. This confusion about the spelling of his nickname, which he did little to clear up, reinforced his image as a cosmopolitan person with a mysterious name. In the coming years, the multiple spellings reinforced his enigmatic personality.

Once Oppie arrived in the Netherlands, Leiden reminded him more of the proper Cavendish Laboratory than the lively Göttingen. After studying at Leiden, Oppie intended to go to Copenhagen to work with Niels Bohr, but Ehrenfest doubted that Bohr's genial nature would provide the rigorous training in mathematics that Oppie needed. Instead, Ehrenfest sent Oppenheimer to Wolfgang Pauli in Zurich, Switzerland "for more discipline and schooling."

An additional reason to send Oppie to the Alps for the mountain air was his persistent cough which had worsened in the cold damp climate of northern Europe. By this time, Oppenheimer smoked heavily, a habit he had first picked up on the horseback rides in New Mexico. Ehrenfest suggested that the IEB place Oppie under medical care for the cough, but when questioned, Oppie somewhat romantically said, "Rather than take care of the cough, I prefer to live while I am alive." With this live-for-the-moment attitude, Oppie headed to Switzerland and its higher elevations, both in altitude and in physics.

Under Pauli's guidance in Zurich, Oppenheimer cultivated close collaborations with experimental physicists. From discussions about their experiments, Oppie wrote papers that explained the inner workings of the atom. He unraveled the mysteries of some of the characteristics of x-rays and the penetration of the atom by specific types of radiation. The year at Zurich focused Oppenheimer's attention on some of the most fundamental questions of physics. In one of his most important speculations about atomic structure, Oppie suggested that the proton was an independent elementary particle and had to be balanced by its own antiproton.

CALIFORNIA BOUND

In July 1929 Oppenheimer returned to the United States. After having spent three of the last four years in Europe, Oppie would not leave the United States again until after World War II ended, a gap of more than nineteen years. Physics would consume his life for the next decade, and then world events would further control his destiny.

Back in the States, Oppie went straight to Perro Caliente. Frank and other friends joined him, and in addition to recovering his health, Oppie also prepared for his teaching responsibilities at Berkeley, which would begin in August. They rode horses over the high mountains of the Land of Enchantment. Possibly during this trip, they rode through and camped out on the Pajarito (Little Bird) Plateau. About ninety miles west of Perro Caliente, the area lies at eight thousand feet above sea level. Deep canyons cut through the plateau and large ruins of ancient American Indian dwellings are hidden in the canyon bottoms and mesa tops. Amid these ruins and also scattered in unlikely places, pottery shards lie on the ground, a testimony to the people who lived there until the sixteenth century. Riding up and down the steep canyons, over pueblo ruins, and among the forests and wildlife, Oppie and his friends communed with nature and witnessed the remains of ancient civilizations.

At the end of their New Mexican vacation in 1929, Oppie and Frank continued west to California by a road trip that almost ended in disaster. On the way, they came close to rolling their Chrysler roadster over and, another time, accidentally drove up the steps of a courthouse. As often happens on road trips, tempers flared. Frank later recalled, "When I drove up to the edge of the Grand Canyon, [my brother] yelled 'STOP!'" Oppie feared that Frank would plunge them into the gorge. When Robert finally staggered into the Physics Department at Berkeley, his coat sported large holes eaten by battery acid from the car. As bad as the brothers' battered Chrysler looked, it still looked better than Dr. J. Robert Oppenheimer, the new assistant professor of physics.

THE UNIVERSITY OF CALIFORNIA AT BERKELEY

Riding into Berkeley as if he were careening down a mountain on horseback, Oppenheimer's brashness brought theoretical physics west of the Mississippi River with a unique force. In a short time, he established a world-renowned center for the new discipline in the hills above San Francisco Bay and energized the Physics Department at Caltech. At Zurich, Oppie had learned the latest theories and experimental results in the rapidly changing field of atomic physics. At UC Berkeley, he started his own program and within five years had created one of the best theoretical physics departments in the country. The westward tilt of theoretical physics that began with Oppie's arrival in California first changed the academic field of physics and then history itself.

The same year that Oppenheimer arrived at Berkeley, another newly hired scientist in the Physics Department had an inspiration that aided this revolution and inspired Oppie. Dr. Ernest Lawrence, an experimental physicist fresh out of Yale University, developed a machine that hurled various particles of matter at the atom at tremendous speeds to see what would come out of the collisions. Because scientists could not see an atom, they studied what resulted from these bombardments. In a way, atomic physicists conducted experiments similar to smashing a car into another car and then speculating on how cars worked by studying what pieces fell out as a result of the collision. For example, if a carburetor flew out, how did that part help a car go? If a tire bounced out, what role did it play?

Atomic physicists hampered by the invisibility of the atom had to compensate for their blindness by studying what flew out of the high-speed collisions. Like all scientists, Lawrence built on the experiments of others who paved the way with their own atom smashing and paradigm shifts.

During World War I, Nobel Prize–winner Sir Ernest Rutherford had used naturally occurring alpha particles to bombard atoms. During the bombardments, Rutherford observed alpha particles changing direction as they bounced off various materials. He concluded that their directions diverged from straight-line paths because of the electrical repulsion between the particles and the atomic nucleus.

After Rutherford used naturally occurring sources of radiation to explore the structure of the atom, others sought stronger methods to smash particles into atoms. Throughout the 1920s, scientists created laboratory equipment that accomplished this by accelerating particles along linear paths using electrical or magnetic power. Using such an accelerator, one of Rutherford's colleagues, James Chadwick, discovered another component of the atom in 1932. When crashing alpha particles into the atom, Chadwick shook out the neutron, which had the same mass as a proton but without any electrical charge. With this discovery, the basic structure of the atom was set.

Through the experiments in European laboratories during the first part of the twentieth century, theoretical physicists created a model of what the atom's structure looked like. The nucleus at the atom's center held a proton and a neutron. The proton accounted for the positive electrical charge of the nucleus, counterbalanced by the negatively charged electron circling the nucleus. The balanced electrical charge of all atoms, composed of equal numbers of protons and electrons, equals the atomic number of every element. For example, uranium, which has an atomic number of 92, has ninety-two protons and ninety-two electrons. The neutron in a nucleus adds more mass to the atom and accounts for the weight in excess of the atomic number. Thus, uranium has an atomic weight of 238. Although the mass and the weight of the atom reside in the nucleus, the size of an atom comes from the electrons that orbit the nucleus. An atom is ten thousand to one hundred thousand times as large as its tiny nucleus as a result. These discoveries, which began in the late 1910s, resolved some of the anomalies of atomic structure but also created other questions as scientists tried to understand the results of their increasingly sophisticated experiments.

In 1929 Ernest Lawrence at Berkeley revolutionized these experiments by spiraling particles, accelerating them with magnets and electronic boosters, and increasing their speeds beyond those possible with the straight-line accelerators. Once the particles attained a maximum velocity, Lawrence smashed them into different lumps of matter to see what atomic pieces spun out of the crash. The result of these collisions gave him a brief glimpse of the subatomic particles. Lawrence dubbed his new machine the cyclotron.

Over the next decade, Lawrence's cyclotrons provided vital data for theorists like Oppenheimer who speculated on the structure and functions of the atom's various parts. Together, Lawrence's experiments and Oppie's explanations of those results built the department at Berkeley into one of the premier places in the nation to study physics. To be sure, atomic scientists around the country and the world conducted important experiments in those heady days, but the ones at Berkeley and Caltech conducted by Lawrence and analyzed by Oppenheimer played key roles in this scientific revolution.

Despite their close collaboration, Oppie and Lawrence were a mismatched pair. While Oppie was ethereal, cryptic, and cosmopolitan, Lawrence was pragmatic, enthusiastic, and provincial. Lawrence's stout body dwarfed Oppie's slight frame. Lawrence came from a Lutheran family; his parents were schoolteachers in South Dakota. Oppie was a secular Jew from New York City. However, they did share two qualities: both had gifts of keen insight and even intuition that propelled them onto the frontiers of science — Lawrence with his experiments on the cyclotron and Oppie with his insights into the workings of the atom. And both were ambitious.

STRUGGLING AS A NEW PROFESSOR

Oppenheimer's first years teaching in California proved difficult. His lectures often confused his students. He talked too fast, jumped from one subject to another with little advanced warning, and did not react kindly to questions he considered frivolous. German-born theoretical physicist Hans Bethe later commented, "Robert could make people feel they were fools." As an insecure new professor, Oppie sometimes lectured more to confirm that he knew the complex material than to impart the difficult subject matter to his students. He later admitted that during those first few years, he was lecturing to himself.

Among those students who could keep up with him, Oppie gained a loyal following. From his time spent at the European centers of science, his readings of scientific journal articles, and his correspondence with other nuclear physicists, he kept up to date on the latest advances in atomic theory. Robert Serber, one of Oppie's teaching assistants, later observed, "Many facets of Oppenheimer's character contributed to his greatness as a teacher: his great capacity as a physicist, his wide intellectual interests, his astonishing quickness of mind, his great gift for expression, his sensitive perception, his social presence, which made him the center of every gathering." For those who entered his inner circle, Oppie's wide range of interests integrated science, art, literature, and religion. Once accepted into that fellowship, students were intellectually stimulated with diverse topics, invited to Oppie's house for parties, treated to dinners at expensive restaurants, and influenced by his charismatic personality.

Two years after Oppie arrived at Berkeley, in the middle of the fall term, he had to rush back to New York. His mother's health, which had declined over the summer, had worsened. At the beginning of October, Oppie rode the train across the country and went to her bedside. On October 17, 1931, Ella Friedman Oppenheimer died. Her final words to Robert were: "Yes — California." After her death, Oppenheimer declared, "I am the loneliest man in the world." For the remaining six years of their father's life, Oppie and Frank had him spend winters with them in California.

By the mid-1930s, the University of California at Berkeley attracted national attention as it became a center for the advanced studies of physics. Robert Serber is an example of this. He had planned on going to Princeton as a National Research Fellow after he received his Ph.D. in physics from Wisconsin. But at a summer institute in Michigan, he met Oppenheimer, who made such a deep impression on him that he changed his mind. As Serber later recalled: "I went to Berkeley in 1934 and when I got there I discovered that three of the five people who had won National Research Fellowships were students of Oppenheimer's at Berkeley. . . . That was an extraordinary center of theoretical physics. It was the first great one that existed in this country, the one that Oppenheimer had created for his students." Within his first five years in California, Oppie had transformed the Physics Department at Berkeley and, along with Lawrence, had established a national reputation that attracted men and women from around the country. This quick establishment of Berkeley as a national center illustrates Oppenheimer's success in tilting the center of physics westward. In the 1930s, led by Oppie, Lawrence, and others, California moved into the forefront of the fast-paced world of nuclear physics. Victor Weisskopf, who was at Göttingen University at the same time as Oppenheimer and later played a leading role in the development of atomic weapons, commented about Berkeley in the 1930s that "Oppenheimer and his group were completely on par with European physics."

Oppie's personality had such a powerful influence on people that his students even began imitating him. One of them, Robert Wilson, remembered: "So all of his students would come, in their grey suits and blue shirts and blue ties. . . . They would say, 'Ja, ja,' the way Oppie did. He had just come back from Germany and he affected a German mode, he'd say 'ja, ja,' and all the students would say that, and they would all walk with their feet splayed out. It was fantastic how they emulated Oppie." Some students even copied the way Oppie smoked his cigarettes, flicking the ash off with their little fingers. In those days, professors and students smoked during classes.

Ed Gerjuoy, who attended Berkeley as a graduate student in physics from 1938 to 1942, recalled Oppie's teaching style. Oppie always came to class well prepared, never gave final exams or any other tests, and assigned numerous homework problems that he graded himself. Oppie never assigned reading in textbooks, mainly because they did not contain the latest theories. His lectures outpaced the textbooks, as he explained the newly formulated and still-developing theories about quantum mechanics and atomic structure. He lectured each class at high speed and scribbled equations on a chalkboard, also at high speed. To understand these lectures, Gerjuoy rewrote his hastily jotted notes as soon after class as he could. Despite the lack of a text and Oppie's rapid delivery of material, Gerjuoy admitted, "I undoubtedly learned far more physics from each of Oppenheimer's courses than I did from any of the other graduate courses I took."

Some students, however, did not. One commented: "I did not like Oppenheimer as a teacher. . . . He was unaware, I think, of how little the students were understanding what he was talking about. As you know, he never gave any examinations and so he never knew how much students learned." For those graduate students who kept up with Oppie, grasping his rapid-fire lectures gave them a foundation for tackling the complicated issues of nuclear physics.

Oppenheimer contributed even more to the education of his students outside the classroom. One student recalled that "when you took questions to him, he would spend hours — until midnight perhaps — exploring every angle with you. At that personal level he was an excellent teacher although he always overestimated what others knew or could learn." Oppie also held daily sessions with his graduate students. Each afternoon, they would cram into an office, sit on chairs, tables, even the floor, and wait until Oppie strode in. Each would describe the status of his or her research problem, and the group would discuss possible solutions. Oppie's assistant, Robert Serber, recalled: "All were exposed to a broad range of topics. Oppenheimer was interested in everything, and one subject after another was introduced and coexisted with all of the others." After advising all the students on how to proceed, Oppie left. Then Serber had to "explain to each what Oppie had told them to do." This daily grilling exposed students to a wide range of topics and sharpened their ability to think under pressure as well as to come up with innovative ways to solve problems.

Oppie also interacted with his students on a more informal basis. He held parties at his house and treated his students to dinners after seminars or meetings. The parties at his house entailed eating spicy food, including one Indian dish nicknamed the "Nasty Gory." Oppie also mixed a strong martini. Some participants later recalled that there was more drink than food at these gatherings, and if one were not used to spicy cuisine, one would grab a martini in the mistaken belief that it would help wash down the fiery food.

Through these formal and informal sessions, Oppie took his inner circle of graduate students to the frontiers of atomic theory and, through curricular and extracurricular contexts, challenged them to grapple with the latest experiments or respond to the newest theories on how the atom worked. During this time, he wrote his brother: "The work is fine. . . . There are lots of eager students, and we are busy studying nuclei and neutrons and disintegrations; trying to make some peace between the inadequate theory and the absurd revolutionary experiments. . . . We have been running a nuclear seminar, in addition to the usual ones, trying to make some order out of the great chaos, not getting very far with that." Despite his doubts, Oppie taught his students the latest in the rapidly changing fields of nuclear physics and quantum mechanics.

OPPENHEIMER'S NUCLEAR RESEARCH

Although Oppenheimer took his teaching duties seriously, his main scientific focus in the 1930s revolved around making order out of the chaos of nuclear physics. Using the experimental data coming from Lawrence's cyclotron, which was the largest in the nation at the time, Oppie helped revolutionize the field of atomic physics. He made significant discoveries in two areas at the opposite ends of the physical world: one concerning the infinitesimal parts of the atom and the other dealing with cosmic rays that emanate from the nuclear combustion of stars.

Delving into the mysteries of the atom, Oppie, with his colleagues and students, tackled some of the anomalies that arose from the frontier of atomic theories. As experimental physicists discovered more sophisticated ways to shake up the atom and dislodge its intimate particles, theorists like Oppenheimer explained what happened as these particles mysteriously appeared and disappeared and as high energies transformed the basic structures of nature. Theorists investigated the results of the experiments, questioned the explanations of other theorists, and arrived at their own understandings of the workings of the atom. During such scientific revolutions, conflicting explanations can pit scientists against each other, and arguing about what happened can become a blood sport.

For example, Paul Dirac, a respected theorist with whom Oppie worked at Göttingen, speculated that an imbalance of energy in atoms came from the protons in the nucleus. Oppie disagreed and speculated that whatever created the imbalance had to have the same mass as electrons. This opened the door for Carl D. Anderson to discover the positron in 1932, an achievement for which he won the Nobel Prize in 1936. A positron is an antimatter electron. It has the same mass as an electron but the opposite electrical charge. Offering explanations that other scientists debate and either accept or reject is how credible theories emerge in times of revolutionary change. It also is a way to make enemies.

Another puzzling phenomenon that Oppie helped explain was the occurrence of electron showers that came from outer space. Cosmic rays burst from the sun as part of the naturally occurring solar nuclear reaction that showers the earth. Composed of protons, electrons, and gamma rays, cosmic rays are fast moving and invisible to the eye. When they enter the earth's atmosphere, they collide with atoms in the air and "showers" occur. In the 1930s, physicists explored the different types of showers. Oppie and his colleagues at Berkeley and Caltech developed an elegant theory that explained most of the observations. Their theory remains credible to this day. This work gave rise to the discovery of "mu mesons." Key components in radiation, mu mesons are heavy electrons with a half-life of only one microsecond.

While investigating the physics of stellar phenomena in outer space, Oppenheimer was also one of the earliest physicists to work on what would later be known as black holes. Black holes are collapsed stars with such an intense gravitational field that everything, including light, is pulled into their centers. If Oppie had continued this research into cosmic theory, some colleagues have suggested that he might have won a Nobel Prize in Physics for the work.

Others, however, have expressed doubt about Oppenheimer's ability as a scientist. Edwin McMillan, who worked with Ernest Lawrence and succeeded him as director of what is now the Lawrence Berkeley Laboratory, recalled that Oppenheimer worked "in darts and spurts, you know. He was somewhat intuitional. He rarely worked anything out in the way Bethe did. He rarely would carry through a long detailed calculation." Throughout Oppenheimer's career, some associates maintained he did not have the mathematical expertise to be a really good physicist.

To recover from his hectic teaching schedule and research activities as well as his dual appointment at two prestigious universities, Oppie retreated to his ranch in New Mexico every summer during the 1930s. Accompanied by Frank, scientific colleagues, and an assortment of friends, he would rest in nearby Santa Fe for a few days to acclimate to the higher elevation as well as to prepare for roughing it at Perro Caliente. Staying at the renowned La Fonda hotel on the plaza in Santa Fe, they gathered supplies for the mountain retreat, which had neither electricity nor indoor plumbing. From the Perro Caliente base, they launched excursions by horse and by car into the mountains and deserts of the Southwest. They rented horses for camping trips over the high mountain peaks and passes and into the back country. They drove to ceremonial dances at the American Indian pueblos along the Rio Grande. While in New Mexico, they sometimes worked on physics problems and laid the foundation for future research. The combination of the high altitude, rugged outdoor activities, lack of modern amenities, good company, and stiff martinis renewed Oppie.

THE GREAT DEPRESSION

As Oppie helped explain the inner workings of the atom in the 1930s, he lived in a world that struggled to cope with the worst economic disaster in modern history. In the same year that he joined the faculty at Berkeley, the Great Depression struck and devastated the United States and many other countries. The stock market crash in October 1929 started a vicious cycle of bank failures, business closings, and severe unemployment. From 1929 until the early 1940s, the Great Depression destroyed the financial well-being of the United States. Thousands of banks closed; 25 percent of all Americans were out of work, with another 25 percent underemployed. As grim as these statistics sound, however, they are misleading. A man selling pencils or apples on a street corner was counted as employed.

When thousands of banks started failing in 1929, all the money held in them disappeared. Overnight, people discovered that the money in their checking and savings accounts was gone, leaving many without their lifelong savings as well as their latest paycheck. Additionally, some people continued to work but were not paid. Teachers in Chicago did not receive salaries even though they still taught. The city had run out of money to pay them. Many of these teachers lost their homes because they could not keep up with their mortgage payments.

The rapidity of the financial collapse caught most people by surprise. The trigger of the Great Depression, the stock market crash, wiped out the fortunes of those who had invested in stocks. Even though only 10 percent of Americans played the stock market, the crash aggravated an already weak economy. So by March 1930, within six months of the crash, the country had fallen into a troubling state of individual economic suffering. The federal government did little to alleviate the hardship, and consequently, a growing number of protests and strikes erupted into societal chaos.

In Oppenheimer's home state of California, agricultural wages fell by more than 50 percent. As a result, in 1933 alone, fifty thousand farmworkers went on strike. In 1934, longshoremen at California's ports walked off the job to protest how men were chosen for the work groups and over limiting the workday to fifteen hours. The conflict grew, and soon, all along the West Coast, labor strife prevented ships from being loaded and unloaded. By mid-May, more than thirty-four thousand maritime workers had gone on strike. The *San Francisco Examiner* reported that on May 16, not a single freighter had left a Pacific Coast port. Tensions escalated into a full-fledged riot in San Francisco in July with running battles between police and the strikers. After two men died from police gunshot wounds and thirty others were injured, the National Guard arrived to restore order. Teaching in the San Francisco Bay area, Oppie had to know of this labor unrest.

In the chaos and turmoil of the Great Depression, the right and left-wings of the nation's political and economic forces battled against each other, sometimes in the negotiating rooms and sometimes on the streets. The left-wing, with its advocacy for the working class, often had the support of the Communist Party (CP). As the domestic economic crisis grew and as fascists began goose stepping across Europe, communism seemed for many people to offer an alternative to the financial disaster and political turmoil. Consequently, university students and their professors began joining the CP in the United States to work on ways to alleviate the suffering of the Great Depression and to counter the fascist tide in Europe.

Coming from a wealthy family, Oppie was insulated from the Great Depression, and in truth, he barely felt the impact. He later claimed that he learned of the crash on Wall Street only six months after the fact while on a walk with Ernest Lawrence. As Oppie scrambled in the 1930s to find his teaching style, work with graduate students, and unravel the mysteries of the atom, he at first could ignore the financial meltdown that swirled around him. He finally became concerned when his graduate students could not secure employment because of the Depression. In response, he became politically active in left-wing causes. Some of his friends and even family members became Communist Party members.

OPPENHEIMER AND THE COMMUNIST PARTY

The suffering and agony of those without jobs who could not provide for themselves or their families struck some people as an indictment against the capitalistic system. During the first part of the Great Depression, the federal government did not help those in need. It offered no social security, no unemployment benefits, no welfare payments, no safety net for those who had lost everything. Once Franklin Delano Roosevelt became president in 1933, he instituted the New Deal, which provided jobs and support for many Americans. In addition to the New Deal, other alternatives to the crumbling capitalist system arose as people advocated fascist or communist methods of dealing with the economic crisis. In Germany, many embraced fascism. With fascism, the national government joined with corporations to run the country, ruled by a single political party like the National Socialist Party (Nazis) in Germany. In fact, Adolf Hitler took over the national government of Germany in the same month that Franklin Roosevelt became president of the United States. Some people advocated for a fascist solution to alleviate U.S. suffering, as well.

At the same time, others turned to communism to fix the broken economic machine. Particularly for those in colleges and universities across the United States, communism offered a hope for correcting the nation's economic ills. Communism called for a system in which individuals could not own private property. The state owned the resources of the country for all. As explained by German philosopher Karl Marx in his books on communism, in capitalistic societies, workers produce wealth through their labors, but owners accumulate the wealth by exploiting the workers. Ideally, then, a communist state would create a workers' utopia where wealth is evenly distributed to the workers, those who created the wealth.

In the 1930s, communism and fascism's political and economic systems opposed each other. Beginning with the Spanish Civil War in 1936, communist forces fought against the rising fascist tide in Europe. In the late 1930s, the communist opposition in Germany, Spain, and Italy seemed the only strong challenge to the fascists in those countries. Seeing the communists fight the fascists in Spain and listening to their promises of a new economic system that would abolish the suffering of the Great Depression, people across the United States supported the Communist Party. Some even worked to bring about the end of capitalism in the United States.

The Bay Area, with its large working class at the docks and elsewhere, had strong unions that supported communist causes such as workers' rights and the Loyalists' fight against the fascists in the Spanish Civil War. Surrounded by failing businesses, destitute neighbors, and worldwide fascist military aggression, Oppie experienced a social and political awakening as the Great Depression dragged on.

In addition to his political awakening, Oppenheimer also grew concerned about Germany's surging anti-Semitism, which he had first witnessed as a graduate student in Göttingen. In 1934, he pledged 3 percent of his annual salary to support the scientists (many of them Jewish) who sought refuge in the United States from the fascists. In 1937, Oppie and Frank helped rescue their father's younger sister, Hedwig Stern, her son Alfred, and his family from Nazi persecution in Germany.

Unfortunately, Julius, Oppie's father, died only days before his relatives landed in New York. Consequently, the German relatives moved to Berkeley, and lived close to Oppie's home.

Oppie's growing activism against the nation's economic woes and the rise of fascism led him to support left-wing and communist organizations. He found like-minded colleagues among the faculty at Berkeley. In 1936 Oppie met Jean Tatlock at a benefit for the Spanish Loyalists organized by his landlady. Jean, the daughter of a professor of medieval literature at Berkeley, was working on her doctorate in psychology at Stanford. They began a tempestuous romance that lasted three years. Twice during that time they almost married. She was tall and slender with green eyes and auburn hair, and her combination of beauty and intelligence entranced Oppie. Some of Oppie's students said that she had a humanizing effect on him. She introduced him to the poetry of John Donne.

Jean also introduced Oppie to communism. She rebelled against her father's well-known right-wing politics and actively worked for several left-wing organizations at Berkeley, including the Communist Party. Through her, Oppie met people who fervently believed in communism and who strived to create a workers' utopia in the United States. The couple's tumultuous relationship, complicated by Jean's bouts of depression and Oppie's intellectual impatience and ineptness with women, ended in 1939. This first long-term adult liaison and his increasing confidence as a professor helped Oppie overcome the social awkwardness that had plagued him since childhood.

Another person who changed the course of Oppie's life also became a close friend of his during this time. In 1937, Haakon Chevalier, a professor of French literature at Berkeley, met Oppenheimer at a benefit for the Spanish Loyalists. Haakon, born in New Jersey to parents of Norwegian and French descent, embraced life with a passion. As a young man, he served as a deckhand on a four-masted schooner that sailed around the world. In the early 1930s, he traveled to New York and Paris and, while in France, became attracted to communism. As a new professor at Berkeley, he attended Bay Area CP meetings and raised money for the Spanish Loyalists, for California farm-workers, and for other left-wing causes.

Oppie and Haakon shared many interests. Together with Jean, they raised money to buy an ambulance that they sent to the Loyalists in Spain. The two men founded a Berkeley branch of the American Federation of Teachers. In 1940, they wrote and distributed two editions of *Report to Our Colleagues*, a newsletter that supported the CP's position to keep the United States out of the European war. By that time, Germany and the Soviet Union had signed a mutual nonaggression pact so that the Nazis could focus on conquering western Europe. The *Report to Our Colleagues* complained of President Roosevelt's growing support for the Allied nations as a way to preserve the old order in Europe "with the wealth and lives of this country." The second *Report* strongly stated, "There has never been a clearer issue than that of keeping this country out of the war in Europe." In the late 1930s, the conversation at Oppie's dinners and parties with his friends and students shifted away from physics and toward politics and world affairs.

During this period of intensifying emotions about the growing war in Europe, Oppie and Haakon began holding meetings with other professors and labor organizers to discuss politics. Later, the two men had very different memories of what happened at those meetings. Oppie claimed the group consisted of naive people who innocently and informally met at one another's houses to discuss current events and politics. Haakon disagreed, and years later called the group a "closed unit," a clandestine cell of the CP for professionals who wanted to keep their party membership secret. Whatever the purpose of these meetings, they would come up later to cast doubt on Oppie's loyalty to the United States and eventually help to destroy his life.

Oppie's attendance at left-wing meetings attracted the interest of the Federal Bureau of Investigation. Through its surveillance of the various CP meetings and fund-raisers in the Bay Area, the FBI started to build a file on J. Robert Oppenheimer. Notorious for its suspicion of progressive causes and left-wing organizations, the FBI in the 1930s and early 1940s actively investigated individuals around the country for their liberal political views. Oppie first came to the FBI's attention in the fall of 1940 when he attended a meeting at Haakon's house. Others at that meeting included William Schneiderman, secretary of the Thirteenth District of the CP of California, and Isaac Falkoff, a financial supporter of the party in the Bay Area. Because Oppie attended the meeting, the FBI began watching him and in March 1941 put him on a national list for "custodial detention . . . in the event of a national emergency." That spring of 1941 was about the same time that Oppenheimer began his work that led to the creation of the atomic bomb.

Oppenheimer had familial company in his support of left-wing causes. In addition to Jean Tatlock and Haakon Chevalier, Oppie's brother, Frank, grew active in left-wing causes. In 1936, Frank married Jacquenette (Jackie) Quann, partly against Oppie's wishes. Jackie, majoring in economics at Berkeley at the time, was also active in the Young Communist League. Although in later years Frank described his joining the CP as more of a lark than a strong political commitment, he and Jackie did work on party activities like organizing and performing at a benefit concert for Spain and putting together a rally to racially integrate a municipal swimming pool in Pasadena. Oppie, who attended that rally, later called it a "pathetic" demonstration. In the politically charged climate of the late 1930s and early 1940s, Oppie, his brother and sister-in-law, their friends, and colleagues searched for answers to the economic crisis of the Depression and the growing threat of fascism. They found their answers in liberal causes, sometimes championed by the Communist Party of the United States.

OPPIE STARTS A FAMILY

During this heady period of camaraderie in the fight against the Great Depression and fascism, Oppie found his future wife. Not long after he broke up with Jean, Oppie met Katherine (Kitty) Puening Ramseyer Dallet Harrison in Pasadena. Kitty, born in Germany in 1910, had moved with her family to Pittsburg at the age of two. In the early thirties, Kitty went to universities in France and Germany and witnessed Hitler's rise to power firsthand. In 1932, she married Frank Ramseyer in Europe, a musician who she quickly discovered was a drug addict and a homosexual. She divorced him within the year. When Kitty returned to the States for Christmas in 1933, she met Joe Dallet, a dashing Communist organizer of the steel mills around Pittsburg. Joe came from a wealthy family and had attended Dartmouth College. Like Oppie, he did not come from a working-class background. Kitty and Joe married and moved to Youngstown, Ohio, where they lived in poverty with Gus Hall, a future leader of the CP in the United States.

Married to a man dedicated to the communist cause, Kitty's life overflowed with meetings, organizing drives, and comrades passing through her home in Youngstown. Kitty joined the Communist Party herself. With her dark hair and a radiant smile, the petite and vivacious woman helped Joe with his union organizing and work with the legions of unemployed in the Ohio Valley. She also supported his difficult decision to volunteer as a member of the Abraham Lincoln Brigade to fight against Gen. Francisco Franco and the fascists in Spain.

Once in Spain, Joe served as the political commissar for his unit. On the night before the Battle of Saragossa, Abe Osher-off, a soldier who served under Joe, along with some other soldiers "raked him over the coals" for his authoritarian leader-ship style. The next day, he tried to rescue a fallen comrade on the field of combat, perhaps to counter the complaints made against him the night before. Joe died in the field, felled by fascist machine-gun fire. In Paris, Kitty was ready to join Joe in Spain, where she planned on driving ambulances. Just before she left on the dangerous journey to the front, a friend, Steve Nelson, intercepted her. Steve told Kitty that Joe had died and spent some time with her as she grieved. Kitty returned to the States, stayed with Steve and his wife in New York for a while, and then went back to school at the University of Pennsylvania. Steve would resurface several years later and again change Kitty's life — as well as Oppie's.

Sitting next to his mother, Ella, Robert had an intensity even at this early age. Notice Ella's glove, which hides an early prosthetic device. *(Courtesy of J. Robert Oppenheimer Memorial Committee)*

Four-year-old Robert posed with his father, Julius Oppenheimer, in August 1906. *(Courtesy of J. Robert Oppenheimer Memorial Committee)*

Robert sits by his younger brother, Frank, who was born in 1912, in this 1915 portrait. *(Courtesy of J. Robert Oppenheimer Memorial Committee)*

In 1939, Katherine (Kitty) Puening Ramseyer Dallet Harrison fell in love with Oppie. They married on November 1, 1940. *(Courtesy of J. Robert Oppenheimer Memorial Committee)*

In their backyard in Berkeley in 1942, Oppie feeds Peter, who was born in May 1941. *(Courtesy of J. Robert Oppenheimer Memorial Committee)*

At the university, Kitty met Richard Stewart Harrison, an older man from Great Britain who was a physician and medical researcher. Offering her stability, Harrison married Kitty, and they moved to Southern California. Kitty later admitted that the marriage was "unsuccessful from the start." In August 1939, while at a garden party thrown by a professor from Caltech, she met Oppie. She later recalled, "I fell in love with Robert that first day, but hoped to conceal it." Nonetheless, their relationship quickly blossomed into an affair that scandalized the community, and the next summer, she traveled to Oppie's ranch in New Mexico without her husband. In the fall of 1940, she went to Nevada for a month to establish residency so she could receive a quick divorce from Stewart. On November 1, the same day she received her divorce, Kitty married Oppie. She was already pregnant and gave birth to Peter in May 1941. They nicknamed him "Pronto" due to his speedy arrival after their marriage.

The brilliant physicist and the widow of an anti-fascist war hero found many common interests. Both were cosmopolitan, having lived in the 1920s and 1930s in Europe. Both supported communism and actively worked to fight fascism and alleviate the sufferings caused by the Depression. And like Oppie's earlier comment about his persistent cough, both preferred to live while they were alive.

They bought a house at 1 Eagle Hill Road in the foothills above Berkeley and began to raise their young son, Peter. Steve Nelson, who had comforted Kitty in Paris, had left the East Coast and was now serving as a CP organizer in the Bay Area. He reconnected with Kitty, brought his young family to the Eagle Hill house for picnics, and grew to know Oppie. Soon, Oppie began giving money to Steve for CP matters, like fighting fascism and aiding California's migrant workers.

Some of Oppie's family and friends found themselves unwelcome at 1 Eagle Hill. Frank's wife, Jackie, had few kind words about Oppie's new wife: "Kitty was a schemer. If Kitty wanted anything, she would always get it. . . . She was a phoney. All her political convictions were phoney, all her ideas were borrowed. Honestly, she's one of the few really evil people I've known in my life." Some felt that Kitty had seduced Oppie as part of a scheme to marry him. Others felt that his running off with another man's wife showed that he was just as human as everyone else. Despite others' reservations, this marriage — Kitty's fourth and Oppie's first — lasted for the rest of their lives, through their crushing responsibilities during World War II and the vicious public attacks and humiliations afterward.

By the time he married Kitty in November of 1940, Oppenheimer's scientific path had also changed. In January 1939, Danish physicist and Nobel Prize–winner Niels Bohr burst into a conference Oppie was attending in Washington, D.C., and announced that two German scientists had split the atom. This announcement ignited the imaginations of the gathered scientists, who quickly speculated on both civilian and military uses of the new form of energy. Most of the scientists also voiced fear about how the Nazis might use the revolutionary discovery. The first atomic arms race had begun.

CHAPTER THREE

Chasing the Atom

When the time is run, and that future becomes history, it will
be clear how little of it we today foresaw or could foresee.
                                    J. Robert Oppenheimer, *Atom and Void*

FOR Niels Bohr to attend the Washington conference, he had
to steam across the Atlantic on an ocean liner, disembark in
New York City, and then take a train down to the nation's
capital. People who traveled between Europe and the United
States in the late 1930s took a week to sail across the Atlantic.
This long ocean voyage allowed Bohr to think through many of
the consequences of the Germans splitting the atom. Lounging
in his stateroom without the ordinary distractions that can oc-
cupy a Nobel Prize–winning physicist, Bohr thought about the
implications of atomic energy and weapons. By the time his
ship nudged into its berth in New York, Bohr had a lot to talk
about at the physicists' conference.

Oppie also headed to the conference, although for him to get
to Washington, D.C., he took trains from the West Coast. In the
1930s, commercial air travel was still in its infancy, so traveling
across the United States took three to four days on trains that
rocketed at speeds of up to seventy miles per hour. The trip might
have been on a new luxurious streamliner, the railroad companies'
response to the decline in riders due to the Great Depression and
private automobiles. These sleek trains had comfortable sleeping
cabins, formal dining cars, and domed observation cars. Due to
the days of travel necessary to cross the country, Oppie, like Bohr,
had time to leisurely think and read. Colleagues from the West
Coast also joined him on parts of the trip for animated discussions, and concentrated periods of intense problem solving occurred in their smoke-filled sleeping cabins.

THE GERMANS SPLIT THE ATOM

The Germans who split the atom had built on the experiments and theories of previous physicists. By the turn of the twentieth century, scientists were exploring how to shake up the atom. During the 1930s, experiments in England, France, Italy, Germany, and other countries began unraveling the atom's secrets. James Chadwick in England discovered the neutron in 1932. Irène and Jean-Frédéric Joliot-Curie (the daughter and son-in-law of the famous physicists Pierre and Marie Curie) unleashed artificial radiation in 1934. That same year, Italian Enrico Fermi bombarded uranium with neutrons and produced several different artificially radioactive elements. He won the Nobel Prize in Physics in 1938 for this work.

As Germany invaded its neighboring countries, research in atomic energy quickly progressed at its universities. In Nazi Berlin in 1938, physicists Fritz Strassmann and Otto Hahn bombarded a lump of uranium with neutrons. The uranium broke down into a different element, barium, with a release of a substantial quantity of energy in the form of heat. Befuddled by these results, Strassmann and Hahn sent a letter describing the experiment to Lise Meitner, a colleague of theirs who had fled her shared laboratory with Hahn in Berlin because she was Jewish. On Christmas Eve 1938, Meitner and her nephew, Otto Frisch, sat on a stump in the snowy woods of southern Sweden and discussed the puzzling experimental result.

To their astonishment, Meitner and Frisch realized that Strassmann and Hahn had split the atom. They had no word in physics to describe the event so they borrowed "fission," a word from biology, to explain what had happened. Fission is the splitting apart of an organism into two distinct units. At the time, no one knew how to pronounce the verb, so "to fission" was pronounced like "to fishing."

Frisch returned to the Institute for Theoretical Physics in Copenhagen after Christmas and told Niels Bohr (who had won the Nobel Prize for his theory on atomic structure) about their explanation of the Berlin experiment. Bohr at once grasped the meaning and interrupted Frisch, exclaiming: "Oh what idiots we have all been! Oh but this is wonderful! This is just as it must be!" Bohr then crossed the Atlantic to attend the scientific conference in Washington, D.C., where he spread the news of the successful fission experiment conducted in Nazi Germany. Word spread like wildfire through the atomic physics community, and scientists on both sides of the Atlantic began speculating, first on the process of splitting the atom and then on whether they could make an atomic bomb as a result. If Germany obtained such a revolutionary weapon first, many feared that the Third Reich might indeed rule for a thousand years, as Hitler intended.

Scientists rushed back to their laboratories around the world to confirm the experiment. In a letter to *Nature* magazine in the spring of 1939, the Joliot-Curies reported that every split atom produced 3.5 neutrons. A chain reaction then occurred when neutrons released from divided atoms hit and fissioned more atoms, throwing off even more neutrons. If a lump of uranium were bombarded so that its atoms broke apart and released more and more neutrons, a potent explosion could result.

THE ALLIES CHASE THE BOMB

During the first seminar back at Berkeley after the Washington meeting, one of Oppenheimer's fellow professors, Glenn Seaborg, noted, "I do not recall ever seeing Oppie so stimulated and so full of ideas." This excitement, coupled with anxiety about the Nazi discovery, fueled a rush of experiments and speculation. With the Germans ahead of everyone else in atomic research, concern grew about whether they were pursuing creation of an atomic bomb. Hungarian physicist Leo Szilard, a refugee living in the United States, persuaded Albert Einstein to appeal to President Franklin D. Roosevelt and to alert him of the Nazi threat. The August 2, 1939, letter warned FDR: "It may become possible to set up a nuclear chain reaction in a large mass of uranium, by which vast amounts of power and large quantities of new radium-like elements would be generated. . . . It is conceivable — though much less certain — that extremely powerful bombs of a new type may be constructed." After reading the letter, Roosevelt ordered the U.S. government to support atomic research, and an Advisory Committee on Uranium formed to coordinate research. Later, Einstein deeply regretted his action, which set in motion the United States' pursuit of making an atomic bomb. Despite Roosevelt's order and the creation of the Uranium Committee, the United States did little for the next two years.

Lack of funds and an obsession with secrecy hampered the work. Some of the members of the original Advisory Committee on Uranium did not even know they were working on creating an atomic bomb. Dr. Sam Allison from the University of Chicago recalled: "We weren't told. I thought we were making a power source for submarines." Money to conduct the research also was scarce. From the fall of 1939 to the fall of 1941, the United States government spent only fifty thousand dollars on atomic bomb research.

On the other side of the Atlantic, the British put their atomic physicists together with refugee scientists fleeing the Axis countries and created the top-secret "Tube Alloys" project to aggressively pursue the atomic bomb. Disappointed with lackluster American progress, the British sent several physicists to the United States to try to inspire their counterparts in July 1941. They met with Ernest Lawrence, Oppenheimer's colleague at Berkeley, who was receptive to their arguments that the Germans posed a real threat in securing an atomic weapon.

Lawrence persuaded James Conant, the senior scientist connected with the Advisory Committee on Uranium, to reorganize the committee and press for greater progress. Allied with Vannevar Bush, President Roosevelt's key scientific adviser, Conant met with FDR at the beginning of October 1941 to convince him that the Germans were making great strides in creating an atom bomb. Spurred by this information, the president authorized more support for the U.S. effort. Part of the motivation involved preparing for America's entry into the war, but Bush and Conant had a farther-reaching goal — they wanted the United States to emerge from the conflict as a superpower for the rest of the twentieth century. They sought to create the American Century, a Pax Americana to replace the Pax Britannica Britain had in the nineteenth century. An atomic weapon and a perpetual source of power fueled by the atom would ensure postwar domination by the United States and speed the creation of the American Century.

As a result of the growing interest in an atomic weapon, the Advisory Committee on Uranium (code-named the S-1 Committee) reorganized to coordinate atomic weapons research. Part of this research occurred at Berkeley, where Lawrence converted his cyclotron from experimental work and began producing larger quantities of uranium for atomic bomb research. Still, the amount of uranium that Lawrence produced only fit on the head of a pin. Lawrence also began recruiting his colleagues to weapons work. In October 1941, he arranged for Oppenheimer to accompany him to a secret meeting at the General Electric headquarters in Schenectady, New York. Oppie provided the calculations on how much enriched uranium would be needed for an atomic weapon. Using these figures, the meeting attendees concluded that "a fission bomb of superlatively destructive power would result from assembling quickly a sufficient mass of Uranium-235."

Uranium occurs naturally in a yellow-tinged earth that crumbles easily. Such uranium ore provides the raw material for atomic bombs but, as found in nature, remains unsuitable for making a weapon. The nuclear material in the yellow earth contains several forms of uranium — mainly uranium-238 (U-238), with only a trace amount of the isotope uranium-235 (U-235). An isotope is a slightly different form of an element, in which the number of protons in the nucleus is the same, but the number of neutrons is different. To trigger an atomic explosion, uranium-235 proves more unstable and thus, easier to fission; however, this isotope is only found in less than one percent of naturally occurring ore. Thus, uranium ore has to be processed to extract the U-235, a difficult process that "enriches" it into weapons-grade nuclear material.

WORLD WAR II ERUPTS

Most people in the United States knew that the country would enter the war sooner or later. Governmental agencies, businesses, universities, and individuals all geared up for the impending conflict. In the 1930s, the Axis powers of Japan, Germany, and Italy had invaded neighboring countries, beginning with Japan's attack on China in 1933. In September 1939, Germany invaded and quickly defeated Poland. In April 1940, German soldiers stomped through Denmark and Norway. Denmark's king surrendered immediately, while the Norwegians resisted for a month. Then the Nazis turned south and west. During that summer, the blitzkrieg swept through Belgium and the Netherlands and then slammed into France. To the surprise of many, the German military accomplished in 1940 what its predecessor in World War I was unable to do — it conquered France quickly. By June, France had fallen. The rapid defeat of first Scandinavia, then the Low Countries, and finally France shocked the rest of the world. Could anything stop Germany's military machine? For Britain, the answer was vital since Germany's air force had started attacking England.

As German bombers destroyed English cities, scientists working at British laboratories struggled to make an atomic bomb. Their Tube Alloys project gathered physicists from England's elite universities as well as refugees from Germany and Italy. As the Battle of Britain escalated and a possible invasion of the islands loomed, pressure intensified to move the atomic research to the safe shores of the United States. Exchanges between Britain and the United States also fostered greater cooperation on building the bomb, and refugee scientists sometimes found work at American universities involved in such weapons research. For example, Enrico Fermi took his family to Sweden to accept the Nobel Prize in 1938 and, since his wife was Jewish, did not return to Fascist Italy. First at Columbia University in New York City, then at the University of Chicago, Fermi conducted nuclear experiments and initiated the first controlled chain reaction in December 1942 on the south side of Chicago. Although some of the émigré scientists found work in the United States, many were unemployed until the United States entered the war.

OPPENHEIMER JOINS THE BOMB TEAM

Throughout the fall of 1941, Oppie attended more and more meetings and conferences concerning atomic weapons. Because of his participation at the October meeting in Schenectady, Oppie won the appointment to head the "fast neutron" research undertaken at Berkeley that took a closer look at how uranium fissioned. In May 1942, a vacancy on the S-1 Committee allowed Oppenheimer to join the group and contribute at the highest levels in the collaboration between the governmental and university researchers.

By the time that Oppie joined S-1, the United States had entered World War II. On December 7, 1941, Japan launched a surprise attack on one of the key U.S. naval ports in the Pacific. At Pearl Harbor in Hawaii, two waves of Japanese planes flying off of aircraft carriers sunk eight battleships, three light cruisers, and three destroyers, and smashed 292 American airplanes. Within minutes, the attack killed 2,403 Americans and wounded another 1,178. The only good news that came from Hawaii that day was the fate of the nation's aircraft carriers, which were out on maneuvers and thus escaped the surprise attack. The next day, President Roosevelt asked Congress for a declaration of war against Japan, which quickly passed. On December 11, Germany declared war against the United States, and the potential nuclear rivals lined up against each other.

The United States entered the war scrambling to mobilize its soldiers and war matériel and also searching for new weapons to counter the successes of the formidable militaries of Germany and Japan. From his early involvement in weapons discussions in 1941 to his selection as the director of a yet-to-be-created central laboratory in October 1942, Oppenheimer grew to become a de facto leader of the theoretical work conducted around the country. He started coordinating atomic bomb research in May 1942, and by June, Oppie and John Manley, who became a key experimental physicist on Oppie's team, were organizing atomic weapons research in at least nine university laboratories spread around the country. That summer, Oppenheimer invited a small number of scientists to a seminar at Berkeley to discuss various paths to take in building a bomb. The scientists grappled with estimating how much nuclear material they needed in order to create an explosive chain reaction, how to initiate such a reaction, and how much destruction such an explosion would wreak.

Part of the theoretical team at the summer session was Dr. Edward Teller. A brilliant nuclear physicist born in Hungary who had been educated at universities around Europe, Teller latched onto the idea of a more powerful bomb than one that used fission. In 1941, Edwin McMillan and Glenn Seaborg had discovered a new man-made element, which they named plutonium, as a by-product in a nuclear reactor while working at Lawrence's cyclotron. Plutonium offered promising characteristics for weapons work, and during the summer retreat, Teller argued that a fusion bomb using plutonium would fuse elements together. He proposed that a fusion bomb—as opposed to a fission weapon, in which atoms split apart—could possibly produce an even more powerful detonation. From that point on, Teller became obsessed with the idea of creating a fusion bomb. This started a decade of competition and conflict between Teller and Oppenheimer that altered the course of the Atomic Age and culminated with Oppie's downfall in 1954.

One of the issues explored at the summer seminar was the difficulty of conducting research at universities and laboratories scattered around the country. Oppenheimer wrote Robert Bacher at the Massachusetts Institute of Technology: "It seems certain that on some of the projects which are being pursued simultaneously along parallel lines in more than one laboratory, we shall want to get together the people involved for a critical discussion at not too infrequent levels." With work conducted at the scattered labs, colleagues could not easily discuss their top-secret research or share the results of their experiments and theories over the phone or in letters. Thus, progress occurred in fits and starts.

As the massive scope of the effort to build an atomic bomb solidified from the fuzzy calculations of Oppie and others, senior scientific advisers Vannevar Bush and James Conant scrambled to keep the project on track. They had heavy responsibilities beyond the creation of atomic weapons. On June 14, 1940, President Roosevelt had created the National Defense Research Committee (NDRC) with Bush as director. A year and a half before the United States entered the war, Bush began organizing the civilian research projects undertaken around the country to come up with new weapons and defense systems. These innovations—like the proximity fuse, radar, and the atomic bomb—brought technology on board to fight for the Allies. The advances helped wrench the balance of power away from the Axis militaries and helped the Allies defeat the fascists in Europe and Asia.

THE MANHATTAN PROJECT

Bush and Conant realized that they could not handle all of the details in developing the atomic bomb. So they turned to the U.S. Army. In June 1942, the Army Corps of Engineers established the Manhattan Engineer District (MED) to oversee the development of the atomic bomb. The MED's first military commander, Col. James Marshall, had his office in Manhattan, thus the initiative's code name, the Manhattan Project. As a colonel, Marshall had little success in acquiring scarce matériel in a war-rationed country. He also was slow in picking locations for the various facilities and in choosing the civilian director for a central laboratory. To succeed, the Manhattan Project needed a new commanding officer.

On September 16, 1942, Col. Leslie R. Groves discovered that he would replace Marshall as head of the Manhattan Project. He later recalled, "I was probably the angriest officer in the United States Army." As deputy chief of construction for the entire army, Groves had just finished overseeing the building of

the Pentagon. He felt he had earned a combat assignment overseas and wanted to get away from Washington. He also knew
enough about the bomb project to doubt whether it would
actually produce a usable weapon. He feared that those associated with such a colossal potential failure would put their careers in jeopardy. Nonetheless, a quick promotion to brigadier
general helped persuade him to take over the floundering Manhattan Project.

Groves stood almost six feet tall, with blue eyes sparkling
above his heavy jowls. He weighed more than two hundred and
fifty pounds and had uniforms specially tailored to camouflage
his ample waist. Born in Albany, New York, in 1896, he graduated from the University of Washington in 1914, studied engineering at MIT for two years, and then went to West Point,
where he graduated fourth in his class. Groves got difficult jobs
done. Kenneth Nichols, who served under Groves in the Manhattan Project, remembered him as "the biggest sonovabitch
I've ever met in my life, but also one of the most capable. He
had an ego second to none, he had tireless energy—he was a
big man, a heavy man but he never seemed to tire. He had
absolute confidence in his decisions and he was absolutely ruthless in how he approached a problem to get it done. . . . I hated
his guts and so did everybody else but we had our form of
understanding." The mutual understanding among those working with Groves centered on completing their task.

A decisive administrator, Groves was just what the Manhattan Project needed. Even before his appointment became official, Groves addressed one of the major obstacles that had hob-
bled Marshall. Beset by wartime shortages, Marshall had been
unable to get the highest priority rating, AAA, for the Manhattan Project. To obtain the supplies necessary for operating the
MED's far-flung facilities, Groves wrote a letter granting the
project AAA priority. He then walked it over to Donald M.
Nelson, chairman of the War Production Board, and had Nelson sign it. AAA priority meant the MED could obtain whatever
it needed in goods and services in a country racked by war
shortages and rationing. For example, to build the massive mag-

nets to separate the uranium isotopes and enrich uranium ore, the Oak Ridge, Tennessee, plant needed metal wiring. Copper—a key component of bullets, artillery shells, and other munitions—was scarce, so the MED borrowed fifty-three tons of silver, worth $300 million, from the U.S. Treasury to make the wire. In 1949, the silver was returned to its rightful place in the treasury. Groves quickly approved locations for the uranium-enrichment plant at Oak Ridge and a plutonium-producing nuclear reactor at Richland, Washington; and a plan to create a central laboratory to research and develop an atomic bomb. To choose the central laboratory's director and location, Groves turned to the West.

THE MANHATTAN PROJECT MOVES WEST

The Western mystique fascinated Groves. Since his father had been an army chaplain, Groves had lived on posts established during the American Indian Wars in the nineteenth century. He later recalled: "Here I came to know many of the old soldiers and scouts who had devoted their active lives to winning the West. . . . I grew somewhat dismayed, wondering what was left for me to do now that the West was won. . . . Yet those of us who saw the dawn of the Atomic Age . . . will never hold such doubts again. We know now that when man is willing to make the effort, he is capable of accomplishing virtually anything." The lure of the West—of opportunity, innovation, and invention—made the region seem like a good match for the location of the Manhattan Project's central laboratory as well as the place to find the civilian director to run that facility.

Groves had to pick the civilian director even before a place could be chosen for the lab. Groves prided himself on his ability to quickly gauge a person's character and abilities. Taking command of the Manhattan Engineer District in mid-September, he acquainted himself with all aspects of the project and traveled around the country to the various university laboratories, meeting the scientists and seeing their experiments. While touring the Berkeley facilities, Groves had lunch with Oppenheimer on October 8, 1942, when they talked about the type of central laboratory needed in order for scientists to design and build an atomic bomb. Oppie argued that the lab needed to be in an isolated area, away from urban areas, so the scientists could freely exchange the results of their work. Oppenheimer impressed Groves, who invited Oppie to join him several days later on a train ride from Chicago to Detroit. In a cramped sleeper room as the train sped east, Groves, Oppie, and various military and scientific people expanded on Oppie's ideas about where and how to create a central laboratory. By the time Oppie left the general in Detroit, the basic plan for the lab was set.

As Groves rocketed across the country on trains and even scarce airplanes, the Manhattan Project picked up speed. Groves had learned enough about the project and had met enough of the key people to begin breaking up the logjam that had stymied Marshall. He now started making momentous decisions. Only three weeks after meeting Oppie, Groves picked him as the civilian director of the yet-to-be-constructed central laboratory. Few people in both the scientific and the military establishments agreed with Groves's choice. More prominent scientists, some with Nobel Prizes, had been considered and rejected by Groves. Oppie had little administrative experience since he had not even headed an academic department prior to his appointment by Groves. He also was a theoretical physicist, and some feared he would flounder in the experimental work of creating an atomic bomb.

As serious as those concerns were, the security officers in the military had even graver worries. Since his support for the Communist Party in the late 1930s, Oppenheimer had attracted the attention of agents at the FBI. Now that he was involved with the atomic bomb project, the FBI's interest sharpened. When the FBI warned against using Oppie as a security risk, Groves told the agents to cease their investigation because "the Army has a full time technical and physical surveillance on him." The military was bugging his phones and tailing him wherever he went. Citing Oppie's FBI file, which detailed his left-wing activities and Communist connections, Army Intelligence refused to grant him security clearance for months. In fact, Groves had to directly order the reluctant army security forces to grant Oppenheimer top-secret clearance in July 1943, nine months after he had picked Oppie to direct the lab.

Why then, did Groves go against the scientific community, the FBI, and his own security officers to choose this unlikely candidate for the most important civilian post in all of the Manhattan Engineer District? As with other parts of Oppie's life, no one factor completely answers this mystery. Groves trusted his own instincts about people and saw in Oppie someone who was younger and hungrier than a more senior scientist. A hungrier person would work harder to accomplish something than a more accomplished person. So Groves picked Oppie at least partly because of Oppie's "overweening ambition." A successful Manhattan Project would gain Oppie the recognition that had so far eluded him. Groves also liked Oppie's quick mind and ability to synthesize complex concepts. On the train ride from Chicago to Detroit on October 15, Oppie had patiently answered all of Groves's questions, giving him a basic tutorial in nuclear physics, and showed the general the brilliance that impressed those who came into contact with him. Somewhere west of Detroit, Groves offered Oppie the directorship of the lab. Bush and Conant knew Oppie well, and even though they initially argued with Groves about his choice, they eventually agreed with him. With such powerful people behind the scene as supporters, Oppie won the position as director.

The strongest opposition to Oppenheimer's selection was Groves's own security personnel. Did Oppie impress Groves so much that he ignored the Communist connections? By 1942, the Soviet Union and the United States were allies, so did Groves dismiss the security implications because both countries were fighting on the same side? Or in a Machiavellian way, did Groves want someone who had a skeleton in his closet, so he could better control him? In 1954, Groves told a board that then sought to revoke Oppie's security that the scientist already knew everything about the bomb project and that he thought it was better to keep such a person on the job and under surveillance than to expel him where he could spread his knowledge around. Groves remembered, "In all my inquiries, I was unable to find anyone else who was available who I felt could do the job." Oppie later immodestly commented about his selection as director that Groves "had a fatal weakness for good men." In 1942, however, Oppie later admitted that he felt "worried." "This was before the turn of the war," he said. "The nature of the job was only part known, the nature of the technical job, the rather odd conditions under which we were to live and work in the hope of keeping things secret. . . . Some doubts as to my fitness for getting it done made me worried, also; I had then as I've had throughout the whole thing—I am not completely free of a sense of guilt. I was also very excited to do fast and well what had to be done and very eager to get going." For better or for worse, Oppenheimer began directing the new lab.

THE MANHATTAN PROJECT LANDS IN NEW MEXICO

The disjointed locations of the laboratories around the country prevented the far-flung scientists from fully talking about their work with each other. The need for a central laboratory where scientists could collaborate and freely discuss their research became obvious by the summer of 1942. Once Groves assumed command of the Manhattan Project in September, he pushed for selecting the location of that lab. On November 16, he met Oppenheimer and several MED officers at Jemez Springs, New Mexico, to consider the town for the lab's site; however, Jemez Springs fell far short of the criteria for the lab. At the bottom of a steep canyon, Jemez Springs could not expand readily enough to accommodate all the planned buildings. Oppie thought the place was too gloomy, and Groves saw that security forces would have a difficult time patrolling the cliffs towering above the town. He muttered, "This will never do." As the party mulled over the deficiencies of Jemez Springs, Oppenheimer suggested that they drive to an isolated boys' school forty miles to the northeast, on the eastern side of the Jemez Mountains.

The military convoy bumped along the dirt road that climbed up the southern flank of the mountain range and across Valle Grande, the vast caldera of a once-massive volcano. Descending the eastern slopes of the mountain range, the staff cars drove onto the Pajarito Plateau and stopped outside of the Los Alamos Ranch School, named after the cottonwoods that grew in the area. Founded in the 1910s as an exclusive boarding school for the sons of wealthy families from the East and Midwest, the Ranch School followed Teddy Roosevelt's philosophy of toughening up young men with strenuous outdoor activity. Students wore shorts all year long and had to remain outdoors for several hours each afternoon, even during the bitterly cold winters. As Oppenheimer, Groves, and the others evaluated the site, a light snow fell on the boys playing hockey on the iced-over pond in shorts and knee-high woolen socks.

Even though Los Alamos did not fit the selection criteria for the lab's location, Oppie wanted the site. He had lamented in the 1930s that it was a pity he could not combine two of the loves of his life — physics and New Mexico. Los Alamos fulfilled his dream. Despite Oppie's strong endorsement, the difficulties of the location — like its lack of water, limited electrical capacity, and the dangerous roads up the cliffs to Los Alamos — made it an unlikely candidate for a scientific laboratory. Groves, however, found the isolation attractive, with the plateau easily secured by patrols, and most of the land nearby was already owned by the federal government. Acquisition of the Ranch School site would help in quickly taking possession of the place. Back in Santa Fe that evening, over a steak dinner at La Fonda hotel, Oppie insisted on picking Los Alamos. Groves eventually agreed. The atomic bomb project was already behind schedule in choosing the central laboratory site, so Groves took quick action.

In early December, on the one-year anniversary of the bombing of Pearl Harbor, the army sent a letter to the Los Alamos Ranch School condemning the property and giving the educators until the beginning of February to complete the school year and leave the plateau. Even before the boys left and the

school closed its doors, bulldozers started leveling the landscape. Contractors started pouring foundations for the laboratory buildings, even though some were not yet fully designed.
Los Alamos became a U.S. Army post, built just for the war's
duration with only one purpose — to create an atomic bomb.

A BROTHERHOOD OF SCIENTISTS

At first, Oppie naively thought that only a few people would be
needed to do the work at the lab. In May 1942, he wrote Lawrence: "What we should need is a total of three experienced men
and perhaps an equal number of younger ones. . . . I would think
that any two of these [distinguished physicists] working with
me could get the job done in good order." Quickly though,
Oppie realized that he needed more personnel — indeed, quite a
lot more. So he began an aggressive campaign to recruit the
scientists necessary to create an atomic bomb. He crisscrossed
the country, persuading top scientists to drop whatever work
they were doing and to commit themselves for the duration of
the war to his project. Until they agreed to join the project,
Oppenheimer could not tell them exactly what they would work
on; however, most knew of Oppie's recent work with the S-1
Committee and assumed they would assist with an atomic
bomb project. Oppie not only took scientists away from their
universities but he also scavenged scarce laboratory equipment
from those same institutions.

To persuade sometimes-reluctant scientists, Oppenheimer
argued passionately and convincingly about the importance of
the work. His colleague, I. I. Rabi, remembered, "Almost everyone realized that this was a great undertaking . . . the culmination of three centuries of physics." Although history has
proved Rabi right, at the time, Oppie did not agree with Rabi.
He wrote: "To me, it is primarily the development in time of
war of a military weapon of some consequence. . . . I am asking
that you use [your] influence to persuade [other scientists] to
come." Oppie talked about the vital role that their efforts would
play in winning the war. The promise of destiny, the crucial war

work, and the brotherhood of scientists all proved powerful incentives for recruiting personnel to drop their own projects and travel to a distant and isolated mountain in the West.

In addition to such enticements, Oppie used the lure of the West to attract scientists. He could not mention in his recruitment the location of Los Alamos, but he did say that the laboratory lay in a beautiful location, isolated in the mountains of the West. He hinted at an idyllic setting, a scientific utopia where scientists and their families could contribute to winning the war. Physicist Victor Weisskopf recalled: "There was this element of pioneering, of the first ones, we felt like the maybe twenty-five or thirty young physicists all rough and nobody older than forty you know, rather younger. There was a tremendous atmosphere of adventure in the whole thing." Not everyone Oppie approached joined him, since some scientists balked at Groves's demands.

Originally, Groves wanted to enlist all the scientists into the military. Oppie had even ordered an army uniform to go along with his anticipated rank of lieutenant colonel; however, several colleagues argued that at that rank, he would be too low on the military hierarchy to get much accomplished. They also reminded Oppie that scientists might not come to Los Alamos if they could not bring their families with them. This was a common prohibition in the military. So Oppenheimer argued on behalf of his colleagues, and Groves relented on militarizing the laboratory. Personnel brought their spouses and children, and the character of Los Alamos changed from a stark army post to a town with schools, churches, maternity wards, and other facilities necessary for accommodating married couples and raising children.

Another one of Groves's ideas also hindered the scientists. Most top-secret and military operations dictate a compartmentalization of information, which allows only those who need to know something access to that information. From the beginning, Groves demanded compartmentalization at the laboratory. Oppenheimer argued that scientists grappling with the complex issues of harnessing the power of the atom for a weapon had to know what else was going on around the lab. Problems and solutions in one part of the lab could impact and even speed along work going on elsewhere. Oppie fought against the compartmentalization of information at Los Alamos and eventually won, although Groves and Army Intelligence at the lab never fully accepted the loosening of security restrictions.

Groves did arrange for the University of California to operate Los Alamos. For academic scientists and engineers, this installed a familiar system and helped to smooth over the army's rough edges. The University of California also provided valuable organizational and fiscal expertise. From filling payrolls to ordering scientific equipment to hiding the huge amounts of money funneled to Los Alamos, the university proved essential to the success of Los Alamos. To this day, the university still comanages the operation of Los Alamos National Laboratory for the Department of Energy.

LIFE ON THE HILL

To assist newcomers at Los Alamos, Oppenheimer hired Dorothy McKibben to operate an office in Santa Fe. He had met her during the winter of 1943 in the lobby of La Fonda hotel in downtown Santa Fe. She opened a small office at 109 East Palace Avenue, the official address for the lab given to people coming from around the country. Some of these travel-weary people stumbled into Dorothy's office expecting a posting in Santa Fe for the duration of the war. Instead, she gently directed them to the last forty miles of their journey and issued them temporary passes for the front gate at Los Alamos. For the rest of the war, 109 East Palace was a haven for day-trippers from Los Alamos who got off buses at that address, dropped off their purchases from Santa Fe stores there, stopped by for an encouraging chat with Dorothy, and then stepped back on a bus for the return trip back up to "the Hill."

The secrecy of the project resulted in code names for places, things, and even people. Army Intelligence forbade anyone from using "Los Alamos" in his or her communiqués, so many called it the Hill. The official code name for the laboratory in New Mexico was Site Y and for the facilities in Tennessee, Y-12, X-10, and K-25. Nuclear physicists with easily recognizable names such as Niels Bohr and Enrico Fermi became Nicholas Baker and Eugene Farmer. Fermi's wife, Laura, spent a frustrating time at the train station outside of Santa Fe waiting for someone to pick her up. She did not know that the driver calling for a "Mrs. Farmer" was her ride. Oppenheimer became James Oberhelm and Edward Teller, Ed Tilden. A certain playfulness also surfaced with the choice of some code names. "Physicist" and "chemist" were replaced by "fizzler" and "stinker." Secrecy even extended to official state documents. Children born on the Hill had the post office box for Los Alamos — P.O. Box 1663 — as the place of birth on their birth certificate.

Beginning at the end of February 1943, men, women, and their children started flooding into Los Alamos. They came by train from Chicago, New York, and California. They drove from Arizona, Colorado, and the Midwest. Scientists came and technicians, too. Plumbers, carpenters, and truck drivers also arrived. The military ordered soldiers to go to Los Alamos to provide security, assistance, surveillance, technical support, and weapons expertise. Some of the workers only had to travel from nearby Hispanic villages or American Indian pueblos. However they got there, all flocked to Los Alamos to work in the war effort. Some went to change history, others to devote themselves to winning the war, and still others to earn a good wage in a poverty-stricken part of the country. Whatever the reason, the rush to Los Alamos created a crush of people at Site Y.

The modern pioneers found that the Hill lacked many common comforts. Senior personnel, like Oppie, resided in the old log cabins that had housed the teachers at the Ranch School. For the rest, lodging was primitive, with some newcomers crowding into dorms or trailers, while others lived in tents at the nearby Bandelier National Monument. On some Saturday nights, from tents and trailers as well as apartments and houses, elegantly attired couples walked through the muddy streets past rows of drying laundry to have dinner with world-renowned scientists. After the dessert at some of these dinners, Otto Frisch or Edward Teller played classical piano to end the evening.

As they all assembled at Los Alamos throughout the spring of 1943, person by person, family by family, they created a unique community of Nobel Prize winners, military men and women, engineers, émigré scientists, maintenance workers, truck drivers — all the people necessary to support a scientific laboratory. Los Alamos mushroomed during the war. By the fall of 1945, approximately five thousand men, women, and children lived on the Hill. About two thousand of them worked in the lab, and the rest raised children, went to the post's commissary, attended school, and found releases from the pressure of living at the center of the bomb project.

FAT MAN AND LITTLE BOY

To brief all the scientists on their mission, Oppie, John Manley, and others planned to hold a meeting on the Hill. In addition to inviting the scientists already at Los Alamos, Oppie sent a letter to Enrico Fermi, who had yet to join the central lab, asking him to attend: "The purpose of the conference is to discuss the scientific problems of the Los Alamos laboratory and to define its schedules and its detailed experimental program. The background of our work is so complicated, and information in the past has been so highly compartmentalized, that it seems that we shall have a good deal to gain from a leisurely and thorough discussion." Fermi declined to join the bomb team at Los Alamos at that time.

In April 1943, the scientific staff members gathered at the laboratory's unfinished library for their orientation. The meeting, led by Robert Serber, one of Oppie's top assistants from Berkeley, laid out for the first time the scope of the work. Serber's first sentence told all: "The object of the project is to produce a practical military weapon in the form of a bomb." Serber briefed everyone in the room about the ideas on how to build an atomic bomb that came from the previous summer's meeting in Berkeley and discussed the work accomplished in the various laboratories since then. The scientists' effort to create a weapon would follow two paths. Each path centered on the nuclear material available—uranium for one type of bomb, plutonium for the other. Neither of these materials was available in sizable quantities at the time. Nonetheless, Serber predicted that they would need thirty-three pounds of enriched uranium or eleven pounds of plutonium for a single bomb. These lectures were eventually published as *The Los Alamos Primer*.

One of the biggest challenges of the Manhattan Project— and one outside of Oppie's control—involved the production of this enriched uranium and plutonium necessary for creating a weapon. Eventually, enormous manufacturing plants at Oak Ridge, Tennessee, and Hanford, Washington, produced the uranium and plutonium for the bombs. The first delivery to Los Alamos of plutonium from Hanford arrived in April 1944, but in the spring of 1943, Oppenheimer and the others at Site Y did not know which radioactive element would be ready in time for their bomb. They also did not know what technological difficulties might derail their creation of an atomic weapon. So they followed several different paths to build a bomb.

During Serber's lectures, he freely mentioned the words "atomic bomb." Oppie, concerned about the workmen still swarming around the building to finish it, advised Serber to switch to code when talking about the bomb. From then on, scientists spoke of the "Gadget" when they referred to the weapon. Eventually, other code names for the bomb included "Fat Man" and "Little Boy"—Fat Man for the plutonium model and Little Boy for the uranium weapon.

The two models for a potential atomic bomb utilized radically different techniques to create a critical mass and a chain reaction. Little Boy, the simpler bomb, looked like a conventional bomb, only elongated. This model—also referred to as the gun assembly method—sought to shoot a plug of enriched uranium (U-235) like a bullet from one end of the device into a larger mass of the same material at the other end. When the two masses of uranium collided, the scientists hoped that an explosion would occur.

A plutonium bomb proved more technologically challenging. Calculations showed that plutonium would "fissile" if shot like a bullet — that is, if used in a gun assembly-type weapon, it would detonate early without a chain reaction and the precious material would scatter. So an alternative method of detonating plutonium had to be discovered, one that would not blow the material apart before it could go critical. This method, called implosion, surrounded a grapefruit-sized core of plutonium with a sphere of conventional explosives. The conventional explosives, when detonated, would direct a shock wave inward and compress the plutonium core until neutrons began splitting atoms, throwing off stray neutrons, and starting a chain reaction. If part of the shock wave hit the core a millisecond sooner than the rest, it would blow the plutonium apart before an atomic explosion occurred. Fat Man attracted scientists at the laboratory with what Oppenheimer called a "technologically sweet" problem. In an example of complementarity, Oppie and his lab pursued both of these paths to create a viable atomic weapon.

THE WORK INSIDE THE LAB

For months after assuming the directorship of the lab, Oppenheimer resisted establishing an official organizational structure. Finally, after being badgered by several of his close associates, he threw a piece of paper with an organizational chart at John Manley. The chart organized the widely different fields and functions of the laboratory into four divisions to work on the many difficulties in creating a nuclear weapon. The four divisions and their directors — Experimental (Robert Bacher), Theoretical (Hans Bethe), Chemistry and Metallurgy (Cyril Smith and Joseph Kennedy), and Ordnance (Navy Capt. William Parsons) — tackled the myriad of problems and created a few of their own.

One of these problems haunted Oppie off and on for the next decade and eventually contributed to his security clearance revocation. Edward Teller, who had participated in the summer seminar at Berkeley that laid the foundation for the work on atomic weapons, had joined the project at Los Alamos. He wanted to serve as the head of the Theoretical Division instead of Hans Bethe. Disappointed that Oppenheimer did not pick him and also frustrated that Oppie did not devote the lab to pursuing the Super (or hydrogen bomb), Teller caused problems for Oppie throughout the entire war. Norris Bradbury, who replaced Oppie as director after the war, commented that "Oppie picked Bethe I think correctly, but it's a tough choice. Edward, of course, fought with Oppie constantly." To satisfy Teller and to counter his disruptive presence, Oppie eventually assigned Teller to work solely on the Super, even though it contributed little to the creation of "a practical military weapon" — the MED's mission — by war's end. Teller's animosity and competition drove him to continue to oppose Oppenheimer in future years and then to testify against him during hearings in 1954.

As the civilian director at Los Alamos, Oppie played an indispensable role in creating the atomic bomb. He managed the prima donna scientists, the no-nonsense military officers, the governmental bureaucrats, the laboratory's technocrats, and the town's maintenance workers so that almost everyone worked long hours, six and sometimes seven days a week. Led by Oppenheimer, they sacrificed and did whatever was needed to invent an atomic bomb. Oppie knew all aspects of the theoretical and experimental progress at the lab and integrated the work from one division with that of another. He directed his charm and quick wit to encourage each individual's work at Los Alamos. When people talked with Oppie about their part of the project, they felt that they were the center of this unique and exciting universe, and most came away from their discussions inspired to continue to work hard to achieve success. Hans Bethe, leader of the Theoretical Division, recalled: "He was our leader. It was clear to all of us, whenever he spoke, that he knew everything that was important to know about the technical problems of the laboratory, and he somehow had it well organized in his head. He was not domineering, he never dictated what should be done. He brought out the best in all of us, like a good host with his guests. And because he clearly did his job very well, in a matter all could see, we all strove to do our job as best we could." According to people like Bethe, the bomb might not have been built without Oppenheimer.

Oppie's management style helped ensure the success of the laboratory. When asked to describe his leadership, Norris Bradbury replied that it "must have been Oppie's best." "I don't think anyone believed he had it in him, but he surely did," Bradbury said. "He knew what was going on everywhere, could ask about it, did ask about it, could keep people working in the same line, even keep Edward in line, a little bit. Damndest bunch of prima donnas in the world. . . . I would say a large fraction of the things that I did [as subsequent director of the lab] I copied from him: no compartmentalization, colloquia, staff member meetings, keeping people informed. All these ideas I swiped from him." Even to this day, the morning seminars at Los Alamos National Laboratory begin at 8:15, the time set by Oppenheimer during the Manhattan Project.

DIFFICULTIES IN THE BOMB PROJECT

Many issues surfaced to challenge the successful creation of an atomic bomb. Manufacturing the necessary amount of fissionable material — the thirty-three pounds of enriched uranium or eleven pounds of plutonium for a single weapon — forced Groves to enlist some of the largest corporations in the country to operate the processing plants at Oak Ridge and Hanford. Over the course of the war, the Manhattan Project employed more than two hundred thousand people at all of its facilities and spent approximately $2 billion to build atomic weapons. The majority of the people and money went to making enriched uranium and plutonium. Despite this enormous industrial effort (which rivaled the automotive industry's production of military vehicles), usable quantities of bomb-grade material came slowly to Los Alamos. Scientists depended on estimates backed by dense calculations to determine how uranium and plutonium would behave in a nuclear reaction. The key question rested on how much of this material would be needed for a critical mass to be reached, for a chain reaction, and for a resultant massive explosion.

The serious lack of fissionable material hindered Los Alamos's research. Over the first year or so, scientists stumbled down the two paths toward a workable nuclear weapon. Out of the conflicting views and chaotic opinions on how to create a bomb, Norris Bradbury stated, "There was one great thing that Oppie said about the wartime program: 'Never pick a course of action unless it's a course of action which has the highest probability of success and the least chance of having some unsuspected difficulty turn up.'" Although progress came in jumps and starts, Oppenheimer picked the two paths — Fat Man and Little Boy — that seemed to him to have the best prospects for success.

The instant city at Los Alamos stumbled over other difficulties along the path to creating the bomb. On frontiers throughout history, cities have popped up in the boom and bust cycles of gold rushes, colonizing efforts, and industrial enterprises. At Los Alamos, the crush of personnel and their families strained the ability of the post to carry out its mission. On the one hand, the army could not build residential facilities fast enough to accommodate all of the people streaming to the Hill. The early pioneers at Los Alamos first found temporary housing at nearby ranches and then moved to dormitories, multiple-unit family dwellings, and trailer parks as the population expanded to get the job done. The throng of people taxed the town's utilities such as electricity, water, and sewage treatment. On the other hand, the overcrowding also affected the schools and recreational facilities at Los Alamos. If these difficulties did not present enough of a distraction to the bomb-making efforts, additional conflicts emerged that Oppenheimer had to manage.

"AS IT WAS, WE HAD A VERY GOOD TIME"

Despite the idyllic setting in the pristine mountains of northern New Mexico, the isolation, the security restrictions, the pressure of the work at the lab, and the army's control of the post took a toll on the town's residents. Rings of fences surrounded Los Alamos. The Tech Area, where the scientific offices and laboratories lay, was surrounded by tight security with tall fences and military police controlling access to prevent anyone without proper clearance from entering. The residential area, which encompassed the Tech Area like an oyster shell around a pearl, was similarly fenced. Only people with security passes could come and go from the residential part of Los Alamos. Even young children had to have passes to get into and out of the town. Caught between the fences, the tension of living in a top-secret community acted like a pressure cooker on some residents. They found traditional and nontraditional ways to release their anxieties and frustration.

Although the work in the Tech Area totally engaged the mainly male scientists and engineers, living at Los Alamos proved difficult for many of the families on the Hill. The wives of the Tech Area personnel often felt marginalized at Los Alamos since they were isolated in the instant city and unable to follow their own interests. Many women did work at the labs, assisting with the experiments, serving as human number crunchers, filling in as secretaries, or teaching in the town's school. They also worked hard to invent a community that nurtured their families.

Unlike at many army posts during the war, husbands and wives lived together, and a resultant baby boom occurred, which put further strains on the town's facilities. Groves demanded that Oppie say something to his scientists about this. Oppie declined, stating that it was not his job. At the time,

Kitty was pregnant with their second child. Consequently, a limerick swept the town:

The General's in a stew
He trusted you and you
He thought you'd be scientific
Instead you're just prolific
And what is he to do?

The baby boom at the maternity ward in Los Alamos continued throughout the war.

Immersed in the serious work of building an atomic bomb, perhaps even because of it, residents of Site Y sought ways to escape the stress. They took advantage of outdoor activities like hiking, skiing, and horseback riding. People went to one of the two theaters to watch the latest movies or a play. During a local drama production of *Arsenic and Old Lace*, Oppenheimer delighted the audience when he appeared as the first corpse, followed by other corpses played by Nobel Prize–winner Enrico Fermi, theoretical physicist Hans Bethe, and other men prominent in the Tech Area.

One of the most popular forms of release from the tension and stress of Site Y was to attend parties. As Eleanor Jette recalled, "The pioneers of the new and frightening era escaped their tasks with hard play whenever opportunity offered itself, which was every Saturday night and Sunday." On the Hill, dormitory residents cleared out the furniture from their common rooms, mimeographed invitations, and with alcohol brought in from Santa Fe, mixed a potent punch in bowls borrowed from the Tech Area. As Bernice Brode recalled: "On Saturdays, we raised whoopie. . . . There was always too many people, too much noise, and too much liquor." Jean Bacher, wife of Robert Bacher (who had helped persuade Oppenheimer not to militarize the scientists), later wrote: "Our parties and athletic activities were a healthy escape from the nervous strain of the great Project in which we were involved. Without this release in alcohol and fresh air we would have gone mad.

As it was, we had a very good time." Partygoers at Los Alamos could not always get away from the seriousness of their work, though. As Elsie McMillan remembered, "We had parties, yes, once in a while, and I've never drunk so much as there at the few parties because you had to let off steam, you had to let off this feeling eating your soul, oh God, are we doing right?"

Not everyone on the Hill knew the true purpose of the Manhattan Project. For those who did, some — like Elsie McMillan — voiced misgivings about the moral implications of what they were doing. Oppenheimer himself expressed some doubts. In the fall of 1942, he wrote to Manley about John coming to Los Alamos from Chicago: "I think it will be easy to get you out of that mad house . . . but I am afraid that what you will be getting into will be a good deal worse; at least a good deal grimmer." As scientists worked in their laboratories at Los Alamos, as they lay awake at night thinking about the day's experiments, these scientists also questioned whether they could play God with the fundamental elements of the universe, especially if the result were a single bomb that destroyed an entire city. During the war, only one person, Joseph Rotblat, ever left Los Alamos on moral grounds, but the grim task of creating a weapon that could release destruction on an unprecedented scale did weigh heavily on some people at Site Y.

As the Tech Area and the residents of Los Alamos struggled through its first summer in 1943, Oppenheimer took a trip to the Bay Area to consult with Lawrence and the other scientists at Berkeley. While there, the army placed him under physical surveillance. Army Intelligence agents followed him to his meetings at the university and then tailed him to an old friend's house that evening. In fact, the army agents waited outside of Jean Tatlock's apartment all night for Oppie. He did not come out until the next morning.

CHAPTER FOUR

The Grim Work of the Lab

It did not take atomic weapons to make wars, or to make wars terrible, or to make wars total.

J. Robert Oppenheimer, The Open Mind

FOR the federal agents chasing Oppie, his liaison with a former lover and Communist Party member confirmed that he was a security risk at best and a spy at worst. As for Oppenheimer, he later said that Tatlock had appealed to him while suffering from a deep depression and that he visited her as a concerned friend. Nonetheless, the alarm raised by Oppie's visit with Tatlock turned into a full-blown security emergency on Oppie's next trip to the Bay Area. The alarm began with a comment by Oppie that continues to mystify atomic historians and to haunt his legacy. He told army security personnel about a possible breach in security within the Manhattan Project.

OPPIE WARNS OF SPIES IN THE PROJECT

Returning to the Bay Area later that summer of 1943, Oppie casually mentioned to Lyall Johnson, an army security officer, that if the army were concerned about Communist espionage, it should investigate an engineer by the name of George Eltenton. Johnson immediately called Lt. Col. Boris Pash, the army's expert in the Bay Area on Soviet spies. Boris's expertise came from his experience during the Russian Civil War from 1918 to 1920, when he fought against the Russian Communists. As soon as Pash heard about Oppie's curious comment on August 25, he rushed to interview him. Pash also arranged for an army technician to secretly tape-record the conversation from an office next door.

Oppie told Pash a disturbing tale. He said that several months earlier, a person had approached him who said that if Oppenheimer wanted to let the Soviets know about any top-secret research going on at the university in Berkeley, another person could pass along such information. Oppie told Pash that his response to this inquiry was that he had no problem with the U.S. president passing along such information, but he did not support "having it moved out the back door." He then mentioned to Pash that the contact person approached three other people with similar offers. Oppie named George Eltenton as the person who could transfer the information to the Soviet consulate in San Francisco, but he refused to name the other people involved. He naively claimed that since all three had rejected the invitation and since the contact person had acted in good faith and was a close friend of his, no one had done any harm.

Silently, Pash strongly disagreed. Without letting Oppie know of his alarm, Boris pressed Oppie for the names, but Oppie continued to refuse to give them. He assured Pash that the real person to watch was Eltenton, not the others. That evening, Pash rushed a transcript of the forty-five-minute conversation to General Groves. Army Intelligence then began searching for these mysterious people, two of whom Oppie said had gone to Los Alamos, and the third of whom was destined for Oak Ridge. With Oppie's admission that someone had tried to recruit atomic scientists as informants, Army Intelligence scrambled to counter the threat that Soviet spies might have already infiltrated the Manhattan Project.

In early September, Groves and Lt. Col. John Lansdale (Pash's boss at the Pentagon) shared a sleeping compartment with Oppenheimer on an eastbound train. Somewhere east of Cheyenne, Wyoming, they reopened the investigation, but Oppie again declined to name names. He claimed that there had been no more contacts and that no secrets had been divulged. Oppie did tell Groves that he would tell him the names if Groves ordered him to, but for the moment the general chose not to force the issue.

Lansdale pressed Oppenheimer again later that month when

both were in Washington, D.C., and, like Pash, he secretly re-corded their conversation. Interviewed in Groves's office, Op-pie refused to say who had approached him and who else the person had contacted. Lansdale then switched to asking Oppie the names of Communists he knew who worked at Los Al-amos. Oppenheimer named a few of the people he had earlier mentioned as possible CP members, but he divulged no new information. When Lansdale asked about Haakon Chevalier, Oppie did acknowledge that he was "quite a Red."

Finally in early December 1943, Groves went to Los Alamos to inspect progress at the lab. Groves went to Oppie's office, closed the door, and ordered him to disclose the names. Op-penheimer told Groves that Chevalier had approached the three people with the offer to pass information on to Eltenton. Groves then asked Oppie to name the three men. Oppie said he would name them only if Groves promised not to give the information to the FBI. Groves agreed, thinking that Oppie would name some graduate students already under surveillance by the army and the FBI. To the general's surprise, Oppie did not name three people, but only one — his brother, Frank.

Troubled by these revelations as well as his promise not to tell the FBI, Groves consulted with Lansdale and Maj. William Consodine, the lawyer for the Manhattan Project. Groves feared that if he told the FBI, he would lose Oppie's trust, which would doom the bomb project. On the other hand, if he did not tell the FBI about this possible espionage, he would aid in felonious activity that could compromise national security. Groves decided to have Lansdale informally tell the FBI about Haakon and Frank. The FBI began chasing these possible atomic spies through a variety of surveillance efforts, from wire-tapping their phones to having agents follow their movements. Despite Oppenheimer's belief that his disclosure laid the matter to rest, army security officers also kept him under tight sur-veillance and worked to secure Los Alamos from espionage. The lab at Los Alamos did indeed house Soviet spies, but their true identities did not emerge until years and even decades later.

CREATING THE GADGET

The atomic research that the security agents worked to protect progressed slowly. Pursuing the several paths toward building an atomic bomb, scientists at Los Alamos grappled with the complex issues of creating a rapid chain reaction that would cause a colossal explosion. With scant quantities of either uranium or plutonium available for experiments, scientists at first could only speculate on the results. In a world before high-speed computers, to calculate the various scenarios of what might happen when atoms split proved difficult. As a consequence, women on the Hill worked in the lab as human calculators. They helped figure out how much material would be needed to reach a critical mass. IBM calculating machines — primitive types of computers — arrived on the Hill and started running formulas to predict how many neutrons would be set free by the fission and how much energy would be released. Both predictions proved essential in calculating how much nuclear material would create an atomic explosion.

The early euphoria of working on the Gadget wore off over the summer of 1943, and Oppenheimer ran into difficulties as the lab's director. Through the fall, concerns grew about his ability to manage the lab. When problems arose over using plutonium in a gun assembly, that method was ultimately abandoned. Research into the uranium gun assembly and the plutonium implosion device continued. However, uncertainties surrounding both of these paths to creating an atomic bomb hindered those who worked in the lab. Teller caused further problems as he refused to work on the atomic bomb and insisted on pursuing the Super, or hydrogen bomb. Other scientists including Felix Bloch and Emilio Segrè argued with Oppie over the direction of the research. Some of the arguments concerned valid questions about the best way to create an atom bomb, but others came from turf battles and the inflated egos of those who worked at the lab. Not everyone believed Oppenheimer could successfully bring together all of the key personnel on the Hill and forge a productive research team.

General Groves himself began to have his doubts about Oppie. On December 23, 1943, Groves sent a letter to Oppenheimer ordering him to "thoroughly review [his] organization from the standpoint of good, sound administration." Groves urged Oppie and his assistants to delegate their duties: "I feel it more strongly now as a result of my study . . . [which] showed faulty organization with failure to decentralize authority. . . . Your various assistants and their assistants in turn must decentralize their authorities and responsibilities to the limit. . . . The bigger the job the more essential this is." In closing, Groves sternly ordered Oppie, "At the time of my next visit I would like to have you prepared to discuss in detail your existing set-up together with the changes that you have made and those that you are contemplating." Thus, by the end of 1943, as the lab struggled with its task to create an atom bomb, Oppie came under increasing pressure to show progress.

In response, Oppie reorganized the lab, brought in more experts and personnel, and drove himself and his staff even harder. These were the dark days of World War II, not just for Los Alamos but also for the Allies as a whole. Germany had captured most of western Russia and had advanced to the outskirts of Moscow and Stalingrad. The Nazis occupied most of western Europe and also held large regions in North Africa. The Japanese had swept through Asia, conquering large parts of China and all of the Philippines, and their armies and navies ruled over the western Pacific. An invasion of Australia seemed imminent, and India also appeared threatened. The Axis powers spread their war machines over much of the world, and the Allies seemed unable to stop them.

An atomic bomb could decide the war, either by defeating the Axis powers or, if the Nazis won the bomb race, by allowing Germany to rule the globe. As a result, whatever supplies or personnel that Oppenheimer and Groves wanted for the Manhattan Project, they received. The success of the Allied bomb project was vital for the successful pursuit of the war because if the Nazis obtained the bomb first, they could destroy Western civilization.

PROGRESS AT LOS ALAMOS

A key element for the success of the Manhattan Project was the processing plants for uranium and plutonium at Oak Ridge and Hanford. Until the plants could produce enough fissionable material for the scientists at Los Alamos to experiment with, their work remained merely theoretical. Finally, in the summer of 1944, the Hill received its first shipment of U-235 from Oak Ridge, accompanied by armed guards. Using the enriched uranium, scientists confirmed in August that with enough U-235, a gun assembly bomb would work. The production at Oak Ridge increased through the fall of 1944, and by December, the plant was producing 200 grams a day. A single bomb like Little Boy would need almost 15,000 grams to create a critical mass and the resultant atomic explosion. With Oak Ridge and Hanford beginning to produce usable quantities of weapons-grade material, experiments at Los Alamos to find a way to detonate this material moved more quickly.

One of these experiments tackled the tricky issue of how much uranium-235 would be needed to create a chain reaction. Once adequate amounts of enriched uranium arrived on the Hill, scientists experimented with it in such a way as to produce a critical assembly, a coming together of enough nuclear material to create an explosive chain reaction. This experiment, called "tickling the dragon's tail," dropped a small plug of uranium through a hole in a doughnut-shaped mass of the same material. In that split second as the two masses of uranium-235 interacted, scientists measured how many neutrons escaped their nuclei to get an idea of how many atoms had fissioned. Using these measurements, scientists estimated how much enriched uranium they needed to create an atomic bomb.

By the summer of 1944, the gun assembly team knew that Little Boy would work and the focus shifted to the Implosion device. Oppie then quickly reorganized the lab once again to focus on the implosion bomb. By August, he had created new divisions to study the hydrodynamics of implosion, the critical assembly of plutonium, and the design of the explosive lenses used to focus the conventional explosives in the plutonium bomb. As successes grew in the effort to create a usable atomic weapon, personnel tackled the remaining difficulties. Navy Capt. William "Deak" Parsons, a native New Mexican, returned to the state to lead the Ordnance Division. He had previously helped develop the proximity fuse, which allowed bombs to explode close to their targets. Parsons was a vibrant part of the community at Los Alamos, serving not only as a division director but also as a school board member. He eventually rode on the plane that dropped the first atomic bomb on Japan and thus played a key role in the creation of the Atomic Age.

In a letter in August to Enrico Fermi in which he tried to persuade the Italian to join the work at Los Alamos, Oppenheimer cited the need for a strong experimental physicist like Fermi to help guide the project to its final goal. Perhaps as an incentive to lure Fermi to the Hill, Oppie told him that the "water boiler" nuclear reactor, the first of its kind in the world, "should be completely your baby, if only because it may give you a place to retreat on occasion when the rest of the laboratory becomes too grim." Despite the knowledge that a successful Gadget would end the horrific war, Oppie on occasion fretted over the troubling quest that his lab pursued. He did attract Fermi to Los Alamos, and the scientist then helped bring the grim work at the Tech Area to a successful conclusion.

TENSIONS ON THE HILL

Not all seemed grim to those at Los Alamos. Oppie and Kitty added to their family on the Hill. Kitty gave birth to Katherine on December 7, 1944—the third anniversary of the surprise attack on Pearl Harbor. Raising Katherine (nicknamed Toni) added strains to the Oppenheimers' marriage and household. Pat Sherr, a family friend and psychologist, observed that Kitty "had absolutely no intuitive understanding of the children." By the spring of 1945, Kitty needed a break. She left Los Alamos for a couple of weeks just as the pace and tension in the rush to complete the bomb increased.

As Oppenheimer's wife, Kitty might have taken a lead in coordinating the social life at Los Alamos had she not been ill-suited to serve in such a role. Priscilla Duffield, Oppie's secretary, said this about her boss's wife: "Kitty Oppenheimer was a very charming, vital, intelligent person, who wasn't very strong on interpersonal relations. She didn't get along with a lot of people very well. . . . I think that Kitty was very difficult in many ways for Oppie and for her children and for people she knew."

Oppenheimer, on the other hand, fostered informality at the lab. Take, for example, his interaction with Manual Salazar, a local teenager who worked at the post during the war. At the age of fifteen, Salazar cleaned out the buses that sped around the site. He recalled: "I'd eat at the PX [Post Exchange] at noon and so would Dr. Oppenheimer. He had an English bike with real thin tires, the only one I ever saw around. He rode up to the PX one day and I told him I would like to ride his bike some time. He said: 'Go ahead.' So from then on, I would wait for him at the noon hour and I'd ride all over the tech area. I didn't mind him being a top scientist. I didn't even know. All I knew was that he had a great skinny bicycle."

Not everyone got along so well together at Los Alamos. Civilians chafed against the military's discipline, husbands and wives fought over inadequate housing and community services, and the lab's staffers were forbidden from going home and talking about their top-secret work with their spouses. Consequently, Enrico Fermi's wife, Laura, later wrote that Hill residents "were high-strung because the altitude affected us, because our men worked long hours under unrelenting pressure; high-strung because we were too many of a kind, too close together, too unavoidable even during relaxation hours, and we were all crack pots; high-strung because we felt powerless under strange circumstances, irked by minor annoyances that we blamed on the Army and that drove us to unreasonable and pointless rebellion." Oppie had to juggle these contentious people to get them to live and work together toward the common goal of creating a weapon of mass destruction.

VICTORY IN EUROPE AND THE PACE QUICKENS

In the spring of 1945, as the war in Europe ground to an end, the United States lost its leader. On April 12, President Franklin Delano Roosevelt died in Warm Springs, Georgia. Over the years, he had sought relief from his polio in the therapeutic waters there. As the nation mourned, Oppenheimer addressed those who attended a memorial service for the president on the Hill:

> We have been living through years of great evil, and of great terror. Roosevelt has been our President, our Commander-in-chief and, in an old and unperverted sense, our leader. All over the world men have looked to him for guidance, and have seen symbolized in him their hope that the evils of this time would not be repeated; that the terrible sacrifices which have been made, and those that are still to be made, would lead to a world more fit for human habitation. . . . In the Hindu scripture, in the Bhagavad-Gita, it says, "Man is a creature whose substance is faith. What his faith is, he is."

For Oppenheimer and many others in the United States, Roosevelt had restored their faith.

Harry S. Truman, who succeeded Roosevelt, knew little about the Manhattan Project even as vice president. He received his first full briefing about the new weapon only after Roosevelt had died. As the country mourned Roosevelt, the war in Europe ended. On May 1, 1945, a German radio broadcast announced the suicide of Hitler in his bunker in Berlin, and on May 8, Germany surrendered. Despite the removal of Germany as a nuclear threat and its defeat on the battlefield, the people of Los Alamos continued to work on the atomic bomb. Allied soldiers still fought and died in the Pacific Theater, and Japan remained a formidable foe.

In fact, in late spring the laboratory staff worked even longer hours. Many of them disappeared from the Hill for weeks at a time and returned dusty and accompanied by renowned scientists. More and more military officers appeared on the Hill. Even the residents who knew little about the work at the lab knew that whatever was being done behind the fences with stern security guards would soon conclude.

When lab personnel disappeared during that spring, they usually traveled two hundred miles south of Los Alamos into one of the most inhospitable stretches of desert in the entire United States. Travelers along the Camino Real during the Spanish colonial days had named this part of the Chihuahuan Desert the Jornada del Muerto (Journey of the Dead Man). In the early days of World War II, the army had moved the resident ranchers off their lands on the Jornada. Air crews from the nearby Alamogordo Air Base then practiced dropping bombs on the desert in preparation for flying missions overseas. In August 1944, Oppie chose the Jornada del Muerto for testing the Gadget.

The naming of the site of the first atomic explosion as "Trinity" is shrouded in atomic folklore. Oppenheimer later said it came to him while reading this John Donne sonnet:

Batter my heart, three-personed God, for, you
As yet but knock, breathe, shine, and seek to mend;
That I may rise, and stand, o'erthrow me, and bend
Your force, to break, blow, burn, and make me new.

Ferenc Szasz, who wrote about Los Alamos and the Trinity test in *The Day the Sun Rose Twice*, suggested that Oppenheimer meant to invoke not the Christian Trinity but a Hindu one of Brahma, the Creator; Vishnu, the Preserver; and Shiva, the Destroyer. Atomic historian Gregg Herken speculated that the name was a secret tribute to Oppie's past lover Jean Tatlock, who had introduced him to the poetry of Donne and had committed suicide in January 1945.

Whatever the real truth about the naming of Trinity, Oppie at times shaped history by making retrospective pronouncements about what he had said or thought at previous times. People often remember the past selectively and even creatively;

Oppie did so as well, which has complicated historians' understanding of the atomic past.

The testing of the bomb at Trinity served several different purposes. First, nobody knew with certainty if Fat Man would actually work. Second, the military needed to know how powerful the detonation would be to plan for the use of the bomb on Japan. Third, the nuclear physicists used the test as an opportunity to conduct a large-scale physics experiment. And finally, President Truman wanted a successful test as he negotiated with British prime minister Winston Churchill and Soviet leader Joseph Stalin at the Potsdam conference in defeated Germany. With little diplomatic experience before he succeeded Franklin Roosevelt in April, Truman felt he needed an extra advantage in his dealings with Stalin. All of these factors converged at a desolate spot in the desert of central New Mexico.

FISHING IN THE DESERT

Earlier that summer, Oppie had sent a coded invitation to Arthur Compton, director of the Met Lab in Chicago, where the first nuclear chain reaction had occurred: "Anytime after the 15th [of July] would be good for our fishing trip. Because we are not certain of the weather, we may be delayed several days. As we do not have enough sleeping bags to go around, we ask you please not to bring anyone with you." Compton could not attend but replied, "Best luck to catch the big one." Oppenheimer and the atomic anglers headed into the desert to go "fission."

Numerous scientific groups from the Manhattan Project worked to detonate the implosion device and to record the experiment at Trinity. These groups armed the atomic bomb and prepared to measure the energy release, blast damage, and radiation created by the explosion. Various types of equipment, gauges, and cameras spread out over the test site and were connected by five hundred miles of cables to document all the effects of the blast. Cameras capable of taking more than eight thousand frames per second were invented to record the explosion.

The bomb tested at Trinity was an implosion device of the Fat Man series. The heavy metal sphere with junction boxes and electrical wires woven around its outside encased an intricate assembly of nearly one hundred high-explosive lenses, which encircled the plutonium core. These conventional explosives had to fire within milliseconds of each other to simultaneously compress the plutonium into a critical mass. It took several days to assemble all the components, hoist the Gadget to the top of the one-hundred-foot-high test tower, and connect all the wires. During the night of July 15, summer thunderstorms swept the Jornada. Some nervously wondered whether a lightning strike would prematurely set off Fat Man and the Atomic Age. Despite the technical delays, the timing of the test remained paramount to President Truman as he negotiated with Stalin and Churchill in Potsdam, Germany. The leaders had assembled to plan the end of the war with Japan and map the postwar world. Truman wanted a successful test so that he could face Stalin from a position of strength.

Whether the Gadget actually would detonate remained a contested topic among the scientists from the Hill. When Ed McMillan left Los Alamos for Trinity, he told Elsie, his wife: "We ourselves are not absolutely certain what will happen. . . . We know there are three possibilities. One, that we all [may] be blown to bits if it is more powerful than we expect. Two, it may be a complete dud. Three, it may, as we hope, be a success, we pray without loss of any life." Some scientists at Trinity organized a gambling pool, placing bets on the power of the bomb if and when it detonated.

The closest human observers hid in bunkers six miles from the explosion. Three observation shelters—one north, one south, and one west of ground zero—held the closest observers at ten thousand yards. almost six miles away. In the bunkers and farther away from the bomb test site, men and women nervously bided their time. An additional group of scientists, military officers, and distinguished visitors waited at Compañia Hill, twenty miles to the northwest. Few personnel waited east of ground zero, since the fallout cloud would blow with the prevailing winds and dust them with radioactivity.

"AT THE END OF THE WORLD . . . THE LAST MEN WILL SEE WHAT WE SAW"

Originally scheduled to explode at 4 A.M. on July 16, the Trinity test was postponed until 5:30 A.M. because of the thunderstorms pelting the basin. The last scientists to leave the tower departed at 5:05 A.M. after which the world's first nuclear countdown began. As the countdown approached zero, a local radio station began broadcasting over the same wavelength that the site personnel used. Strains of Tchaikovsky's *Nutcracker Suite* intermixed with the final tense seconds of the countdown.

At 5:29:45 A.M., Fat Man imploded. The flash from the blast lit up the sky, and people in New Mexico, Texas, Arizona, and Mexico saw it. Trinity personnel had been warned to avoid looking at the explosion since they might be blinded by the flash. Nonetheless, ever-inquisitive physicist Richard Feynman covered one eye and looked at the explosion with the other. He was blinded in that eye for several days. In contrast to the visual chaos of the explosion, silence lasted for thirty seconds at the observation posts ten thousand yards away as the sound waves raced across the desert. Then, a shock wave knocked anyone standing outdoors at the closest observation posts to the ground. A seismologist fifty miles away said that it felt like an earthquake. With the shock wave, sound engulfed the observers with a crack and roar that then bounced between the mountains surrounding the plain. Eyewitnesses at Compañia Hill heard nothing for ninety seconds as they watched the roiling mushroom cloud continue to rise. Then the thunder shook them as well.

Many eyewitnesses to the first atomic explosion have described the historic fireball. Joan Hinton, a graduate student in physics from Wisconsin who worked at the Los Alamos nuclear reactor, observed the blast from a hill twenty-five miles away: "It was like being at the bottom of an ocean of light. We were bathed in it from all directions. The light withdrew into the bomb as if the bomb sucked it up. Then it turned purple and blue and went up and up and up. We were still talking in whispers when the cloud reached the level where it was struck by the rising sunlight so it cleared out the natural clouds. We saw a cloud that was dark and red at the bottom and daylight on the top. Then suddenly the sound reached us. It was very sharp and rumbled and all the mountains were rumbling with it."

William L. Laurence, a *New York Times* journalist brought in by General Groves for the event, later wrote: "Up it went, a great ball of fire about a mile in diameter, changing colors as it kept shooting upward, from deep purple to orange, expanding, growing bigger, rising as it was expanding, an elemental force freed from its bonds after being chained for billions of years." Otto Frisch, looking at the developing mushroom cloud, thought of a "red hot elephant balanced on its trunk." After the luminous mushroom cloud rose like the sun, it dispersed, and a little while later, the real sun rose. Some said it was the day the sun rose twice.

Enrico Fermi witnessed the blast from the base camp about ten miles away. After describing the detonation and rising mushroom cloud, he then recalled: "About forty seconds after the explosion the air blast reached me. I tried to estimate its strength by dropping from about six feet small pieces of paper before, during, and after the passage of the blast wave. Since, at the time, there was no wind I could observe very distinctly and actually measure the displacement of the pieces of paper that were in the process of falling while the blast was passing. The shift was about 2½ meters, which, at the time, I estimated to correspond to the blast that would be produced by ten thousand tons of TNT." Other scientists using more precise instruments calculated the power of the explosion as the equivalent of eighteen thousand tons of TNT (or eighteen kilotons). Most scientists at Los Alamos had anticipated a blast of four kilotons.

Raw emotions rose with the mushroom cloud. Groves's assistant, Col. Thomas Farrell, gasped: "Jesus Christ! The long hairs have let it get away from them." James Tuck, a physicist brought over from Britain, exclaimed, "What have we done?" Chemist George Kistiakowsky speculated "that at the end of the world — in the last millisecond of the earth's existence — the last men will see what we saw." Test director Kenneth Bainbridge searched out Oppie to congratulate him by stating, "Well, now we're all sons of bitches."

Oppenheimer's reaction to the explosion reflects his complex and conflicted personality. Around 6:30 A.M., he commented: "My faith in the human mind has been somewhat restored." Interestingly, Oppie's faith was just somewhat restored. Some time afterward, Oppie sagely recounted the event: "We knew the world would not be the same. A few people laughed, a few people cried. Most people were silent. I remembered the line from the Hindu scripture, the *Bhagavad Gita*: Vishnu is trying to persuade the Prince that he should do his duty and to impress him he takes on his multi-armed form and says, 'Now I am become Death, the destroyer of worlds.' I suppose we all thought that, one way or another."

In the *Bhagavad Gita*, the following passage is similar to what Oppie quoted: "Time I am, the destroyer of worlds and I have come to engage all people. . . . All soldiers on both sides here will be slain." In Hinduism, the multi-armed god Shiva is eternally poised to destroy the earth at a moment's notice, but has always relented due to a benevolent action by one of his human devotees. Oppenheimer knew the physics behind the explosion better than anyone, but he had to borrow from Hinduism to fully grasp what he had unleashed in the desert that morning. However, when Oppie actually came up with this quote remains shrouded in uncertainty. He said that it was sometime that morning. Perhaps so, but this may also illustrate how Oppie at times manipulated his version of what he said, did, and thought to match an image of what he thought he should have said, done, or thought.

Frank Oppenheimer, brought to Los Alamos that spring to help calm Oppie as the test neared, later said about Trinity: "In all these things there were mixed feelings. . . . There was that radioactive cloud that seemed to hover a long time. It was bright purple but the astonishing thing was the thunder in that Jornada del Muerto. It just echoed back and forth. It just never seemed to stop. I don't know where or what it was bouncing on even, there was only that one cliff, but it went back and forth and back and forth and never stopped while that great miserable purple thing hung over us." Other eyewitnesses, overwhelmed by the rising fireball, stated that they did not remember hearing any of the booming that rocked the basin.

At Los Alamos, two hundred miles to the north, some of the residents kept vigil into the early morning hours of July 16. Alerted by their husbands, Elsie McMillan and Lois Bradbury shared coffee to keep awake as they waited. At 5:30 A.M. on July 16, a bright flash of light flooded into the baby's south-facing bedroom at the McMillan home, and the women knew something significant had happened. Having heard that the culmination of the project would occur on July 16 in the desert to the south, Dorothy McKibbin drove from Santa Fe to the top of the Sandia Mountains east of Albuquerque in the rain. As she looked south, a full quarter of the sky lit up, and the leaves around her shone like gold. She felt awe at the sight and later said she knew that the world had changed forever. Eric Jette left Eleanor, his wife, with this advice: "You might see something if you stay up all night." From her house, she beheld a sunrise at 5:30 A.M. — in the south.

The post's commissary butcher, George Hillhouse, had heard rumors that something big was about to happen. He sent his wife, Dorothy, and daughter Jean to Kansas right before the event. After the day the sun rose twice, he sent a postcard to his vacationing wife and child, telling them: "The cat screamed all night the night you left." Young Jean was perplexed. They did not have a cat. She did not know that this was a coded signal telling her mother that it was safe for them to return to the Hill.

With the flash seen at Los Alamos, many knew that something big had happened in the desert on July 16. Many people on the Hill worried whether the flash meant success or failure until an Albuquerque radio station broadcast a midday news bulletin that an ammunition dump had accidentally exploded near Alamogordo. This coded news release signaled a successful atomic explosion.

A paragraph on the back page of the Santa Fe newspaper that afternoon read: "Explosion of an ammunition magazine on the Alamogordo Air Base reservation this morning, heard and seen for many miles, was reported by William O. Erickson, commanding officer of the air base. There was no loss of life or injuries to persons."

Beginning in the early evening, men from Trinity straggled back to Los Alamos. Physicist Stanislaw Ulam, who had stayed at Los Alamos, watched them return. Looking at them, he thought: "You could tell at once they had a strange experience. You could see it on their faces. I saw that something very grave and strong had happened to their whole outlook on the future." Led by Oppie, the scientists of the Manhattan Project had opened the Pandora's box of atomic energy. In ancient Greece, when Pandora opened this box, fear, greed, and anger flew out; however, Pandora closed the box's lid before hope could escape. Unable to put nuclear weapons back into the box, many at Los Alamos worried about the peril they had unleashed and worked hopefully toward the future promise of atomic energy.

TARGETING JAPAN

Whatever the future would hold for the development of nuclear weapons, Fat Man worked. The army rushed to get all of the bomb components to the Pacific for an attack against Japan. The bomb casings for Fat Man and Little Boy arrived at Tinian Island on July 26, delivered by the ill-fated USS *Indianapolis*. A Japanese submarine sank the ship several days later as it steamed toward the Philippines, resulting in great loss of life. On July 28 and 29, the uranium and plutonium cores of the bombs arrived by air at Tinian. To drop the bombs on Japan, the Army Air Corps' 509th Composite Group had trained with specially modified B-29 bombers since September 1944. Before Truman had left for the Potsdam conference, he had given final written approval for the atomic bombing of Japan. As Capt. Deak Parsons later recalled, "All orders necessary for carrying out the atomic missions had arrived in Guam well ahead of the active material."

Long before the bombs arrived at Tinian, the government had selected the target cities. The Target Committee, composed of military officers and Manhattan Project scientists, met in Washington, D.C., to consider the choice of Japanese cities. As the nation celebrated Victory in Europe (VE) Day in May, the committee finalized its list of Japanese cities. It chose as the primary target Kyoto, the ancient capital of Japan and the historic center of its civilization for a thousand years. Secretary of War Henry Stimson vehemently dissented. He recognized that Japan needed to become an outpost for United States interests in the Far East after the war. Bombing the ancient capital would create a bitterness that could tilt Japan toward Russia. Stimson declared: "Nobody's going to tell me what to do on this. On this matter I am the kingpin." Stimson successfully struck Kyoto from the list. Consequently, the Target Committee sent to President Truman these cities as potential targets: Hiroshima, Kokura, Niigata, and Nagasaki.

For the next meeting, the committee's members traveled to Los Alamos and met in Oppenheimer's office. They debated various issues, including weather conditions over Japan, status of targets, use of bombs against military objectives, and height of detonation. They concluded that even though they needed to drop the Gadget on a military target, in order to get the full psychological impact on the Japanese rulers and public, the bombs had to hit an urban area full of civilians.

Not everyone who helped create the bombs wanted them used against Japan. A petition circulated among the atomic scientists—especially at the Met Lab in Chicago, where Fermi had created the first controlled chain reaction—asking the president not to drop the bombs on Japan. Leo Szilard—who co-wrote the letter Einstein sent to FDR that started the U.S. participation in the atomic bomb project—petitioned President Truman. Szilard argued: "The development of atomic power will provide the nations with new means of destruction. The atomic bombs at our disposal represent only the first step in this direction, and there is almost no limit to the destructive power which will become available in the course of their future development. Thus a nation which sets the precedent of using these newly liberated forces of nature for purposes of destruction may have to bear the responsibility of opening the door to an era of devastation on an unimaginable scale." He asked for Truman to consider the full moral and future implications of nuclear weapons before using them. More than sixty Manhattan Project scientists, mainly from Chicago, signed this petition.

Some scientists called for a demonstration of the atomic bomb against an uninhabited island with Japanese observers nearby. The Target Committee rejected such a demonstration for several reasons. Negotiating to get Japanese military officers through Allied lines as witnesses for a demonstration seemed difficult if not impossible. If Japanese observers attended a test, the element of surprise would be lost. Additionally, if the Gadget did not work, it would prove more than just an embarrassment; it could fortify the resolve of the Japanese to mount stronger resistance.

At the beginning of July, Szilard sent a copy of the petition to Los Alamos. Oppenheimer did not circulate it. One of Szilard's associates on the Hill, Edward Creutz, explained to him why: "He [Oppie] preferred to have the document go through other channels. . . . He also believed that, since an opportunity has been given to people here to express, through him, their opinions on the matters concerned, the proposed method was somewhat redundant and probably not very satisfactory." On July 17, the day after the Trinity detonation, Oppie forwarded to Groves a copy of Szilard's petition and Creutz's letter to Szilard, commenting, "The inclosed note is a further incident in a development which I know you have watched with interest." With the test a success and the war continuing to rage in the Pacific, the petition held little power in Los Alamos and, more importantly, in Washington, D.C. Even though some of the Manhattan Project's personnel had qualms about using the device against Japan, the decision had never truly been in the scientists' hands.

Debate continues even today over whether the atomic bombing of Japan was necessary to end the war. Some argue that the bomb was the first shot of the Cold War, aimed more at the Soviet Union than at an all-but-defeated Japan. Some in the government, like Bush and Conant, realized that owning a revolutionary new weapon such as an atomic bomb would give immeasurable power in foreign affairs to the country that possessed it. They hoped that power would help the United States to create the American Century.

At the same time, some members of the Japanese government had started negotiations with the Soviets to surrender. With Japan close to collapse, whether these Japanese could have persuaded their military counterparts in the government to surrender remains uncertain. Oppenheimer later recalled that "the actual military plans at that time for the subjugation of Japan and the end of the war were clearly much more terrible in every way and for everyone concerned than the use of the bombs. . . . [An invasion of Japan] would have involved a half million or a million causalities on the Allied side and twice that number on the Japanese side. Nevertheless, my own feeling is that . . . there could have been more effective warning and much less wanton killing. . . . That is about all that I am clear about in hindsight."

Despite the notion that the atomic bombing of Japan was a warning shot across the bow of the Soviet state, and thus the first shot of the Cold War, the Target Committee did want to end the war as quickly as possible. The Allied conquests of the islands of Iwo Jima and Okinawa in the spring of 1945 revealed not only a determined Japanese military that fought to the death but also civilians who committed suicide instead of surrendering. On Iwo Jima, 20,000 Japanese defenders died, and the Allied forces captured only 1,083 Japanese military personnel. On Okinawa, 70,000 Japanese died, including the commanding general, who committed suicide instead of surrendering. The Japanese launched 1,900 planes against the Allied forces on Okinawa in ten waves of kamikaze attacks. None of the pilots survived. Thousands of Japanese civilians threw themselves to their deaths off the island's cliffs to avoid capitulating to the Allies. At the end of the eighty-two-day battle for Okinawa, one-third of the Allied invasion force members had been killed or injured. The human cost of invading the home islands of Japan could cause large numbers of both military and civilian casualties.

With such determined and stiff resistance by the Japanese military and the commitment of both its soldiers and civilians to die instead of surrender, an invasion of Japan would prove bloody. U.S. military planners estimated that at least 50,000 Allied casualties would occur, and some thought that 1 million Allied soldiers might die in the conquering of all the Japanese islands. The planners did not estimate a figure for Japanese dead, but with civilians trained to defend their beaches with hay forks and children fighting against armored tanks, the total might have reached the millions. Faced with such numbers, the Target Committee dismissed any demonstration tests for Fat Man and Little Boy and prepared to drop them on the cities of Japan.

In examining the atomic bombing of Japan, two complementary truths exist: First, the bombs were deployed to bring a swift end to the most horrendous war in human history. Second, the United States dropped the bombs to better position itself for the postwar world, in which its wartime ally the Soviet Union might quickly become a potential enemy. Rarely do momentous events in history have only one cause and effect. The first combat use of nuclear weapons is such an event.

HIROSHIMA AND NAGASAKI

To get close enough to Japan to deliver the atomic bombs by airplanes, the Manhattan Project and the 509th Composite Group took over the northern part of Tinian Island. The previous summer, U.S. forces had captured Tinian as part of the amphibious assault to secure the Mariana Islands, fifteen hundred miles away from Tokyo. The Army Air Corps quickly converted the small island into a sprawling air base and sent waves of bombers every day to pound Japan with conventional bombs. As the United States hammered Japanese cities, Air Corps bombers avoided several targets to preserve them for a future atomic attack.

To deliver Fat Man and Little Boy by airplane, the Air Corps had to invent new methods for dropping the bombs. The 509th Composite Group trained in Wendover, Utah, for more than a year with specially modified B-29s. Led by Col. Paul Tibbets, the air crews dropped replicas of Fat Man and Little Boy from thirty thousand feet, and then banked sharply to quickly escape the target area. By the summer of 1945, the 509th and its B-29s had transferred to a fenced and guarded airstrip on northern Tinian. The crews continued to train and wait for both the bomb components and the approval to launch their attacks.

On July 31, the uranium bomb on Tinian was ready to use; however, weather over the target cities prevented a clear view of the ground, a necessary condition for observing the bomb's devastation. On August 5, 1945, at 4:15 A.M., Gen. Curtis Le-May, commanding officer of the Twentieth Air Force in the Pacific, gave final approval for the mission. Later that day, Little Boy was loaded onto the *Enola Gay* (named by pilot Tibbets for his mother). Once the bomb was aboard, Brig. Gen. T. F. Farrell, Groves's deputy, signed a receipt for a "projectile unit containing [censored] kilograms of enriched tubealloy [uranium] at an average concentration of [censored]." Immediately below this description, Farrell wrote: "The above materials were carried by Parsons, Tibbets & Co. to Hiroshito as part of 'Doomsday' leaving Tinian."

The *Enola Gay* took off at 2:45 A.M. on August 6 and flew north to Japan. Navy captain William Parsons, who had headed the Ordnance Division at Los Alamos, rode on the *Enola Gay* to conduct the final arming of Little Boy in flight. At 8:15:17 A.M. Hiroshima time, Little Boy cleared *Enola Gay*'s bomb bay doors and dropped toward the city. In less than a minute, the device exploded nineteen hundred feet above Hiroshima. The *Enola Gay* and two other accompanying B-29s took pictures and observed the cloud, which quickly rose to more than forty thousand feet. They lost sight of the towering mushroom cloud

a little before 11 A.M. when they were 363 miles away from
Hiroshima.

On August 6 at 9 A.M. Los Alamos time, the White House
announced the atomic bombing of Hiroshima. The headlines of
Santa Fe's afternoon daily, the *New Mexican*, told all: "Los Alamos
Secrets Disclosed by Truman; Atomic Bombs Drop on Japan."
Front-page articles described the destruction of Hiroshima by a
single bomb with the force of twenty thousand tons of TNT.
Comparing the bomb's strength to the equivalent of "2,000 times
the power of the Great Grand-Slammers dropped on Germany,"
the stories detailed how this "one bomb pack[ed] the wallop of
the bomb loads of 2,000 Superforts [B-29 bombers]."

That day, Los Alamos figured prominently in newspaper stories about the atomic attack on Japan. Some Hill residents
learned about the true purpose of the Tech Area and their community at the same time as the rest of the world. The articles
described the community through population figures, building
descriptions, social activities, and profiles of key men at Site Y.
These stories came from the Manhattan Engineer District, prepared ahead of time for press releases. Overnight, Los Alamos
lost its secrecy and isolation and burst onto the national and
international scene. Through information released by Site Y
and printed in newspapers around the world, the secrecy partly
lifted, and people outside of the fence discovered Los Alamos.
The first newspaper stories about an atomic weapon, this potential doomsday bomb, came not from independent reporters
but from army publicists.

Residents of Los Alamos gained a perspective about Hiroshima not found in the usual media. Five-year-old Ellen Wilder
Reid recalled hearing a tape recording of the approach, release,
and detonation of the Hiroshima bomb broadcast over the
local radio station KRS. Since her family had no radio at home,
her father shepherded them into the car where they listened to
the crew as it approached Hiroshima, to the countdown and
release of the bomb, and to the exclamations: "There's the
cloud. There's the mushroom cloud."

The Japanese government rushed investigation teams to

Hiroshima since little information escaped the atomic devastation. As the Japanese scrambled to ascertain what had hit Hiroshima, the 509th Composite Group prepared for a second run. The order to drop an atomic bomb on Japan also stated, "Additional bombs will be delivered on the . . . targets as soon as ready by the project team." To knock out Japan, Truman, Groves, and others felt a second bomb would prove decisive.

Three days later, a Fat Man bomb exploded over Japan. By chance, the primary target, Kokura, was obscured by ground haze and smoke, so *Bock's Car*, the B-29 carrying the bomb, diverted to Nagasaki. At 11:50 A.M. on August 9, the plutonium implosion device was released. The *Bock's Car* flight log noted, "The bomb functioned normally in all respects." The destruction of the two Japanese cities by single bombs forced the Japanese government to concede defeat. On August 14, Japan accepted the Allied surrender terms, and World War II finally ended. Representatives of the Japanese government and its armed forces signed the surrender accord aboard the USS *Missouri* in Tokyo Bay on September 2.

On August 9, 1945, at the same time that newspaper stories reported the Nagasaki bombing, more details about the destruction of Hiroshima appeared in print. Little Boy had leveled a 4.7-square-mile area (about 60 percent of the center of Hiroshima). Radio Tokyo broadcast that "practically every living thing there was annihilated." In truth, people did survive the atomic attack, but casualties quickly mounted. Later estimates put the number of dead from the Hiroshima bomb between 70,000 and 80,000, with an equal number of people injured out of the population of approximately 250,000.

The approximately 150,000 men, women, and children who died at Hiroshima and Nagasaki brought to an end the bloodiest war in human history. The stark statistics tell the grim truth from World War II. The Soviet Union lost the most — at least 13 million soldiers and 7 million citizens. Germany's war dead totaled 3.2 million military personnel and 3.6 million civilians, including Jewish victims of the Nazis' "Final Solution." Japan lost 2 million people, and China suffered 10 million deaths,

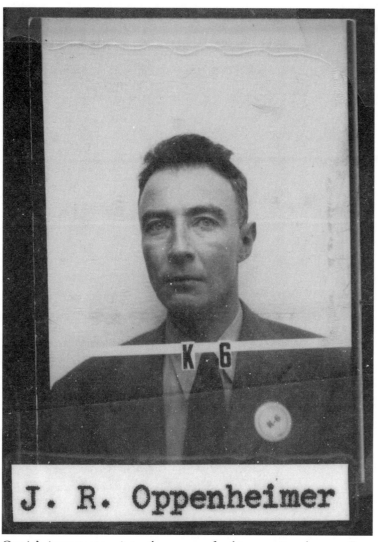

Oppie's intense stare into the camera for his security photo at Los Alamos in the spring of 1943 hints at the "grim work of the lab" that awaited him. *(Courtesy of Los Alamos National Laboratory Archives)*

At a party on the Hill in 1944, Oppie, *center right,* visited with, *left to right,* I. I. Rabi, Dorothy McKibben, and Victor Weisskopf. *(Courtesy of J. Robert Oppenheimer Memorial Committee)*

In New Mexico in the 1940s, Oppenheimer checks out the leg of his horse, Crisis, before a ride in the mountains. *(Courtesy of J. Robert Oppenheimer Memorial Committee)*

This official portrait of Oppenheimer as the director of the Manhattan Project laboratory during World War II still hung in some offices at the Los Alamos National Laboratory long after he left New Mexico. *(Courtesy of J. Robert Oppenheimer Memorial Committee)*

On July 16, 1945, at 5:30 A.M., the world's first atomic explosion rocked the predawn desert floor at Trinity Site in southern New Mexico. The Fat Man bomb unleashed explosive power equivalent to eighteen thousand tons of TNT. *(Courtesy of Los Alamos National Laboratory Archives)*

IM-4: 90-384

The gun assembly bomb (a.k.a. Little Boy) worked by shooting a plug of uranium into a bigger mass of enriched nuclear material to cause a chain reaction and an atomic explosion. This type of bomb detonated over Hiroshima. *(Courtesy of Los Alamos National Laboratory Archives)*

At 8:15 A.M. on August 6, 1945, a Little Boy bomb devastated Hiroshima, Japan. The mushroom cloud seen here quickly rose to forty thousand feet. Notice the churning dust and smoke swirling around the base of the cloud only minutes after the detonation. *(Courtesy of Los Alamos National Laboratory Archives)*

The Little Boy bomb flattened 4.7 square miles around ground zero at Hiroshima. In addition to the massive blast that blew apart buildings, firestorms swept through the city, destroying many of its wooden residences. This photograph was taken on October 26, 1945. *(Courtesy of Los Alamos National Laboratory Archives)*

Between seventy thousand and eighty thousand people died within days of the atomic bombing of Hiroshima, the deaths equaling approximately 30 percent of the city's population. This photo was taken on November 27, 1945. *(Courtesy of Los Alamos National Laboratory Archives)*

On November 27, 1945, life continued in Hiroshima as survivors walked, pedaled bicycles, and rode trolleys through the city's atomic landscape. *(Courtesy of Los Alamos National Laboratory Archives)*

The implosion bomb (a.k.a. Fat Man) created an atomic explosion by compressing plutonium within imploding blast waves to cause a chain reaction. *(Courtesy of Los Alamos National Laboratory Archives)*

In this view taken from *Bock's Car* (the B-29 bomber that dropped a Fat Man bomb on Nagasaki), a mushroom cloud rises swiftly after the 11:50 A.M. detonation on August 9, 1945. *(Courtesy of Los Alamos National Laboratory Archives)*

Because of Nagasaki's rolling hills, the area of total destruction was smaller than at Hiroshima. Still, the death toll rose to forty thousand people within days of the bombing, and more than seventy thousand by the end of 1945. *(Courtesy of Los Alamos National Laboratory Archives)*

The burned-out buildings of the Mitsubishi Steel Works in Nagasaki testify to the destructive power of the atomic bomb. As a result of the two atomic bombs, the Japanese surrendered on August 14, 1945, finally ending the most horrific war in human history. *(Courtesy of Los Alamos National Laboratory Archives)*

Left to right, Oppenheimer, General Groves, University of California
Chancellor Sproul, and Captain Parsons accept the Army-Navy E
Award for Excellence for the laboratory's success in creating the atom
bomb. *(Courtesy of J. Robert Oppenheimer Memorial Committee)*

In September 1945, Oppie and Groves visited the remains of the tower that held the first atomic bomb at Trinity Site in New Mexico. The physical toll of directing the laboratory during the war can be seen as Oppenheimer's suit hangs loosely on his already thin frame. *(Courtesy of J. Robert Oppenheimer Memorial Committee)*

mainly civilian. The United States' death toll equaled the 500,000 soldiers and sailors who were killed in action. Poland, with its large Jewish population and location between Germany and Russia, lost 6 million people, 17 percent of its prewar population. In total, at least 52 million people died around the world during World War II. The atomic bombs brought a final end to this worldwide nightmare.

With the signing of the peace treaty, the islands of Japan opened to Allied forces. A team from Los Alamos quickly headed to Hiroshima and Nagasaki to study the effects of the nuclear explosions on these communities and the people who lived in them. What they found shocked even the veterans of Trinity.

The creation of the atomic bombs at Los Alamos gained New Mexico and the American West a distinction that would grow during the postwar period. Not only did Los Alamos figure prominently in publicity about the end of the war, but the West also moved into the forefront of nuclear enterprises after the war with new laboratories, testing grounds, and military bases to support the nation's growing nuclear weapons arsenal.

The success of the Manhattan Project and the swift ending of the war also brought instant fame to Oppenheimer. Powerful men and women sought his counsel, universities recruited him, and ordinary people rushed to hear his lectures and buy those lectures when they were turned into books. Oppie attained celebrity status, and he attempted to use that status to influence the postwar world. He tried to mold the Atomic Age into one without war. The history of this new age and of the world owes a debt to Oppenheimer for his efforts; however, he ultimately failed in using nuclear weapons as a fulcrum to change human nature. In the end, too many of those powerful people he advised disliked his opinions. Some just disliked Oppie.

CHAPTER FIVE

Promise and Peril

There is only one future of atomic explosions that I can regard
with any enthusiasm — that they should never be used in war.
                    J. Robert Oppenheimer, *The Open Mind*

THE atomic bombs that destroyed Hiroshima and Nagasaki
and ended World War II came from the American West. They
were invented in the mountains and deserts of the West and
shipped to the Pacific battlefield from the ports and airfields of
the West. The spirit that flowed through the work at Los Alamos, Hanford, and other Manhattan Project sites had deep
roots in the West. Although some of the scientists and military
personnel came from more urbane regions, including the greatest cities in Europe, the headlines about the atomic bombing of
Japan focused on the top-secret post at Los Alamos and the
men and women who worked there. The Manhattan Project
thus contributed to the westward tilt of the United States as
people, industry, and power vaulted over the Mississippi River
and migrated toward the West Coast.

To be sure, atomic weapons did not start this westward tilt.
Over the first half of the twentieth century, the western section
of the United States had shed its frontier and colonial status and
grown in prominence as a vibrant region. The creation of atomic
weapons, supported by the federal government and marshaled
by Oppenheimer, cemented this change and opened up a new
era for the West as technologically sophisticated enterprises
found a home in the region. In the postwar period, atomic
energy fueled the economic and political machines that shifted
influence and power to the West. Having lived one American
dream by finding fame and international recognition in the
West, Oppie tried to decide what his future after Los Alamos

held. He chose to travel a well-worn path — he returned to the East and its centers of political power, distinguished scholarship, and cosmopolitan living.

THE EARLY ATOMIC AGE

At war's end, celebrations swept through the Manhattan Project and rocked the entire country. At Oak Ridge, an employee commented that scientists "were running around town, shouting 'Uranium!' 'Atomic!' All these things they had never been able to say before, they were shouting out like dirty words." At Los Alamos, children grabbed pots and pans from their kitchens and paraded around the streets, banging them in delight. During festivities at the nearby American Indian pueblo of San Ildefonso, coworkers from the pueblo and the Hill performed traditional Indian dances intermixed with western square dances. At one point, as dancers weaved around a room, an elder of the pueblo jumped up on a table and, in time with his drumming, chanted, "This is the Atomic Age, this is the Atomic Age."

In September 1945, as the celebrations subsided, an investigative team from Los Alamos arrived in Japan to survey the atomic devastation at Hiroshima and Nagasaki. The destruction overwhelmed even those who had witnessed the blast at Trinity. At Hiroshima and Nagasaki, the atomic bombs had ushered in a quantum leap in destructive capability. In Hiroshima, Little Boy flattened 4.7 square miles. In Nagasaki, the area of total devastation amounted to 1.8 square miles because of the city's rolling hills, which deflected part of Fat Man's blast. In both cities, all buildings within a half mile of ground zero suffered severe damage, as did 99 percent of all buildings within a mile radius of the hypocenter. More than 15,000 people died for each square mile in the central part of Hiroshima, and in Nagasaki, the total equaled 20,000. By comparison, in the massive firebombing of Tokyo on March 9, 1945, the mortality rate per square mile amounted to 5,300. Thus, the atomic bombs greatly multiplied the mortality rate of conventional bombs. In the Tokyo firebomb raids, 279 planes dropped 3.334 million pounds of explosives. With Hiroshima and Nagasaki, two planes delivered one bomb each. Fat Man, the heavier of the two, weighed a mere 10,000 pounds.

The number of human casualties astonished the investigating team from Los Alamos. At Hiroshima, between 70,000 and 80,000 people (about 30 percent of its residents) died immediately or within a few days, and an equal number were injured. A variety of deadly forces killed the people of Hiroshima and Nagasaki. Flying glass, collapsing buildings, and raging firestorms accounted for 50 to 65 percent of the fatalities. Flash burns from the initial blast caused another 20 to 30 percent of the deaths. Radiation sickness killed the final 15 to 20 percent of the residents who died. The true number of people who received a fatal dose of radiation is unknown because most of those residents died from more immediate injuries dealt by the blast or firestorms. By November 1945, 130,000 people in Hiroshima had died, and by 1950 an additional 70,000 inhabitants had perished from the effects of the bombing.

Eyewitness accounts from Hiroshima help bring the human suffering into focus. As atomic historian Ronald Takaki related, a young girl, Yoshihiro Kimura, asked her father, "Where is mother?" "She is dead," he answered. Then the girl noticed that a five-inch-long nail had been stuck into her mother's head, killing her instantly. Richard Rhodes offers the next two accounts in *The Making of the Atomic Bomb*. A six-year-old boy remembered: "Near the bridge there were a whole lot of dead people. There were some who were burned black and died, and there were others with huge burns who died with their skins bursting, and some others who died all stuck full of broken glass." Another young boy recalled, "That day after we escaped and came to Hijiyama Bridge, there were lots of naked people who were so badly burned that their whole body was hanging from them like rags."

On her way to school, thirteen-year-old Shigeko Sasamori was knocked unconscious by the blast in Hiroshima. When she regained her senses, she could see nothing through the pitch-black cloud. Eventually, the darkness dissipated, replaced by a fog that covered everything. She saw people covered in dust, bleeding and moving in slow motion. Lifeless bodies floated away in the river. Shigeko saw a baby nearby, burned and crying. Its mother tried to nurse it, but the infant's scorched skin peeled off. The blast burned one-third of Shigeko's body. For five days, she lay in a makeshift hospital at a school dormitory. Finally, her parents found her and carried her back home. With her face black from the burns and swollen, she could no longer open her eyes to see, but those carrying her commented on how Hiroshima still burned five days after the bombing. Eventually, Shigeko Sasamori came to New York City and received reconstructive surgery to repair her scarred face; however, her fingers remained mere stumps ending at the first joint.

Overwhelmed by the sheer magnitude of the death and destruction, survivors of the atomic bombing initially struggled just to stay alive. As *New Yorker* reporter John Hershey observed: "In general, survivors that day assisted only their relatives or immediate neighbors, for they could not comprehend or tolerate a wider circle of misery. The wounded limped past the screams." The atomic bomb greatly multiplied the ability of the human race to inflict pain, suffering, and death on one another.

The atomic bombs that Oppenheimer helped create unleashed a new force onto the battlefield: radiation. Radioactive energy fuels the sun and is present throughout the world; however, the concentrated radiation released by such bombs can harm and kill humans over both short and long periods of time. Composed of a variety of atomic forces including gamma rays and x-rays, the burst of radiation that occurs at the moment of detonation is deadly for people close to ground zero. These types of rays can pass through one foot of steel, three feet of concrete, or five feet of earth. When such radiation penetrates a human body, it burns internal organs and prevents them from functioning properly. A slow and painful death results. Penetrating, or burst, radiation lasts only through the immediate aftermath of a nuclear detonation.

The other form of deadly radiation generated by an atomic

blast is not immediately fatal. A detonation scatters small bits of unexploded uranium and plutonium, as well as by-products of a nuclear reaction like alpha and beta particles. A mushroom cloud carries this radioactive material aloft and spreads it with the prevailing winds before the material falls to the ground, possibly thousands of miles from the detonation. Unlike the short-lived gamma and x-rays that fly out from the burst of an atomic weapon, this lingering radiation cannot penetrate a person's skin; however, it can remain toxic for up to twenty thousand years. If it does get into the human body, this radiation can cause health problems that might not surface for decades. Consequently, Japanese victims of the atomic bombings not only died from collapsing buildings, flying shrapnel, firestorms, and burns but also from the effects of penetrating radiation in the first month after the detonations. The people of Hiroshima and Nagasaki continued to succumb to illnesses for decades as a result of the lingering radiation.

The number of casualties weighed heavily on some of the Manhattan Project's personnel, including Oppie. At the end of August, in 1945, he and Kitty withdrew to their Perro Caliente mountain retreat to recover from the chaotic and grim work of the previous two years. Oppenheimer replied to a congratulatory letter from Herbert Smith, his former teacher at the Ethical Culture School, on August 26: "You will believe that this undertaking has not been without its misgivings; they are heavy on us today when the future, which has so many elements of promise, is yet just a stone's throw from despair. Thus the good which perhaps this work has contributed to make in the ending of the war looms very large to us, because it is there for sure."

Oppenheimer wrote other letters from Perro Caliente that reveal his thoughts of the future, both for himself and for an atomic America. Concerning his return to the West Coast, he sent this comment to California colleague Charles Lauritsen: "In these days in the mountains we have had a chance to think a little of the personal things of the future. More and more we recognize how strong the personal arguments are for coming to

[Caltech in] Pasadena." Universities across the country had already started recruiting the atomic scientists of the Manhattan Project, and Oppie rose to the top of many lists. In the letter to Lauritsen, Oppie asked: "Would [Caltech] welcome and support, if in conscience we thought it right, my advisory participation in future atomic policy? I am plenty worried about this, far more of course than about the personal things; and if there were a real chance of helping, [I] would want to feel that this was welcome." As one of the creators of the Atomic Age, Oppenheimer hoped to help shape future official policy concerning nuclear energy. Any university that recruited him needed to allow for these anticipated activities.

To Ernest Lawrence, his close colleague at Berkeley, Oppenheimer wrote: "I emphasized of course that all of us would earnestly do whatever was really in the national interest, no matter how desperate and disagreeable; but that we felt reluctant to promise that much real good could come of continuing the atomic bomb work just like poison gases after the last war." The future of atomic weapons weighed heavily on Oppie, and he hoped that the use of such weapons would be outlawed like poison gas was after World War I.

Oppenheimer's thoughts centered on the hope that the horror of atomic bombs would make war obsolete. Toward the end of his family's stay at Perro Caliente, Oppie wrote a friend of his father's: "This work on the atomic bomb, coming after these terrible years of war, may serve as a real instrument in the establishment of peace. This is almost the only thing right now that seems to matter." Like many atomic scientists, Oppie hoped that nuclear weapons would bring an end to war.

Oppenheimer and other people connected with the Manhattan Project had grappled with the implications of an atomically armed world in advance of the rest of the country. While most of the nation celebrated the end of World War II and the atomic bombs that had brought such a conclusion, some people in the Manhattan Project and the government worried about a nuclear future.

LEAVING LOS ALAMOS

The future of atomic weapons, the future of Los Alamos, the future of Oppenheimer and his family — all these concerns greeted the physicist as he returned to the Hill after the short break at Perro Caliente. He quickly made an important decision. He would take his family back to California as soon as possible. As Oppenheimer prepared to leave Los Alamos, both the government and the staff at the laboratory honored him. At a public ceremony on October 16, he accepted on behalf of the entire lab the Army-Navy E Award (a certificate of excellence for industrial productivity from the Department of War). In his acceptance speech at Los Alamos, Oppenheimer predicted: "If atomic bombs are to be added as new weapons to the arsenals of a warring world . . . then the time will come when mankind will curse the name of Los Alamos and Hiroshima. The peoples of the world must unite, or they will perish. . . . By our works we are committed to a world united, before this common peril, in law, and in humanity." To counter the threat created by nuclear weapons, Oppenheimer called for a united international effort in controlling the atomic peril.

Before Oppie and his family left Los Alamos and returned to his position at the University of California at Berkeley, his colleagues saluted him with this testament:

> He selected this place. Let us thank him for the fishing, hiking, skiing, and for the New Mexico weather. He selected our collaborators. Let us thank him for the company we had, for the parties, and for the intellectual atmosphere. . . . He was our director. Let us thank him for the way he directed our work, for the many occasions where he was the eloquent spokesman of our thoughts. It was his acquaintance with every single little and big difficulty that helped us so much to overcome them. It was his spirit of scientific dignity that made us feel we would be in the right place here. We drew much more satisfaction from our work than our consciences ought to have allowed us.

Without Oppenheimer, an atomic bomb might not have been created. At the very least, the bombs would not have been

ready for use against the Japanese in August 1945, and consequently, World War II would not have ended then. Oppie did
not dwell on this more positive result of his work but looked to
the future, a future in which atomic bombs could fall on American cities, a possibility that he had helped to create. He began
working to prevent atomic bombs from ever devastating American cities.

THE ATOMIC WEST

After Oppenheimer and his family left Los Alamos in October
1945, the community continued to serve a vital role in national
security. Even though the work at Los Alamos was supposed to
last only for the duration of the war, the settlement's laboratories
remained open after Hiroshima and Nagasaki with many personnel continuing their research on the revolutionary source of
energy. Quickly, the federal government made Los Alamos a
permanent facility, which assisted in further revolutionizing the
American West. At the premier atomic research laboratory in
New Mexico and at the other Manhattan Project installations in
the West, nuclear energy helped transform the region.

After World War II, atomic facilities around the country attracted money and influence like a nucleus captures stray electrons. With Cold War facilities such as two research laboratories
in New Mexico, a lab each in California and Idaho, plutonium
reactors in Washington, a weapons test site in Nevada, and
military bases, uranium mines, and processing plants in Colorado, Arizona, Texas, Utah, and Wyoming, the influx of money
and talent into the West secured the region's standing as an
essential part of America in the second half of the twentieth
century. To be sure, change had occurred in the American West
throughout the first half of the twentieth century with economic
development through natural resource extraction and manufacturing, with the New Deal programs during the Great Depression, and with the vital role that the region played in fighting
World War II. The Manhattan Project helped cement the American West's change from being on the periphery of national

affairs to being at the center. The West, boosted by its atomic enterprises and its focus on national security, started to lead the country in producing advanced technology and postwar prosperity. As a result, the region garnered a stronger position in the national economy, had a more powerful voice in politics, and served as an integral part of the nuclear military establishment. By taking a leading role in nuclear research and in the development of spin-offs from the labs like computers, lasers, and nuclear power–generated electricity, the American West played a key role in leading the country into the Atomic Age. In the 1930s and early 1940s, the West had transformed Oppenheimer as a young man. Now, what Oppie had started at Los Alamos helped transform the region even more dramatically.

The postwar, westward tilt of the United States was accelerated by the arrival of nuclear laboratories; production plants; military bases built to test, store, and disperse atomic weapons; uranium mines and mills; and nuclear power plants that eventually dotted the arid landscapes of the region. From the Great Plains to the Pacific Ocean, from the deserts of the Southwest to the rain forests of the Northwest, nuclear enterprises spread across the West and brought jobs, businesses, and technological advancement to the region. These atomic energy–focused places revolutionized the West and the nation.

THE COLD WAR BEGINS

Along with the rest of world, Oppenheimer faced a postwar environment full of uncertainty and danger. Even though World War II ended with the atomic bombings of Japan, an uneasy truce existed among the victorious Allies, especially between the United States and the Soviet Union. Despite President Truman's belief that atomic weapons would secure the United States' superiority over the Soviet Union, Fat Man and Little Boy strained their relations even more.

The Soviet Union had lost 25 million to 30 million people during the war, with many Russian civilians losing their lives to the German invasion and subsequent starvation. To protect itself from further aggression, the Kremlin expanded the USSR's borders into neighboring countries, creating a buffer zone between itself and western Europe in violation of the newly forged Allied agreements concerning those countries in central Europe. With the Soviet Union breaking its accords and carving Soviet client states out of the previously sovereign countries of Poland, Czechoslovakia, Hungary, Romania, and Yugoslavia, the other Allies nervously considered how to counter the Russian expansion. With atomic weapons in the U.S. arsenal, an arms race loomed.

Although the United States and the Soviet Union had joined forces to defeat the Axis powers, they were odd partners. As victors, the capitalistic democracy of the United States and the Communist dictatorship of the USSR faced off, and their differences quickly emerged into a Cold War that lasted forty-five years. Each country sought to extend its economic and political clout over spheres of influence that would contribute to its own prosperity as well as provide additional opportunities for expansion into new areas and markets. Combat did occur during the Cold War in such places as Korea, Vietnam, Afghanistan, and Angola, but the military forces of the two superpowers never directly engaged and fought each other. In conjunction with the contest for economic and ideological dominance, the United States and the USSR engaged in an arms race for military superiority. Nuclear bombs promised to be the ultimate weapon, one that could quickly and effectively destroy an enemy's key cities and military installations, reducing them to radioactive and inhospitable rubble. The devil's bargain countries with nuclear weapons made was that such powerful bombs could also be used against their own cities. A full-scale nuclear exchange between belligerent nations could not only wipe out both countries but also bring about a nuclear Armageddon, ending all human life on Earth. In the high-stakes race for political and military superiority after the war, anyone calling for reasoned debate and even sharing the secrets of nuclear weapons seemed to take on an impossible task.

ONE WORLD STRATEGY

Oppenheimer had struggled with the postwar implications of the creation of atomic weapons as early as 1944. He was not alone. The senior scientist in nuclear physics, Niels Bohr, came to Los Alamos in late 1943 after a harrowing escape from Nazi-occupied Copenhagen. Recovering from his journey — which entailed being smuggled across the Baltic Sea to Sweden and then hidden in the wheel well of a British airplane, where he lost consciousness due to lack of oxygen — Bohr started calling for a One World strategy. Bohr hoped that such a strategy would avoid a competition of nuclear armed countries by uniting all nations in utilizing the beneficial aspects of atomic energy while controlling its destructive forces. He predicted a postwar atomic arms race between the United States and the Soviet Union if the Manhattan Project achieved success. To prevent such an arms race, Bohr wanted to share the secrets of the project's aims with the Soviets — before a bomb was even used. By following this strategy, the USSR would know about the weapon and, hopefully, not feel threatened by it. Bohr also put great faith in the international community of scientists to avert an atomic arms race. Later, Bohr said: "That is why I went to America. They didn't need my help in making the atom bomb." At Los Alamos, Bohr found a receptive audience in Oppenheimer.

After Trinity, Hiroshima, and Nagasaki, the Pandora's box of atomic energy was open. Oppenheimer knew he could not put the atomic bomb back in the box, so he latched onto the hope that atomic energy could make the world a better place. In 1945, this hope centered on the belief that the outcome of using an atomic bomb was so horrendous that the weapon's existence would bring an end to all wars — no one would start a war if the final result would mean the end of the human race. So, to prevent a nuclear catastrophe, Oppenheimer believed the nations of the world needed to unite to control these new weapons.

The issues involved with controlling nuclear weapons grew more complicated as more became known about their destructiveness, about the postwar world, and, in particular, about the Soviet Union's intentions. Powerful figures in the U.S. government also worried about the future and offered their own solutions for the postwar era. Secretary of War Henry L. Stimson wrote a memo to President Truman on September 11, 1945, calling for the United States to invite the Soviet Union into an atomic partnership. Stimson maintained if the Russians were blocked from involvement, "such a condition will almost certainly stimulate feverish activity on the part of the Soviet toward the development of this bomb in what will in effect be a secret armament race of a rather desperate character." This desperate arms race played an integral role in the intensifying Cold War between the United States and the Soviet Union.

CONGRESS TACKLES THE ATOM

In an October 3, 1945, address to Congress, President Truman warned that "the release of atomic energy constitutes a new force too revolutionary to consider in the framework of old ideas." The day after Truman's speech, Senator Edwin C. Johnson of Colorado and Rep. Andrew J. May of Kentucky introduced a bill into Congress to answer the question of who would take postwar domestic control of atomic energy. The May-Johnson bill called for the creation of a nine-member commission that answered only to the president. This alarmed many atomic scientists who had chafed under and been silenced by General Groves during the war. Since Groves had helped write the bill, these scientists feared that he and the military would continue to dominate atomic affairs for the foreseeable future.

After Hiroshima, the atomic bomb was no longer secret, so atomic scientists broke their silence about it and organized to educate the public about the bomb, to advocate for their vision on what to do with it, and to counter the military's ownership of the weapon. Manhattan Project scientists and personnel founded local chapters of concerned citizens that quickly evolved into a national organization called the Federation of Atomic Scientists

(FAS). FAS's position on the May-Johnson bill was "Let's pass something that gets it out of the hands of Groves." Thus the scientists derailed Groves and helped defeat the May-Johnson bill, halting its rapid march through Congress.

Originally, Oppenheimer supported the bill. As a newcomer to the corridors of power in the nation's capital, Oppie wanted to accomplish two objectives by supporting the May-Johnson bill. First, he wanted to show that he was a team player who would not rock the boat. His success as the director of Los Alamos opened doors to the inner sanctums of the most powerful country in the world. His creation of the bomb helped boost the United States to the position of a postwar superpower, and Oppenheimer wanted to be in that inner circle to help formulate policy. Additionally, Oppie had his eye on the bigger prize of international control of atomic energy. He wanted to resolve the issue of domestic control quickly so the nation could grapple with the thornier problem of making sure that atomic bombs would not arm the warring nations of the world.

"I DON'T WANT TO SEE THAT SON-OF-A-BITCH IN THIS OFFICE EVER AGAIN"

The fall of 1945 proved a trying time for Oppenheimer. He and his family left Los Alamos, the FAS mounted a successful attack opposing the May-Johnson bill, and Oppie had an audience with President Truman that went horribly wrong. At their meeting, they talked about the efforts to pass the May-Johnson bill, which both the president and Oppie supported, and how to achieve international control of the new weapon. On that topic they had differences. Usually eloquent and persuasive, Oppie found his charm and charisma fleeing him. Into an awkward silence, Truman asked Oppenheimer when he thought the Russians would obtain a nuclear weapon. When Oppenheimer replied that he did not know, Truman responded with his own take on the timeline: "Never!" Shocked by the president's failure to grasp the threat to national security and world peace that atomic weapons posed, Oppie let his own insecurity flood over him. He uttered, "Mr. President, I feel I have blood on my hands." A disgruntled Truman quickly ended the meeting, telling Oppie, "Don't worry, we're going to work something out and you're going to help us." But the damage was done with the president. After Oppie left, Truman muttered, "Blood on his hands dammit, he hasn't half as much blood on his hands as I have." The president later told Assistant Secretary of State Dean Acheson, "I don't want to see that son-of-a-bitch in this office ever again." Although Oppie wanted to have access to power to help shape policy concerning atomic energy, he had said precisely the wrong thing to President Truman.

For someone like Oppenheimer, who prided himself on being articulate and finding the right word or phrase for the occasion, it is surprising that he botched the meeting with the president so badly. But his words show the great strain that he felt in needing to atone for the destruction of Hiroshima and Nagasaki immediately after the end of the war. They also reveal a flawed belief on his part that he could pass off his guilt to the person who actually ordered the bombings. In reality, the exchange discredited Oppenheimer with the president. As the conscience and voice of the atomic scientists, Oppie lost an opportunity to be heard at one of the real seats of power in Washington — in the Oval Office.

THE ATOMIC ENERGY ACT OF 1946

Despite the bungled meeting with Truman, Oppie continued to help create policy on national and international levels. After the May-Johnson bill was withdrawn, largely due to the public outcry of atomic scientists and the FAS, Senator Brien McMahon of Connecticut introduced a substitute bill. The McMahon bill sought to create an Atomic Energy Commission that was less influenced by the military and that would also support freedom of research into atomic matters by the nation's scientists. In the draft of the McMahon bill, released at the end of December 1945, the opening passage stated, "It is hereby declared to be the policy of the people of the United States that the development and utilization of atomic energy shall be directed toward improving the public welfare, increasing the standard of living, strengthening free competition between private enterprises so far as practicable, and cementing world peace." The bill foresaw that peaceful uses of atomic energy could be just as important as military applications.

After six months of intense debate and political maneuvering, the McMahon bill passed the Senate on June 1, 1946, and the House in mid-July. President Truman signed the Atomic Energy Act into law on August 1, 1946. The act created the Atomic Energy Commission (AEC), with five civilian commissioners appointed by the president and approved by the Senate. A military applications committee, a military liaison committee, and a scientific and industrial committee were formed to advise the AEC. Thus, civilian control existed, but the military continued to play a major role in production decisions and the overall direction of the atomic program. Additionally, the measure allowed the military to take control of the atomic weapons stockpile in times of national emergency.

A serious issue arose with the creation of the AEC. It had conflicting duties and goals. On one hand, it had the charge of developing America's nuclear enterprises. At the same time, the AEC held the regulatory responsibility over nuclear matters and, thus, safeguarding American families from the toxic, radioactive by-products of the nuclear industry. The AEC had to choose between expanding atomic enterprises and restricting these projects due to safety and health concerns. At times, expansion won.

In addition to the five-member commission and military committees, the AEC established a General Advisory Committee (GAC). Oppenheimer became the first chair of the GAC, which assisted the commissioners with the complex scientific, industrial, and at times ethical issues that swirled around atomic energy. John Manley, the experimental physicist at Los Alamos who helped Oppie guide the creation of the atomic bomb, was appointed secretary of the GAC. He later recalled:

"Many who know Oppenheimer's service to the nation at Los Alamos do not know it continued at the same magnificent level for the next four or five years after the war. This time around, everything he did had to be done against selfish and short-sighted hysterical pressures."

As chair of the GAC, Oppie was close to the seats of power, but he did not force his views on the committee or the AEC. I. I. Rabi, his friend and fellow GAC member, explained: "He was not an original. Most of the real ideas came from others but he could open doors and present them. . . . Far from bending us to his viewpoint, he took other people's views. . . . Then he'd make them more acceptable, more clear, more persuasive and this sort of thing made him a wonderful front." Rabi's comments might have addressed one of the charges later leveled against Oppenheimer — that he unduly influenced other GAC members and, by doing so, undermined the national security of the country; however, most of those who served under Oppie on this committee praised his consensus-building leadership. More importantly, GAC members were usually distinguished leaders in their respective fields and could think for themselves.

CONTROLLING THE ATOM

One of the most popular movies released right after the war, *The Best Years of Our Lives*, shows how quickly popular culture accommodated the new atomic peril. In the 1946 film that won seven Oscars for its portrayal of returning World War II veterans, Hoagy Carmichael consoled double-amputee Harold Russell, who was having problems adjusting to civilian life. Carmichael advised: "Don't worry about it, kid. It'll all work out unless we have another war, and then we'll all be blown to bits the first day." From the earliest days of the Atomic Age, the specter of one's backyard becoming ground zero in an atomic attack caused concern and, in many cases, outright fear in the American public.

Two strategies evolved in the United States to address the growing concerns. On one hand, members of the government, led by the military, initiated an arms race cloaked in secrecy. In response to the worsening relationship with the Soviet Union, the United States continued to develop and stockpile nuclear weapons. The secrecy that hid the advances in nuclear weapons technology at first prevented the Soviets from catching up to America's lead. However, the secrecy also prevented the American public from knowing about the magnitude of destruction that atomic bombs inflicted on civilian populations. A sustained public debate on nuclear weapons failed to develop due to the national security cloak that hid atomic affairs. On the other hand, some people called for sharing how to make nuclear weapons with other countries and for the creation of an international agency to control the research and production of atomic bombs to prevent their use. This movement, called One World or None, gathered many prominent scientists, Oppenheimer among them.

In the winter of 1946, right after the atomic dust settled, Oppenheimer contributed a short article for the book *One World or None*. Rushed into print and released to the public in March 1946, *One World or None* discussed from scientific, military, and political viewpoints the future of atomic weapons. In his chapter, Oppenheimer stated, "It is clear that in a very real sense the past patterns of national security are inconsistent with the attainment of security on the only level where it can now, in the atomic age, be effective." He argued that how nations protected their security in the past was obsolete and in fact invited disaster.

The revolutionary strategy that nations now needed to employ to ensure security was laid out by Albert Einstein in another chapter in the book. Einstein said there was only one way out of potential atomic catastrophe: he wrote that an international organization should oversee the resolution of conflicts between individual states and that each individual state should "be prevented from making war by a supranational organization supported by a military power that is exclusively under its control." Such powerful voices calling for an international organization to control nuclear weapons seemed ideal to some and a foolhardy attempt at utopia by others. Oppie joined the group of scientists and politicians who tried to figure out how One World could work in the real world.

In a speech to the Westinghouse Centennial Forum — which was quickly published as "The Atom Bomb as a Great Force for Peace" in the *New York Times Magazine* on June 9, 1946 — Oppenheimer declared, "There is only one future of atomic explosives that I can regard with any enthusiasm: That they should never be used in war." To ensure that an atomic war would never occur, Oppenheimer said that "the heart of our proposal was the recommendation of an international atomic development authority, entrusted with the research, development, and exploitation of the peaceful applications of atomic energy, with the elimination from national armaments of atomic weapons." To prevent atomic bombs from being used in war, Oppie called for a complex combination of international safeguards and national sovereignty. During this period, he called for several initiatives, including an international police force to monitor uranium mining and refinement, a pledge by nations not to make nuclear weapons, and transparency so that all nations could rest assured that other countries were not secretly building the weapons.

As a prominent player in the creation of atomic weapons, Oppenheimer gained stature as a spokesman and a visionary for this new era. From Berkeley, he often traveled to Washington and New York to discuss atomic matters. Both military officers and governmental officials sought his opinion on nuclear weapons, and his quick mind impressed many of these policy makers as they grappled with the complex and life threatening issues of the Atomic Age. To transform his dream of an international organization to control atomic enterprises into approved policy, Oppenheimer became one of the main forces behind the Acheson-Lilienthal Report.

THE ACHESON-LILIENTHAL REPORT

In January 1946, President Truman, in response to the creation of the United Nations Atomic Energy Commission, appointed

a committee to draft a proposal for the control of atomic weapons. Assistant Secretary of State Dean Acheson chaired the
committee, which included such prominent figures from the
Manhattan Project as General Groves, Vannevar Bush, and
James Conant. David Lilienthal, a lawyer and former head of
the Tennessee Valley Authority, chaired the advisory group,
which included Oppie. Cobbled together during meetings in
hotel rooms in New York and Washington, D.C., and on tours
to Oak Ridge and Los Alamos, the Acheson-Lilienthal Report
reflected many of the revolutionary ideas that Oppenheimer
and other atomic scientists had hit upon as they grappled with
the implications of what they had created. Oppie wrote the
original draft, which Lilienthal and other members of the committee edited and revised. The report proposed that the Atomic
Development Authority (ADA), an international agency,
should take over all of the enterprises connected with the splitting of the atom and that the potential benefits of atomic energy should be used to reward countries that abided by the
authority's rules.

As recommended by the report, the ADA would monopolize
and own all facilities involved with the mining, research, and
production of both the civilian and military applications of
nuclear energy. From uranium mines to research laboratories to
future power-production plants around the world, the ADA
would control everything. Additionally, any building of atomic
weapons would be outlawed. To accomplish this, the ADA
would control all nuclear material to prevent it from becoming
used in weapons.

One aspect of the Acheson-Lilienthal Report was especially
radical. To internationalize atomic energy and counter the distrust of other nations, the ADA would operate nuclear reactors
and laboratories around the globe. As the report remarked,
"The real protection will lie in the fact that if any nation seizes
the plants or the stockpiles that are situated in its territory,
other nations will have similar facilities and materials situated
within their own borders so that the act of seizure need not
place them at a disadvantage." An intellectually sweet concept,

this radical idea of sharing nuclear technology and materials
with other nations caused alarm bells to go off at the Pentagon
and in the halls of Congress.

While the members of the committee worked on the report,
Oppie took a lead role. Lilienthal wrote of Oppie after their
first meeting: "He walked back and forth, making funny 'hugh'
sounds between sentences or phrases as he paced the room,
looking at the floor—a mannerism quite strange. . . . I left
liking him, greatly impressed with his flash of mind, but rather
disturbed by the flow of words." In the end, with regard to
Oppie, Lilienthal felt that it "is worth living a lifetime just to
know that mankind has been able to produce such a being."

Once the committee completed the report, President Truman appointed Bernard Baruch to usher it through the United
Nations. Baruch, a conservative Wall Street financier who had
advised previous presidents and statesmen as well as made generous contributions to their political campaigns, focused on the
peril that the plan posed to national sovereignty. For Baruch,
who had accompanied the American delegation to the peace
talks in France after World War I, military force was a necessity.
As he mentioned, "World peace is impossible without the force
to sustain it." Baruch took the Acheson-Lilienthal Report and
created the Baruch Plan, which called for harsh punishments
against all violators of the agreement to control atomic weapons. To ensure adequate and forceful retribution, Baruch insisted on the suspension of the United Nations Security Council's veto clause. For the Soviet Union, this was a deal breaker.
In response to the Baruch Plan, the USSR advocated for "immediate and universal nuclear disarmament without inspec-
tion." In fact, the USSR was feverishly working on its own
atomic bomb.

When Oppie heard that Truman had appointed Baruch to
handle the plan at the UN, he muttered, "We're lost." Lilienthal
wrote after he heard the news: "I was quite sick. . . . We need a
man who is young, vigorous, not vain, and who the Russians
could feel isn't out to simply put them in a hole." At the United
Nations, the Acheson-Lilienthal/Baruch Plan needed the So-

viet Union's approval. But with Baruch pitching a hard line against the Soviets and the Soviets demanding that the United States disarm without equal verification that they were not creating their own nuclear weapons, the early United Nations effort to control atomic energy failed. Baruch, Truman, and many others in the U.S. administration rejected the Soviets' proposal of getting rid of the United States' atomic weapons without the ability to inspect possible bomb-making in the Soviet Union.

CHASING OPPIE IN THE POSTWAR WORLD

Oppenheimer's role in the making of atomic policy attracted the attention of many people in the country, including some who had been watching him since before the war. As early as 1940, the FBI had collected information on Oppie. During the war, Groves told the FBI to leave Oppie alone, but in the early postwar period, that protection evaporated. Then, FBI Director J. Edgar Hoover launched a many-pronged investigation into Oppenheimer. The FBI reopened the case in which Oppie had told Army Intelligence in 1943 that Haakon Chevalier had approached him about passing atomic secrets on to the Soviets. After the war, the FBI now gathered information on what Oppenheimer was doing and whom he saw as he traveled around the country crafting bills and discussing policy with congressmen, atomic energy commissioners, fellow scientists, and members of the media.

Haakon Chevalier held the key to Oppenheimer's security status. Chevalier had tried to serve the government during the war, but because of Oppenheimer's warning of his talk of espionage, Chevalier could not obtain security clearance. After the war, Haakon served as a translator at the Nuremberg war crimes tribunal in Germany. On June 26, 1946, a month after Chevalier had finished his work for the government and as he was home in the Bay Area working on a novel, the FBI knocked on his door and escorted him to the bureau's downtown San

Francisco office for questioning. Agents pressed him for details about his visit with Oppenheimer in the winter of 1943 when he suggested that atomic secrets could be passed on to the Soviet Union. Eventually, Chevalier admitted that he had approached Oppie. The FBI also asked about the other scientists he contacted. Chevalier denied that there were any other contacts. At times, the agents would leave the room only to return with more questions. Unbeknownst to Chevalier, George Eltenton — the man Oppie identified as the conduit to pass information to the Soviet consulate — had also been detained by the FBI for questioning at the same time across the bay in Oakland. The agents left the room to call their counterparts at the other interrogation session to corroborate the information that was surfacing in both interviews.

Chevalier and Eltenton told similar stories. At the behest of the Soviet consulate in San Francisco, Eltenton had contacted Chevalier to ask Oppenheimer if he would share atomic information with Soviet scientists. After Chevalier talked with Oppie, he told Eltenton that "Dr. Oppenheimer did not approve." They both denied that they had contacted any other scientists. A month or two later when they met by chance at a luncheon, Chevalier and Eltenton discovered to their surprise that they had been interrogated at the same time. They also wondered how the FBI had found out about their failed attempt at espionage. A couple of weeks later, the Chevaliers came early to a cocktail party at Oppenheimer's house so that the old friends could talk before the other guests arrived. Haakon mentioned the FBI questioning and Oppie, fearing that his house was bugged, took Chevalier outside to talk further. As Haakon described the day-long interview, Oppie grew more and more upset. At one point, Kitty called out from the porch, "Darling, the guests are arriving and I think you'd better come in now." Despite the waiting guests, Oppenheimer had Chevalier recount his story again. Kitty reappeared, saying that Oppie must come in. Chevalier later recalled, "Opje let loose with a flood of foul language, calling Kitty vile names and told her to mind her goddamn business and to get the . . . hell out." Oppenheimer did not confess to Chevalier that he was the source of the FBI's information.

Not surprisingly, the FBI next visited Oppenheimer on September 5. During his interview, Oppie told the agents that Chevalier had only approached him and not the three scientists he had mentioned to Colonel Pash in 1943. No one really knows why Oppie told a different version of the encounter this time, but several possible explanations arise. Perhaps Oppenheimer wanted to protect the friends and family involved in the incident. Chevalier was one of his closest friends and it is possible Oppie's brother, Frank, is really the person Haakon had approached. So by concocting this story of multiple contacts, Oppie might have hoped to throw the military off of the scent of his friend and brother. Or, perhaps Chevalier had told Oppie that Eltenton had asked him to contact three scientists, but, after being rejected by Oppie, Chevalier did not approach anyone else. Or Oppie might have overreacted during his initial interview with Pash and embellished the story to impress the authorities with his ability to ferret out security risks. Whatever his reason for telling contradictory accounts of the potential security breach, Oppenheimer raised serious doubts about his own loyalty. Oppenheimer also had put his good friend Chevalier at considerable risk. The FBI dogged Haakon for the rest of the 1940s until he moved to France in 1950.

Despite the FBI's concerns about Oppenheimer as a security risk, he received a new clearance in 1947 for his work as chair of the General Advisory Committee. He had access to top-secret reports, talked with atomic scientists and policy makers, and gave counsel to the Atomic Energy Commission. Oppenheimer was a powerful voice for both the administration and for the nuclear scientists concerning atomic energy. As a key figure in the early Atomic Age, Oppie helped shape atomic policy. As an outspoken authority, he attracted both interest and animosity for his views. Some of those people he angered waited until the time was right to strike.

THE INSTITUTE FOR ADVANCED STUDY

The years after the war were a heady time for Oppenheimer. He returned to California to teach a new generation of nuclear physicists, he walked the halls of power in Washington, D.C., on atomic business at the request of the government and the military, and he often spoke to the public about nuclear matters. His face even graced the cover of *Time* magazine in November 1948. His strenuous schedule of teaching, travel, and atomic advising taxed his ability to do all three well. The solution arrived when Lewis Strauss, a commissioner of the AEC and a trustee of the Institute for Advanced Study (IAS) in Princeton, New Jersey, invited Oppie to accept the directorship of that institution. Oppenheimer would replace Albert Einstein. Founded in 1930 by department store magnates Louis Bamberger and his sister Caroline "Carrie" Fuld, the IAS was heralded as "a small university in which a limited amount of teaching and a liberal amount of research [were] both to be found." Fashioned after European institutes that created utopias for scholars, the IAS was a perfect match for Oppie's blend of activism and erudition. He envisioned doing for the IAS what he had done for UC Berkeley in the 1930s — to create an internationally renowned institution for some of the best and brightest minds in the world. Initially, Oppie sought out prominent physicists, but eventually he recruited poets, artists, writers, historians, and other humanists.

In July 1947, Oppie, Kitty, Peter, and Toni left the West and returned to the East. For almost twenty years, Oppenheimer had lived in the West, and he had started his family in the region. Although Oppie now left the West, its effect stayed with him, and his impact on the West only grew as nuclear facilities and advanced technology sites transformed the region into a leader in the Atomic Age. Like many Americans, Oppie had gone west to create a name for himself. And like some of those previous immigrants, Oppenheimer returned triumphant, an internationally known scientist whose thoughts on atomic energy and policy were revered by many.

Lewis Strauss, one of those who initially revered Oppie, played a key role in his life over the next decade. As the person who offered him the IAS job, Strauss dramatically shifted Oppie's life away from teaching and enabled him to live close to Washington, D.C. Strauss, who started out as a shoe salesman, had helped Herbert Hoover distribute food to war-ravaged Europe after World War I. During the Roaring Twenties, he joined and quickly became a full partner in Kuhn, Loeb, one of the bigger investment banking firms on Wall Street. During World War II, Strauss served as a special assistant to the navy secretary, James Forrestal, and received an honorary title of rear admiral. Strauss's unique background in government and finance positioned him to assume a powerful role in the postwar period. Originally, he supported Oppenheimer; however, some of the later interactions between them soured this initial relationship, and with the advent of a smear campaign by the FBI against Oppie, Strauss began to entertain doubts.

THE REAL SOVIET SPIES

During the early postwar period, the Soviet Union consolidated its borders in the satellite states of Eastern Europe and challenged its former allies as it expanded its spheres of influence. As the USSR rearranged the map of postwar Europe for its own national security, it also engaged the United States in a race in politics, economics, and arms. With information stolen from Los Alamos even before the Trinity test, the Soviet Union initiated a crash program to build its own nuclear weapons. The warnings of politicians and scientists about an atomic arms race came true, even as the atomic dust settled over Japan.

The Soviet spies at Los Alamos had transferred the blueprints for Fat Man to Russian agents in the spring of 1945. Three spies are known of at Los Alamos: David Greenglass, Klaus Fuchs, and Theodore (Ted) Hall. Even though Greenglass and Fuchs were Communist Party members before they arrived at Los Alamos, they did not know each other and worked in different parts of the lab. An enlisted man in the army, Greenglass helped assemble the explosive lenses for Fat Man and passed on some crude drawings about that part of the project. Fuchs came to Los Alamos as a member of the British Mission. Originally from Germany, Fuchs hid his Communist Party roots from the British authorities when he fled the Nazis in 1933. By the time he arrived at Los Alamos, he was a deep-cover agent for the Soviet Union who had already divulged secrets about the British atomic bomb program. Fuchs worked day and night on the implosion bomb. As Hans Bethe later said, "He contributed very greatly to the success of the Los Alamos project." Through his espionage, he also contributed greatly to the creation of a Soviet bomb.

In the spring of 1945, the Soviet Union received vital information from Los Alamos. Harry Gold, a Soviet agent from the USSR's consulate in New York City, took the Super Chief train to New Mexico and met Fuchs in Santa Fe. On a drive to the outskirts of town, Fuchs gave Gold a briefcase full of detailed plans on how to build an implosion bomb. On the same trip, Gold went to Albuquerque and knocked on the apartment door of Ruth, David Greenglass's wife. He was greeted by David. When Gold produced a box of Jell-O, cut in half, Greenglass produced the other half. He then passed over the drawings he had made. Fuchs's scientific information greatly surpassed Greenglass's drawings in usefulness for the Soviets. Gold rode the train back to New York and sent the package to Moscow. Even before the Trinity test, Soviet scientists knew that their allies were close to having an operable nuclear weapon.

Ted Hall, on the other hand, was not a Communist spy. As a brilliant young technician at Los Alamos, he worked on the difficult calculations required to create an implosion device. He leaned toward socialism but had never joined the Communist Party. In conversations during the fall of 1944, including ones with Niels Bohr, Hall grew alarmed that an American atomic monopoly could destabilize the postwar period and jeopardize world peace by perpetrating a nuclear conflict. On a trip to the East Coast, Hall walked into a Soviet trade office and handed staffers a report that detailed what the Manhattan Project was building and who was working at Los Alamos. He continued to pass atomic secrets about Fat Man to the Soviets throughout the winter of 1945.

In 2007, an additional Soviet spy involved with the Manhattan Project surfaced. George Koval, born in Iowa in 1913, immigrated to the Soviet Union with his family in the 1930s. There, he received espionage training from the GRU, the USSR's feared military intelligence agency. Back in the States during World War II, Koval worked at Oak Ridge. As a health safety inspector, he had the run of the uranium enrichment plant. Koval transferred that vital knowledge to the Soviet Union, which needed it to process weapons-grade uranium for its fledging bomb efforts. After the war, Koval fled the United States for the Soviet Union. On November 2, 2007, he was posthumously made a Hero of the Russian Federation, the highest award by that country. As the only known Soviet-trained intelligence officer to infiltrate the Manhattan Project, he was one of the most important spies in the early Atomic Age.

Oppenheimer knew nothing about the spies among the Manhattan Project personnel. Nonetheless, he had little illusion that the United States would enjoy its atomic monopoly for very long. The scientists at Los Alamos had unlocked the secret of the binding energy of the atom and applied it to military purposes, making what had been a secret of nature merely one of humans. It was only a matter of time before other nations unlocked the secret as well. Oppie advised governmental officials that he did not know when the Soviets would detonate an atomic weapon, but from the outset, it would take them at most a decade to develop their own bomb.

THE SOVIET BOMB

The Manhattan Project spies spirited the atomic secrets they gathered out of the United States in Soviet diplomatic pouches. The head of the Soviet Union, Joseph Stalin, forwarded the information to Lavrenty Beria, the ruthless director of the NKVD, the dreaded Soviet secret police. Beria argued with

Pyotr Kapitsa, a senior Soviet nuclear scientist, about how best to utilize the stolen secrets. Beria pushed for creating a bomb as soon as possible, even if the blueprint for it came from the United States. Kapitsa argued that to jump ahead of the United States, the Soviets needed to develop their own original device and not merely a copy of the American one. Stalin sided with Beria, who placed Kapitsa under house arrest for eight years. As a result, the Soviet bomb project used the blueprint from Los Alamos.

The Soviet effort to build an operable atomic bomb faced many of the same challenges as the Manhattan Project, from the design of the explosive device to the manufacture of nuclear material. In addition to the information provided by the spies, the Soviets also benefited from official publications printed by the United States. On August 12, 1945 (just days after the atomic bombing of Japan), the U.S. War Department published *A General Account of the Development of Methods Using Atomic Energy for Military Purposes* (a.k.a. the Smyth Report). Without revealing any of the top-secret discoveries that went into making an atomic bomb, the report was an in-depth history of the industrial and scientific efforts to build a bomb. Many of the problems and solutions related to processing uranium and assembling the bomb were explained. Released as a combination of national pride and One World spirit, the Smyth Report alerted the Soviet scientists to some of the dead ends encountered by the Manhattan Project. Quickly translated into Russian, the report showed the Soviets what not to do and allowed them to make more rapid progress in their own bomb development.

The Soviet atomic bomb laboratory resided at the top-secret town of Sarov, home of an old monastery 240 miles southeast of Moscow. Like Los Alamos, the Soviets' atomic city had many code names: Base-112; KB-11; Kremlev; Centre-300; the Volga Office; and Arzamas-16. Arzamas-16 became its official title, purposely named after a town forty-five miles to the north. For Andrey Sakharov, who created the Russian hydrogen bomb there, Arzamas-16 was a "curious symbiosis between an ultramodern scientific research institute . . . and a huge labour camp." Some prisoners did work at Arzamas-16, although no political prisoners were allowed at the site. Most Soviet scientists re- ferred to the atomic city merely as Sarov and even humorously as Los Arzamas.

With help from both atomic spies and the Smyth Report, the capable Soviet physicists came under considerable pressure from their government to make rapid progress in exploiting atomic energy. By August 1949, the Soviets were ready to test their bomb, which they dubbed the Manufacture. On the train ride to the testing ground at Semipalatinsk, some of the person- nel jumped onto the station platform during a short stop and started playing volleyball. A colonel went over to stop them, while a superior fumed: "They're supposed to be serious peo- ple. . . . They're on a responsible mission and they behave like a bunch of eighteen-year-old kids." Using the blueprints that had come from Los Alamos, the Soviets detonated a bomb compa- rable to Fat Man at the end of August.

On September 3, 1949, a U.S. weather reconnaissance plane in the northern Pacific took an air sample that showed an ele- vated level of radioactivity. Called in to consult on this finding, Oppenheimer went to Washington on September 19 to join others in reviewing data collected not just from the weather plane but from other sources around the northern hemisphere. They concurred with the air force's conclusion that the USSR had detonated a plutonium bomb sometime between August 26 and 29 in the eastern part of the Soviet Union.

President Truman informed the American public about the Soviet bomb on September 23. In a statement released by the White House, he said: "I believe the American people, to the fullest extent consistent with national security, are entitled to be informed of all developments in the field of atomic energy. That is my reason for making public the following information. We have evidence that within recent weeks an atomic explosion occurred in the USSR. Ever since the atomic energy was first released by man, the eventual development of this new force by other nations was to be expected. This probability has always been taken into account by us." The president concluded his statement with an appeal for international control of atomic energy: "This recent development emphasizes . . . the necessity for that truly effective enforceable international control of atomic energy which this Government and the large majority of the members of the United Nations support." Despite the president's nod to international control, he had missed the opportunity to secure it by his actions earlier in his administration. His boast to Oppenheimer that the Soviets would never create a bomb now seemed foolish.

Two days later, the Soviet news agency TASS released its own statement. After verifying that the USSR had exploded a nuclear bomb, the release concluded: "It must be said that the Soviet government, despite its possession of atomic weapons, still maintains, and in the future will continue to maintain, its former position on the unconditional banning of the use of nuclear weapons." Two of the victorious allies from World War II now faced each other as enemies — both armed with nuclear weapons.

From Los Alamos to Princeton, from becoming director of an unknown top-secret lab to becoming a world-renowned spokesman for the Atomic Age, Oppenheimer had dramatically changed his life since the grim work during the war. He could have remained teaching in a physics department but instead he took a leadership role in planning for an atomic future. Between gracing the cover of *Time* magazine, meeting with the president, writing the Acheson-Lilienthal Report, directing the Institute for Advanced Study, and being shadowed by the FBI, Oppie became known in the postwar period as an influential spokesperson on nuclear matters. After the Soviets detonated their own bomb, the Cold War ratcheted up with the possibility that a U.S. neighborhood might be the next ground zero. As the new decade of the 1950s began, fear gathered over the country like an ominous cloud and targeted people at universities, in Hollywood, and in the State Department. For those who had waited, the time to strike against Oppie had arrived.

CHAPTER SIX

Targeting Oppenheimer

> If we err today — and I think we do — it is in expecting too
> much of knowledge from the individual and too much of
> synthesis from the community.
>
> J. Robert Oppenheimer, *Atom and Void*

IN the late 1940s and early 1950s, Robert Oppenheimer continued to play an important role as an adviser on atomic policy. He attended Atomic Energy Commission meetings, helped to formulate a response to the Soviets' creation of an atomic bomb, and provided guidance for a nervous citizenry. Along those lines, Oppie gave public lectures that helped shape the public debate about nuclear energy and national security. For many Americans, Oppenheimer symbolized the conscience of the atomic scientists, the expert who increasingly questioned some of the atomic policies of the government and the military. To be sure, he had led the effort to create the first atomic weapon, but he started publically doubting the direction of the AEC and the development of new generations of nuclear weapons.

When Oppie spoke, lecture halls overflowed. Millions listened to him on radio and then on television as he grappled with such topics as science, the creative mind, and the modern world. Several of his lectures reached an overseas audience through the British Broadcasting Corporation (BBC). Some listeners said that they did not understand much of what he said, but they felt uplifted nonetheless. As a charismatic speaker, Oppenheimer influenced many who heard him while he also angered those who crafted alternative paths for nuclear development. His opponents did not simply debate whether or not to silence Oppie. They debated how to do it with the least disruption to the Cold War and the arms race.

THE SUPER

After the Soviets cracked the United States' atomic monopoly in 1949, the American public looked to the federal government for reassurance. For some, such comfort came hard to find. At Santa Fe, which is near Los Alamos, one man on the streets asked: "Why should we worry here in Santa Fe? We're all in danger wherever we are. I'd feel no different in Los Angeles or New York than I do here." A fear of atomic bombs, if shared by enough of the American public, could derail the country's nuclear weapons program at the precise moment when it faced its first real international challenge. President Truman and his atomic advisers huddled to decide how best to react to the challenges posed both by the Soviet bomb and the American public's fear of an atomic attack. For nuclear expertise, Truman turned to the AEC's General Advisory Committee, chaired by Robert Oppenheimer.

Now that the Soviet Union had attained parity with the United States by exploding its own nuclear weapon, how should the country respond? In an arms race, nations respond by creating a bigger, more powerful weapon. Even at Los Alamos during the war, some scientists had focused on creating not just an atomic bomb, but a hydrogen bomb, nicknamed the Super. Edward Teller had led this effort — sometimes to the frustration of other scientists, who felt that it delayed the timely development of Fat Man and Little Boy. During the Manhattan Project, Teller's dislike and even distrust of Oppenheimer began, partly because Oppie selected Hans Bethe over him to head up the Theoretical Division and partly because the director would not divert scarce resources for Teller to work on the Super. As Bethe later remembered, "That I was named to the head of the [Theoretical] division was a severe blow to Teller and who . . . considered himself, quite rightly, as having seniority over everyone at Los Alamos, including Oppenheimer." Oppenheimer also contributed to Teller's animosity. J. Carson Mark, who worked with both of the men at Los Alamos, later recalled: "Now Oppie was not blameless. . . . Oppie had privately heaped scorn on Edward and his ideas, and Edward had privately and publicly given his views of Oppenheimer." In part because of professional reasons but also due to personality clashes, Teller and Oppenheimer held scant regard for each other.

As far back as September 1945, Oppenheimer had expressed strong reservations about the Super. Members of the Scientific Advisory Panel on which he participated wrote: "We feel that the development [of the H-bomb] should not be undertaken, primarily because we should prefer defeat in war to victory obtained at the expense of the enormous human disaster that would be caused by its determined use." However, with the 1949 detonation of the Soviet bomb, nicknamed Joe 1 in the United States for Communist leader Joseph Stalin, the American government quietly debated whether the Super could protect the country from a Russian nuclear attack. The GAC met on October 28, 1949, to debate whether the United States should begin a crash program to develop a hydrogen bomb. In a letter to Conant right before the October 1949 GAC meeting, Oppie reaffirmed his misgivings: "What does worry me is that this thing [the Super] appears to have caught the imagination, of both congressional and of military people, as the answer to the problem posed by the Russian advance [in atomic weapons]. . . . That we become committed to it as the way to save the country and the peace appears to me full of dangers."

Theoretically, such a weapon could be more than one thousand times more powerful than an atomic bomb. At the time, some of the people who had helped Oppenheimer with the Manhattan Project—I. I. Rabi, Enrico Fermi, and James Conant—along with Oliver Buckley (president of Bell Telephone Laboratories) served on the GAC. Oppie's close assistant from Los Alamos, John Manley, worked again as his assistant as the secretary of the GAC.

Truman's administration experienced intense pressure to respond to the Soviet bomb with iron resolve. As a result, the GAC felt rushed to support a hydrogen bomb program. Although many in the government and the military dismissed any alternative except pursuing a Super, the GAC seriously weighed the implications of such a move: First, the committee asked if such a weapon could be created. Second, would it indeed protect national security? And third, was a weapon of such massive destructive capabilities morally acceptable?

After deliberating these issues under Oppenheimer's leadership for three days, the GAC released its opinions. First, the Super could probably be built, but the effort would take away from increasing the atomic (as opposed to the hydrogen) bomb stockpile. Second, if the United States successfully created a hydrogen bomb, the Soviets eventually would also discover how to build one, and in the long run, the United States would be even less secure. Third, the GAC concluded that since atomic bombs were powerful enough to easily destroy an enemy's ability to wage war, using a hydrogen bomb, with its dramatic increase in mass destruction, was not morally defensible. Although Oppie chaired the committee, the members later claimed that he did not coerce them to arrive at these opinions. They came to these conclusions on their own, independent of Oppenheimer.

In its unanimous decision, the GAC recommended to the AEC commissioners that the United States should not embark on a crash program to create a hydrogen bomb. The AEC accepted this recommendation and on November 9 voted three to two not to endorse an effort to create a hydrogen bomb. In a congressional hearing, Oppie told the senators: "If the Russians have the weapon and we don't, we will be badly off. And if the Russians have the weapon and we do, we will still be badly off. . . . By going down this path ourselves, we are doing the one thing that will accelerate and insure [the Russians' Super bomb] development." Although Oppie thought that the committee had successfully thwarted the rush to create the Super, the final decision rested with the president.

Many in the United States believed that having a hydrogen bomb would deter the Soviet Union from proceeding. Of course, Edward Teller, who had worked on the Super during the war, supported it. He offered to bet John Manley, an associate director at Los Alamos, that "unless we went ahead with his Super . . . he, Teller, would be a Russian prisoner of war in the United States within five years!" With this type of reasoning, President Truman could ignore the GAC and the AEC recommendations and forge his own path toward creating more massive nuclear weapons.

On January 31, 1950, President Truman met with AEC chair David Lilienthal, Secretary of State Dean Acheson, and Defense Secretary Louis Johnson. Truman wasted little time at the meeting and asked, "Can the Russians do it?" When everyone nodded yes, the president then said: "In that case, we have no choice. We'll go ahead." On the radio that evening, Truman announced that the United States would launch a crash program to develop the hydrogen bomb. At a birthday party for Strauss held that evening, Oppie could not hide his dismay. In a jubilant mood, Strauss tried to introduce his son and daughter-in-law to Oppenheimer. Oppie did not turn around to greet them, but rudely only offered his hand over his shoulder and then walked away. Strauss added this insult to a growing list of slights he felt Oppenheimer had dealt him.

The moment when Strauss first turned against Oppenheimer had perhaps happened nine months before the birthday party snub. At a congressional hearing convened to debate the shipment of radioactive isotopes abroad, Strauss adamantly argued against sending something that he thought could be used in an atomic bomb overseas. When Oppie spoke at the hearing, he countered: "You can use a shovel for atomic energy. In fact, you do. You can use a bottle of beer for atomic energy. In fact, you do. . . . My own rating of the importance of isotopes in this broad sense is that they are far less important than electronic devices but far more important than, let us say, vitamins. Somewhere in between." Laughter swept the meeting room. Strauss clenched his jaw, and his face turned bright red at the public humiliation.

With Truman's decision to proceed with a crash program to create a hydrogen bomb, scientists at Los Alamos accelerated their research. Even though Edward Teller bragged for decades afterward that he had created the Super, in truth others played key roles in solving the technological challenges of harnessing the power of the sun for a weapon. Unlike the atomic bomb, which split uranium atoms (some of the biggest atoms in the universe), the Super would fuse hydrogen atoms (which are the smallest atoms, with only one electron and one proton each). A key person in this work was Manhattan Project veteran Stanislaw Ulam. Still at Los Alamos, he looked out on his dormant garden in December 1950 and had an inspiration on how to create and sustain a fusion reaction in an explosion. By using an atomic bomb as a trigger and reflecting the nuclear explosion back onto itself, a hydrogen or thermonuclear explosion could result. After Ulam's key realization, Teller added to this essential concept, but without Ulam, Teller would likely have remained as stymied as he had been since 1944. With Ulam's insight, the hydrogen bomb team at Los Alamos made rapid progress on the Super.

The work on the Super achieved success on November 1, 1952, when an island in the South Pacific vaporized as the first hydrogen bomb, code-named Mike, detonated with the power of 10.4 million tons (10.4 megatons) of TNT. By comparison, Little Boy's explosion yielded an equivalent of only 12,500 tons (12.5 kilotons) of TNT. Thus, the hydrogen bomb multiplied the explosive power of the atom by almost a thousand times. The first H-bomb fireball shot up to 57,000 feet within a minute and a half after detonation, and the cloud rose higher than 100,000 feet in just two and a half minutes. The stem of the mushroom cloud eventually spanned thirty miles, and the upper canopy of the cloud had a diameter of more than one hundred miles. As nuclear historian Richard Rhodes wrote, "Mike's fireball alone would have engulfed Manhattan; its blast would have obliterated all of New York City's five boroughs." Los Alamos radiochemist George Cowan witnessed the Mike shot and recalled: "I was stunned. I mean, it was big. . . . As soon as I dared, I whipped off my dark glasses and the thing was enormous, bigger than I'd ever imagined it would be. It looked as though it blotted out the whole horizon, and I was standing on the deck of the *Estes*, thirty miles away." The hydrogen bomb inaugurated a new and more powerful way for humans to kill themselves and destroy their own history.

A NERVOUS NATION

Several severe shocks rocked the American people during the period from 1949 to 1952, from when the Soviets exploded their own atomic weapon to the successful test of the United States' hydrogen bomb. In February 1950, Klaus Fuchs, a physicist who had worked at Los Alamos as part of the British Mission, was arrested in England and charged with passing atomic secrets to the Soviets during World War II. Fuchs quickly confessed and furthermore admitted that he had stolen plans for the hydrogen bomb before he left Los Alamos and given them to a Soviet agent as well.

The same month as Fuchs' arrest, Senator Joseph McCarthy shocked the country with his allegations that the U.S. State Department harbored "known Communists" who worked to overthrow the government from within. This startling revelation led to Senate hearings and unsubstantiated accusations that nonetheless destroyed people's careers and lives. Those who questioned McCarthy and his strong-arm tactics often were accused of being Communists themselves and lost their jobs or their political careers. Only when McCarthy attacked the U.S. Army as being soft on Communism in 1954 did the hysterical "Red Scare" tide turn, and the senator lost his following.

As McCarthy started his witch hunt, another shock came in June of 1950. Communist North Korea invaded South Korea and pitted not just that divided country against itself, but the armed forces of the United Nations against the large army of the newly created Communist China. The Korean War lasted until the summer of 1953 and ended just as another scare hit the American public. As a result of the Soviet bomb, the FBI investigated those who worked on the Manhattan Project and discovered another spy in addition to Fuchs. David Greenglass, a mechanic at Los Alamos during the war, had passed crude drawings of Fat Man to the same Soviet agent who had made contact with Fuchs. Greenglass's sister, Ethel Rosenberg, and her husband, Julius, were arrested and tried for espionage. In the Red Scare, atomic hysteria, and McCarthyism that swept the country, they were convicted and then executed in 1953. Oppenheimer realized that because of his past, McCarthy posed a danger to him. He did not suspect that as the investigation into how the Soviets attained an atomic bomb proceeded, the attack upon him would come not from a delusional senator but from colleagues, acquaintances, and even old friends.

Beginning with awareness of the Soviet bomb in the fall of 1949, national and international events battered the confidence of the American public as evidence of atomic spying, claims that Communists had infiltrated the government, and a hot war against Korean and Chinese Communists in northeast Asia unfolded. The Cold War worsened abroad and struck close to home.

THE FIRST STRIKE AGAINST OPPIE

Oppenheimer had argued and voted against the development of the Super. He almost resigned his position on the GAC after Truman gave the go-ahead, but decided against such a radical move. The lure of being at the center of governmental power and helping to shape nuclear policy, even if his advice was at times discarded, appealed to him. Not only did he continue to serve on the GAC, but he also participated in a disarmament panel in 1951. Joining him on the panel were, among others, McGeorge Bundy (future national security adviser to Presidents Kennedy and Johnson), Allen Dulles (the first director of the Central Intelligence Agency in 1953), and Dartmouth president John S. Dickey. The panel deliberated on the future of nuclear weapons and decided that they were not viable armaments since they could never be used. The indiscriminate killing of millions of civilians and the moral burden that came from utilizing such weapons of mass destruction prevented leaders of responsible countries from ever employing them. What then should atomic policy makers do?

For Oppenheimer and those like him, the answer to that question centered on ending the secrecy that prevented the American public from knowing about the increased power of nuclear weapons and that there was no defense against hydrogen bombs. To counter this ignorance, members of the panel called for candor with the public. They advocated letting the public know about the increased destructiveness of hydrogen bombs and the threat that they posed to human existence. Oppenheimer's call for candor as well as his increasing opposition to some of the administration's atomic policies opened him up to a series of attacks that eventually resulted in his removal from influence in nuclear affairs.

The first public attack occurred in California. In 1950, the California State Senate Un-American Activities Committee heard from Sylvia Crouch, a former Communist Party member. Paul Crouch, her husband, had joined the Communist Party in 1925, but he eventually became a double agent, informing the FBI about his fellow party members. Sylvia claimed that she and Paul were present at Oppenheimer's house in July 1941 when Oppie held a "session of a top-drawer Communist group known as a special section, a group so important that its make-up was kept secret from ordinary Communists." After this allegation made front-page headlines in newspapers around the nation, Oppenheimer quickly rebutted the story with this written statement: "I have never been a member of the Communist Party." After he had helped end the war in August 1945, he now began receiving hate mail. One message read: "Why don't both you and your wife go to the Russia that you like so well. Your wife has admitted it, why don't you? We don't want such people as you are in this U.S."

An aggressive FBI investigation of the alleged meeting resulted. Agents escorted the Crouchs to the Oppenheimers' former house in Berkeley and interviewed other supposed members of the secret Communist cell in the Bay Area. The allegation against Oppenheimer fell apart when Oppie proved that he and Kitty had gone to Perro Caliente, their ranch in New Mexico, during the time when the Crouchs claimed they had hosted the party in California. Paul Crouch received $9,675 for his assistance to the FBI, including this testimony against Oppenheimer. At the time, as he and his wife identified Communists for the FBI, he earned the highest payment from the Justice Department of any consultant. Although Oppie dodged this attack, a more serious assault awaited. To succeed, Oppenheimer's opponents realized that they needed a much stronger case against the physicist.

AT HOME IN PRINCETON

As director of the Institute for Advanced Study (IAS) in New Jersey, Robert Oppenheimer and his family lived in Olden Manor, a three-story white colonial house surrounded by woods and lawns. Parts of Olden Manor had been built in 1669, and it had served as a field hospital for General Washington during the American Revolution. Just prior to the Oppenheimers' arrival, it was home to Albert and Mileva Einstein. The house came with a cook and a gardener. The family quickly made the house their home. Kitty had a greenhouse attached for her gardening, Peter secured a room for a photography studio and darkroom, and Toni had a stable built for her pony.

The Oppenheimers, through articles published about them in *Life* and *Time* magazines, created a public image of a happy couple with young children living in an idyllic setting. According to stories in the press, Oppie came home from the institute at 6:30 every evening to play with Peter and Toni; throw a stick to their German shepherd, Buddy; smoke his pipe; and talk with Kitty. Kitty indulged in her avocation of botany and spent many hours tending the garden at Olden Manor; however, the Oppenheimers' family life — especially the marriage between Kitty and Robert — was much more complex.

Perhaps because of Kitty's tragic loss of her previous husband Joe Dallet during the Spanish Civil War, she could be a difficult person to be near. At times, she drank heavily. Every week at her house, she presided over a meeting of a group of women who talked and drank through the afternoon. A wife of a physicist at

Princeton University recalled, "Kitty had a ring of damaged women around her, all of them somewhat alcoholic." Kitty also uttered hurtful comments to those close to her and new friends. She would sometimes embrace a new friend, confiding the most intimate details of her life, and then turn and savage that friend in public. A scientific colleague of Oppenheimer's, Abraham Pais, wrote, "Quite independently from her drinking, I have found Kitty the most despicable female I have ever known, because of her cruelty."

Why then did Oppie stay with Kitty? Several reasons surface. First, he needed her as a confidant and consultant. He talked with her about his work and valued her advice about how to run first Los Alamos and then the IAS. As Princeton theoretician Freeman Dyson recalled: "She was a tower of strength to us as she was to Robert." Additionally, Oppie and Kitty knew from 1946 (if not earlier) that the FBI had them under surveillance. The FBI bugged their phones at Berkeley and chased Robert when he traveled around the country. The pressure that that knowledge created helped to create a bunker mentality. Kitty and Oppie needed each other to withstand the stress of their lives. By accounts of some of those friends close to the Oppenheimers, despite Kitty's harshness and Oppie's distracted aloofness, they were devoted to and loved each other.

Growing up in the famous Oppenheimer family under the best of situations would have been challenging. Peter and Toni faced the additional strain of familial dysfunction caused by alcoholism. IAS colleague Abraham Pais commented: "Oppenheimer's family life looked like hell on earth. The worst of it all was that inevitably the two children had to suffer." Robert Strunsky, a neighbor at Princeton, observed, "I think to be a child of Robert and Kitty Oppenheimer is to have one of the greatest handicaps in the world." Peter grew up from being a shy and sensitive child to being a solemn teenager. As an adolescent, he did not flash the brilliance of his father and at times fought with his mother.

Like many first-born children, Peter had trouble living up to his parents' expectations. Toni, younger than Peter by four years, did not suffer the same parental pressures. A family friend, Verna Hobson, commented: "From when she was six or seven years old, the rest of the family relied on her to be sensible and solid and to cheer them on. . . . Toni was the one you never worried about." She did contract a mild case of polio in 1951, and to help treat her, the Oppenheimers that Christmas rented a seventy-two-foot boat and sailed around the Caribbean islands for two weeks. Robert returned to his childhood passion for sailing, and the whole family frolicked in the warm weather and surf around the U.S. Virgin Islands. They eventually bought a home on St. John and spent weeks there every year sailing, swimming, and relaxing. Even though the family still owned Perro Caliente, their St. John home became their refuge. Oppie and Kitty embraced the Caribbean, just as they had New Mexico. As they incorporated the new aspect of their lives into their individual and familial identities, the West as a part of their identity faded away.

In the early fifties, influential as well as unknown people contacted Oppie for advice and help. George Kennan, the architect of the containment strategy against the Soviet Union, became a friend when they served on committees together. Kennan agreed with Oppie that pursuing the Super provided no real security in an arms race against Russia and indeed might even create more instability. As the hydrogen bomb program progressed in the fall of 1951, Oppie sent this memo about solar energy to Kennan: "It seems to me that we should immediately take the following steps: a) Classify the sun as Top-secret; b) Establish a commission to manage it for the benefit of all mankind; c) Give appropriate high-level indications of a super weapon based on the sun; d) At the same time, make an official policy pronouncement indicating that we wish to use the sun, not for devastation and war, but for the betterment of mankind." Communicating partly tongue in cheek, partly bitterly, Oppenheimer expressed his frustration about the development of the Super.

Sometimes from out of the blue, people wrote Oppie as their last hope. In August 1951, a woman appealed to him: "Others

may pray to a so-called God, burn candles and ceremonial in-
cense . . . but I've always been a long way from any designated
heaven, so I'm taking my appeal to a man of Earth with a godly
brain." Her appeal concerned her two-and-a-half-year-old
nephew who had leukemia. She pleaded with Oppenheimer:
"Won't you try to find a cure for this little boy? Or perhaps with
your easy contact with other brilliant men, you may know a
man (or men) who can do something constructive to help
him." This letter is just one among the many that anonymous
people sent to Oppie seeking his advice and assistance.

STORM CLOUDS GATHER

Having learned from their botched attempt to discredit Oppenheimer in California, his opponents knew that to succeed in
attacking him, they would need to marshal all their forces and
coordinate their strategy and tactics. To destroy the hero of the
Manhattan Project, they would not only have to make a strong
case against him, but they would have to control the proceedings. As a result, powerful people in Washington, D.C., began
to stack the deck against Oppie.

As early as 1945, FBI director J. Edgar Hoover had sent
memos to the White House and secretary of state claiming
Oppenheimer was a Communist and questioning his loyalty. In
1952, the FBI intensified its chasing of Oppie. In January, Director Hoover received a memo advising him "that extensive
investigation has already been conducted concerning J. Robert
Oppenheimer which included periodic physical surveillances,
mail covers, a continuous technical surveillance [listening in on
phone calls] from May 1946 until June 1947, and interviews
with present and former associates, friends, co-workers and
others. Our main case file on Oppenheimer now consists of 11
sections, which does not include bulky exhibits or the MED
[Manhattan Engineer District] investigation." The FBI and the
AEC would build their coming case against Oppie with many
of these documents, some more than a decade old.

The FBI reinterviewed Kitty about her Communist past in

April and again in August. For the April questioning, Oppie accompanied his wife and wondered if there were a particular reason for the timing. He inquired why his wife was not interviewed five years earlier when he received his postwar top-secret clearance. He asked the FBI agents if the interview had something to do with the upcoming McCarran Committee on internal security. Oppie had heard rumors that both he and Kitty would have to testify at those hearings. Oppie told the agents that "his wife was very willing to be interviewed, in as much as her former CP activity was an open book and she had no desire to keep the information off the record." At the end of the questioning, both Oppie and Kitty "stated that they would welcome any additional inquiries for re-interview if desired." Despite such amiable cooperation, the FBI gathered as many incriminating and unfavorable interviews as it could to use in its quest to unseat Oppenheimer.

The FBI also interviewed Dr. Edward Teller. In May 1952, a memo to Hoover summarized Teller's interview: "Teller states subject has opposed development of H Bomb since 1945 and is of the opinion that H Bomb would have been a reality at least one year ago if it had not been opposed by Oppenheimer." Later on in the memo, the report noted: "Teller states he would do most anything to see subject separated from General Advisory Committee because of his poor advice and policies regarding national preparedness and because of his delaying of the development of the H Bomb." In Teller, the FBI found a willing, able, and perhaps most importantly, respectable witness to impugn Oppie. Even though Teller requested that his interview be kept confidential, he let the FBI know that he wanted to help remove Oppie from power. Teller worked behind the scenes for the next two years to remove Oppie not just from the GAC, but from the world of atomic policy making.

Others also wanted Oppie off of the GAC. AEC commissioner Thomas Murray complained to FBI agents in March 1952 about the delay in production of atomic weapons caused by scientists who did not want to make such weapons. For Murray, the main blame lay with Oppenheimer. Murray pointed out "that few people realize the tremendous influence which Oppenheimer has on the Atomic Energy Program, the Defense Program, and all scientific thinking throughout the world." An additional group dissatisfied with Oppie was the U.S. Air Force. Oppenheimer had disagreed with the air force about whether its newly formed Strategic Air Command, with long-range bombers capable of launching nuclear strikes against the Soviets at a moment's notice, was a good use of defense funding.

In May, rumors circulated around Washington that Oppenheimer might be charged with perjury. Then a revelation in an FBI memo cast into doubt Oppenheimer's reappointment to the GAC: "[Senator McMahon] has worked out a plan whereby Oppenheimer would take the initiative and decline to serve another term by an exchange of letters and everybody will be happy." In April, the FBI circulated a memo that stated: "While discussing other matters with AEC Commissioner Thomas K. Murray, Mr. Murray advised [FBI] Agent Bates of the Liaison Unit that his efforts to keep Oppenheimer from being reappointed as Chairman of the General Advisory Committee of the AEC were proceeding very well." All of the other commissioners agreed with Murray, who told Bates that "Oppenheimer would be in Washington in the next few days, at which time they intended to tell him that he would not be recommended for reappointment." Oppie, perhaps fearing the perjury charge, agreed to resign from the GAC, the powerful advisory committee he had chaired since the creation of the AEC in 1946. Even though Oppenheimer was pushed off the GAC by the AEC commissioners, he continued to act as a consultant to the AEC and to hold a top-secret clearance, which allowed him access to the latest documents about atomic weapons.

"BATTEN DOWN THE HATCHES"

In 1953, a key player who would lead the attack on Oppie returned to the AEC. Lewis Strauss, who had grown disenchanted with Oppenheimer as an AEC commissioner, had left the commission soon after the 1950 vote about the Super. He was reappointed as its chair in 1953 by the newly elected President Eisenhower. One of Strauss's conditions for his reappointment involved getting rid of Oppenheimer, and he began a campaign to do so soon after his Senate confirmation.

Under Strauss's reign on the commission, security became the predominate issue. Harold Green, an AEC lawyer who conducted security checks, witnessed the transformation in 1953 and thought that Strauss was conducting a purge of the commission under the guise of tightening security. Soon after Strauss became chair, a close friend of Oppenheimer received a call from a colleague on the staff of the AEC. The colleague warned, "You better tell your friend Oppie to batten down the hatches and prepare for some stormy weather."

In September 1953, only three blocks from the White House, an FBI agent shadowed Oppenheimer. The agent watched him at the Hotel Statler, one of the finest hotels in postwar Washington. Oppie had told Strauss that he could not meet with him that afternoon because he had an appointment at the White House. Fearful about what Oppenheimer might say to the president, Strauss asked for and obtained FBI surveillance of the scientist. According to the FBI report to Strauss, instead of going to the White House, Oppie lounged around the hotel's lobby and restaurant, met with a newspaper reporter from the *Washington Post*, ate, drank beer, and read magazines. This day's chasing of Oppie foreshadowed the full force the federal government would bring to bear against him before the end of the year. Within months, the FBI and the AEC hounded Oppie through the halls of power, removed his responsibilities as a trusted adviser on nuclear weapons, and subjected him to public humiliation. The very man who had led the nation in its creation of atomic weapons was now considered by J. Edgar Hoover, the director of the FBI, as one of the most dangerous men in the country.

Despite the storm clouds on the horizon, Oppenheimer did not hunker down. In fact, he grew more vocal and went more public about the threat posed by nuclear weapons and the impact of secrecy on atomic policy. In a *Foreign Affairs* article in 1953, Oppenheimer lamented: "I must tell [about the arms race] without revealing anything. I must reveal its nature without revealing anything." He also warned that the nation's economy was destined to be skewed by an arms race and that "security" would be used to cover up instances of malfeasance, payoffs, and blunders. In another article, Oppenheimer questioned the sanity of the arms race, comparing the United States and the USSR "to two scorpions in a bottle, each capable of killing the other, but only at the risk of his own life." This was not a perspective Strauss, Teller, and others involved with nuclear weapons wanted broadcast to the American public. Something had to be done before the influential voice on atomic energy and hero for many Americans started eroding public support for the nuclear arms race.

"MORE PROBABLY THAN NOT"

Over the summer of 1953, William Borden, a former lawyer for the AEC, isolated himself at his family's summer cottage on a lake in upstate New York. He read, pondered, and began a report that took another look at Oppenheimer's security status. Over that fall, he continued to grapple with his report. Early in November, he sent it to Lewis Strauss, who forwarded it to the FBI. In his letter, Borden offered three conclusions: "1) Between 1939 and mid-1942, more probably than not, J. Robert Oppenheimer was a sufficiently hardened Communist that he either volunteered espionage information to the Soviets or complied with a request for much information. . . . 2) More probably than not, he has since been functioning as an espionage agent; and 3) More probably than not, he has since acted under a Soviet directive in influencing United States military, atomic energy, intelligence, and diplomatic policy." This letter accusing Oppenheimer of working as a Soviet spy served to ignite the firestorm that led to his downfall.

William Borden was originally hired by Senator Brien Mc-Mahon to work on the congressional Joint Committee on Atomic Energy, when he saw Oppie in action as a member of the General Advisory Council. Borden also knew about modern warfare. Flying in Europe as a bomber pilot in World War II, he saw a German V–2 rocket streak past his plane on its way to blowing up part of London. After the war, he was haunted by the thought that such missiles tipped with nuclear weapons could rain down on American cities. After McMahon died in 1952, Borden came under the influence of Teller and then Strauss. As the conspiracy against Oppenheimer grew, Borden began chasing him. Strauss aided Borden over the summer of 1953 by supplying him with Oppie's top-secret personnel file from the AEC's vault.

In his letter to the FBI, Borden claimed that Oppie contributed to and belonged to the Communist Party, had family members and at least one mistress who were Communists, "had no close friends except Communists," and only recruited Communists into the early atomic bomb project. Borden continued, alleging that after Oppenheimer became involved with the Manhattan Project, he stopped all of his Communist activities and gave false information to Army Intelligence and the FBI concerning his CP activities from 1939 to 1942. Borden also claimed that Oppie turned against the hydrogen bomb after the atomic bombing of Japan and persuaded others not to aid in the further development of nuclear weapons. With his letter, Borden fired the first salvo against Oppenheimer in Strauss's campaign to discredit him. More charges followed.

FBI Director J. Edgar Hoover received Borden's letter and had the charges evaluated. Several weeks passed before he decided that they had enough merit to forward the letter to the White House. Possibly, Hoover was trying to reconcile Borden's letter with the FBI's conclusions in its 1947 report on Oppie. In 1947, when the FBI vetted Oppie for a top-security clearance, the bureau wrote: "Oppenheimer has thus far shown no inclination to be sympathetic with a view of furnishing the Russians information concerning our atomic secret." Armed with Borden's accusations, Hoover felt he could now ignore his own agency's previous evaluation.

President Eisenhower did not see the letter until early December, but once he did, he insisted that Oppenheimer immediately lose any access to classified documents. Eisenhower commented, "The sad fact is that if this charge is true, we have a man who has been right in the middle of our whole atomic development from the earliest days." Fearing that Senator Mc-Carthy might attack his administration with this bombshell about a Communist in the atomic weapons program, the president sent a formal note to Attorney General Herbert Brownell calling for a "blank wall" to be erected between Oppenheimer and all top-secret material. A memo to Hoover on December 3, 1953, detailed Strauss's meeting with Eisenhower concerning Borden's letter. The memo said that: "The President issued instructions that an immediate barrier be placed between Oppenheimer and anything to do with atomic energy. The President said he did not care how this was done, but that it must be done immediately. . . . Strauss advised that he is suspending Oppenheimer's clearance immediately." Strauss set in motion the procedures to permanently strip Oppenheimer of his security clearance.

While Strauss, Hoover, and eventually Eisenhower worked on how to proceed in the security case, Oppie and Kitty traveled through Europe. Oppenheimer gave four talks as part of the prestigious Reith Lectures on the British Broadcasting Corporation's radio network. During these lectures on the radio, Oppenheimer talked about past scientists like Newton and the evolution of atomic physics, and he touched briefly on atomic energy. He talked about how atoms worked and what science brought to humanity. At one point in his lectures, he waxed mystical: "A discovery in science, or a new theory, even when it appears most unitary and most all-embracing, deals with some immediate element of novelty or paradox within the framework of far vaster, unanalyzed, unarticulated reserves of knowledge, experience, faith, and presupposition. Our progress is narrow; it takes a vast world unchallenged and for granted." Millions of people around the world tuned in to BBC Radio to hear Oppie's musings.

After the lectures ended, the Oppenheimers went to Paris. They saw the sights, met people, and had dinner with an old friend, Haakon Chevalier, and his new wife. With the storm clouds building in Washington, a governmental alert went out for U.S. agents to keep track of Oppie and Kitty on their European journeys. Hoover and Strauss feared that if word leaked to the couple about the "blank wall," the Oppenheimers would bolt for the Soviet Union. Ignorant of the blank wall and what awaited them in the nation's capital, the Oppenheimers returned to Princeton as scheduled on December 13.

STRAUSS ACCUSES OPPENHEIMER

In the meantime, Strauss held meetings at the White House on how to proceed against Oppenheimer with Vice President Richard Nixon, several key White House aides, and CIA Director Allen Dulles. They decided the best way to strip Oppenheimer of his security clearance was to convene a panel chosen by Strauss to evaluate the charges against him. In hopes of avoiding using such a panel, Strauss would offer Oppie a choice: he could accept the loss of his security status without protest, or he would have to appeal the security revocation before the panel.

On December 21, 1953, Strauss met with Oppenheimer at the Atomic Energy Commission office in Washington. The AEC chair showed Oppie a letter that detailed the charges against him. This incriminating information had lain in his file for years, thoroughly evaluated during his previous security reviews. Despite the lack of any new damaging evidence, Strauss informed Oppenheimer that the president had called for a further investigation, and until that was finished, Oppie would not have access to classified documents. Strauss then offered Oppie the choice of accepting the loss of his security clearance quietly or appealing it. When asked how much time he had to think this over, Strauss told Oppenheimer that he needed a decision by that evening. After the thirty-five-minute meeting, Oppenheimer left Strauss's office and went immediately to Joe Volpe, a lawyer he had worked with at the AEC. Unbeknownst to Oppie or Volpe, the FBI had already bugged Volpe's office in anticipation of Oppie's visit.

Strauss waited anxiously that evening for Oppie's reply. A lot rested on whether Oppenheimer would accept the loss of his clearance or would appeal the decision. As a respected scientist among most of the physicists working with nuclear weapons, Oppenheimer enjoyed an exalted position as the father of the atomic bomb. As such, the public looked to him for guidance in nuclear affairs. For Strauss and the rest of those interested in removing Oppie's influence from atomic affairs, they hoped Oppenheimer would quietly submit to the revocation.

After considering his options and talking with Kitty and his lawyers, Oppie chose to fight the security clearance revocation. On December 23, Oppenheimer arrived at the AEC headquarters and rejected Strauss's suggestion that he accept the revocation. In a letter, Oppie wrote: "I have thought most earnestly of the alternative suggested. Under the circumstances, this course of action would mean that I accept and concur in the view that I am not fit to serve this government that I have now served for some twelve years. This I cannot do." Oppenheimer and Strauss, and their powerful supporters, squared off to fight a battle that meant more than whether a respected scientist would lose his security access. The fate of the U.S. nuclear weapons program, as well as the course of the arms race, could be impacted by the outcome of this fight. To ensure the desired outcome, Strauss and Hoover employed some unusual and at times illegal tactics against Oppenheimer.

STACKING THE DECK

A memo on January 5 from the FBI's Special Agent in Charge at Newark to Director Hoover confirmed that "technical installation at subject's residence . . . was completed 10:20 A.M. January 1, 1954." In anticipation of the upcoming hearing, the FBI had begun listening to the phone conversations in the Oppenheimer household. On January 5, 1954, an FBI agent who listened to wiretap conversations between Oppenheimer and his lawyer called the central office for guidance. Agent Belmont wrote that Agent "Commons wanted to be sure that the

Bureau desired the technical surveillance [the wiretaps] continued in view of the fact that it might disclose attorney-client relations." Belmont then advised Commons that "our chief concern is to know immediately of any indication that Oppenheimer might flee. Under this set of facts, I think the technical surveillance is warranted." Hiding behind the fear that Oppenheimer might leave the country, the FBI broke the law against listening to a person's conversation with his attorney. Over the next four months, the FBI tape recorded these privileged conversations and distributed them to Strauss and the lawyers for the AEC. Due to these wiretaps, the AEC and its lawyers knew what Oppenheimer and his lawyers had planned for his defense, sometimes as soon as the defense team had decided it.

The charges against Oppenheimer rested on old information and fell into two broad categories. First, the AEC claimed that Oppie had ties to Communists and in fact had been a member of a secret Communist cell in the Bay Area. Second, the commission accused Oppie of delaying the development of the hydrogen bomb. Although Borden stated in his letter that he thought Oppenheimer served as a Soviet spy, this charge surfaced only briefly during the hearing. Thus, the trick for the AEC involved convicting Oppie through hearsay and innuendo about his left-wing past and about his opposition to the creation of the H-bomb.

After four months of intense preparation, the Personnel Security Board (PSB) hearing for Oppenheimer began on April 12, 1954. Strauss had picked three men to judge Oppenheimer — Gordon Gray, a former secretary of the army; Thomas Morgan, a captain of industry who had been president of the Sperry Gyroscope Corporation; and Ward Evans, a retired chemistry professor known for his severe stance in other personnel-related security hearings. Lee Hancock, an ex-FBI agent who helped the AEC with its case, observed that the selection of these three men was "a cold calculating exhibition of trying to stack the deck." By charging Oppie with vague past misdeeds difficult to disprove, listening to his privileged conversations with lawyers, and appointing men to serve as judges who would side with the AEC,

Strauss and his allies felt confident this time that they could finally destroy the reputation and influence of J. Robert Oppenheimer. For people like Strauss and Hoover, this character assassination was the culmination of fifteen years of suspicion, investigation, and personal animosity. From their perspective, their illegal and unethical activities were justified by their genuine conviction that Oppenheimer was a Soviet spy.

"IN THE MATTER OF J. ROBERT OPPENHEIMER"

The Gray Board, named after Gordon Gray, who chaired the Personnel Security Board, held the hearings in a run-down building leftover from war mobilization that was squeezed into the National Mall in Washington, D.C. The hearings ran from April 12 to May 5. Chairman Gray read the general charge against Oppenheimer on the first day of the hearings: "As a result of additional investigation as to your character, associations, and loyalty and review of your personal security file in the light of the requirements of the Atomic Energy Act . . . there has developed considerable question whether your continued employment on Atomic Energy Commission work will endanger the common defense and security and whether such continued employment is clearly consistent with the interests of the national security." With that, the man who had helped the country win World War II now had to defend his loyalty.

Even though this was a hearing, Gray conducted it more like a trial, but without the formal proceedings that protect a defendant. As such, the role of the lawyers for each side proved pivotal. Strauss chose as his lead lawyer Roger Robb, a forty-six-year-old assistant U.S. attorney with a reputation as a fierce prosecutor who shredded the testimony of defendants with intense cross-examinations. On the other hand, Oppenheimer had a difficult time finding the right legal counsel and, ultimately, failed. He chose Lloyd Garrison, the great-grandson of the famous abolitionist William Lloyd Garrison, as his lead lawyer. Lloyd Garrison was a respected lawyer, but for this case, he had two fatal weaknesses: First, he had little actual courtroom experience. He did not counter Robb's sharp assaults and did not protect Oppie from these attacks. Second, he did not have security clearance, which meant that he would not have access to the top-secret documents used to indict Oppenheimer.

Before the hearing began, these weaknesses seemed of little consequence. David Lilienthal, the former AEC head, mentioned, "I had hoped it might be an experienced trial lawyer, but the case against Robert is so weak, really, that choice of counsel isn't as important as if it were." Like Oppie and his lawyers, Oppenheimer's supporters misread the will of his accusers to bend and even break laws and manipulate the proceedings. Choosing Garrison, a politically connected lawyer instead of a hardened trial attorney, played right into the hands of Oppie's opponents.

The list of thirty-eight witnesses — twenty-eight of whom were for the defense — included many key figures in the nation's atomic weapons complex: military officers like General Groves, nuclear scientists, and presidents of corporations. Only a few of the witnesses testified against Oppie, while most praised his wartime work to create an atomic bomb and his postwar efforts to guide the nation's nuclear policies. In fact, the most damning words of the entire proceedings came from only two witnesses: Edward Teller and Oppenheimer himself.

After Garrison submitted his list of witnesses, he asked to see whom the prosecution would call to testify. Since this was not a real criminal trial but merely a hearing, Robb refused to give Garrison his list. Then Robb used the files the FBI had assembled on the defense witnesses to embarrass them when they appeared before the tribunal. Members of the prosecution also did not release to the defense team the thousands of documents they compiled to accuse Oppie. In trying to catch Oppie, they sought to trap him with his own words and actions.

Another questionable strategy of the prosecution was to deny security clearance to Oppenheimer's lawyers. Garrison requested clearance as the trial neared, which Strauss refused. Robb had received his clearance in only a few days. This meant that Oppenheimer at times would be in the hearing without legal representation because his lawyers would have to leave the room when top-secret matters were discussed. So, from the beginning, the Oppenheimer defense team struggled to overcome the handicaps that Strauss and the AEC had placed on them. As the hearings began, Strauss pulled an additional dirty trick that damaged Oppie's standing with the Gray Board for the entire month of the proceedings.

On April 13, the second day of the proceedings, the *New York Times* published a front-page story about the Oppenheimer security hearings. A respected journalist, James Reston, who knew Oppie, had heard of the hearing and wanted to publish a story about it. Under pressure from the AEC, the members of the defense team had promised to try to prevent its publication. So it seemed on April 13 that they had broken their promise in an effort to gain public support for Oppie. In fact, Strauss and James Haggerty, the White House press secretary, arranged for the story to break the day after the hearings began. Chairman Gray was livid, and on that second day of the hearings, he accused Oppie of leaking the story. Gray complained: "I think these stories are very prejudicial to the spirit of inquiry that I tried to establish as an atmosphere for this hearing as we started yesterday. I would very much regret that what would appear to the board [a] possible lack of cooperation in conducting these proceedings in the press." From the second day on, Gray and his fellow hearing officers thought that Oppie had lied when he agreed to try to keep the hearings secret and then the story was leaked. Strauss never admitted that the AEC and the White House had manipulated the release of the story to further damage Oppie's credibility with the Gray Board. Oppie and his defense team never quite recovered from this perceived example of Oppie's untrustworthiness.

Into this poisoned and manipulated atmosphere, Oppie and his lawyers scrambled to answer the charges against him. When Robb questioned Oppenheimer, he attacked on several fronts. On one hand, he grilled Oppie about his support of communist causes and friendship with Communists. In particular, Robb asked about Haakon Chevalier. Robb's other main point of attack focused on Oppie's lack of support for the creation of the hydrogen bomb.

On April 14, 1954, Robb launched in earnest his effort to destroy Oppenheimer, and the next three weeks were probably the worst in Oppie's entire life. Robb asked Oppenheimer if he were a "fellow traveler," a person who was "someone who accepted part of the public program of the Communist Party, who was willing to work with and associate with Communists, but who was not a member of the party." Oppie admitted that he was a fellow traveler in the late 1930s "and then it tapered off, and I would say I traveled much less fellow after 1939 and very much less after 1942." Ignoring Oppie's attempt at humor, Robb established that Kitty, as well as Oppie's brother and sister-in-law, had been Communist Party members.

Having tainted Oppenheimer with his past connections with Communists, Robb then brought up the Chevalier affair. Unknown to Oppie and his defense team, Robb had the transcripts of the World War II interviews from Army Intelligence. Oppie did not know until he was questioned by Robb — who waved the transcripts in his face — that he had been secretly tape-recorded in 1943. On August 25 of that year, Oppenheimer had told Lieutenant Johnson in Berkeley that the army should watch George Eltenton as someone who had offered to pass atomic secrets to the Soviets. The next day in 1943, Lt. Col. Boris Pash interviewed Oppenheimer about his tip. The transcript of the PSB hearing tells the damaging exchange between Robb and Oppenheimer.

ROBB: Did you tell Pash the truth about this thing?
OPPENHEIMER: No.
ROBB: You lied to him?
OPPENHEIMER: Yes.
ROBB: What did you tell Pash that was not true?
OPPENHEIMER: "That Eltenton had attempted to approach members of the project — three members of the project — through intermediaries.

When Robb asked Oppenheimer why he made up this story, Oppie replied sarcastically, "Because I was an idiot." And then he admitted that he did not want to involve his close friend Chevalier.

Robb concluded this part of his interrogation of Oppenheimer with this question: "Isn't it a fair statement today, Dr. Oppenheimer, that according to your testimony now, you told not one lie to Colonel Pash, but a whole fabrication and tissue of lies?" Oppie glumly replied, "Right." Of all the testimony over a month of testimonies, this admission damaged Oppie the most during his Personnel Security Board hearing. He admitted that during the Manhattan Project, he had lied to Army Intelligence about an approach made to him to pass secrets from the atomic bomb project to the Soviets.

To this day, the "cock-and-bull story," as Oppie called it, mystifies historians. Had Chevalier approached three people or just Oppenheimer? Was Oppie protecting his brother, Frank, who might have been the person Chevalier really approached? Was Oppie still involved with Communist activities after 1942? If Oppie truly had something to hide—that he was a member of a secret cell of the Communist Party in the Bay Area in 1943—he surely would not have mentioned any of this to Army Intelligence that August. But from his initial effort to warn the army that Eltenton was involved in atomic espionage, Oppie wove a complicated and eventually disastrous tale that implicated not only himself, but his brother and his best friend. The Chevalier affair, exposed on the first day of Oppie's testimony, turned the Gray Board even more against him. More damaging revelations followed.

On April 16, Robb pushed "the matter of J. Robert Oppenheimer," as the hearing was also called, into discussion of Oppie's opposition to the hydrogen bomb project. Although strained by the five days of Robb's grilling, Oppenheimer had regained some of his composure and began to resist the innuendos that portrayed him as a questionable security risk. Oppie admitted that he had opposed the hydrogen bomb. Robb then asked, "You mean you had a moral revulsion against the production of such a dreadful weapon?" Oppie countered: "That is too strong." When Robb asked if the weapon or his expression were too strong, Oppie replied: "Your expression. I had a grave concern and anxiety." Robb pressed further: "You had qualms about it?" Oppie replied incredulously, "How could one not have qualms about it? I know no one who doesn't have qualms about it." Concerning a weapon one thousand times more powerful than the bomb that ended World War II, Oppenheimer was right. Few people then — or now — could feel comfortable with such a massive weapon.

Easter Sunday came at the end of the first week of the hearings. The Oppenheimers took refuge at a friend's house in Georgetown and, at Sunday dinner, talk turned to the hearing. Along with Garrison and Herbert Marks, who also represented Oppie at the hearing, Joe Volpe — whom Oppie had first turned to when he left Strauss's office after being charged in December — attended. After hearing about how the PSB hearing was being run more like an adversarial trial than an administrative grievance proceeding, Volpe told Oppie, "Robert, tell them to shove it, leave it, don't go on with it because I don't think you can win." Despite his friend's advice, Oppie returned to the hearing room the next day.

After Oppenheimer's five days on the witness stand, prominent people from government, academics, and business appeared who testified mainly in support of his character and loyalty. Vannevar Bush, who helped administer the Manhattan Project, addressed his and Oppie's opposition to the hydrogen bomb when he testified at the hearing: "I think history will show that was a turning point, that when we entered into the grim work that we are entering right now, that those who pushed that thing through to a conclusion without making that attempt [at an agreement with the Soviets] have a great deal to answer for."

John Lansdale, who had been the Manhattan Project's chief of security, confirmed Oppenheimer's loyalty. He then said to Robb, "I am extremely disturbed by the current hysteria of the times, which this seems to be a manifestation." When Robb asked Lansdale if the inquiry were such a manifestation, Lansdale answered: "I think the hysteria of the times over communism is extremely dangerous. . . . I think the fact that associations in 1940 are regarded with the same seriousness that similar associations would be regarded today is a manifestation of hysteria." John McCloy, chairman of Chase National Bank, suggested in regard to Oppenheimer's character and contributions, "I would accept a considerable amount of political immaturity in return for this rather esoteric, this rather indefinite, theoretical thinking that I believe we are going to be dependent on for the next generation." George Kennan, the architect of the containment policy against the Soviet Union, proclaimed that Oppenheimer was "one of the great minds of this generation of Americans."

"UNFROCKING" OPPIE

Although most of the witnesses supported Oppie and vouched for his loyalty and adherence to security, the final week of the hearings allowed those hostile to him to have the last word to influence the Gray Board. In particular, Edward Teller appeared in front of the Gray Board on April 28. Teller had arrived in Washington at least a week before this appointment to coordinate his testimony with the prosecutors. After living in Oppie's shadow for more than ten years and still resentful that Oppie had not appointed him to head the Theoretical Division at Los Alamos during the war, and over other slights, Teller told AEC officials that Oppenheimer's influence over the nuclear weapons program had to end. In a memo to Strauss about Teller's willingness to take the lead in testifying against Oppie, an AEC public information officer said, "Teller feels strongly that this 'unfrocking' must be done or else . . . scientists may lose their enthusiasm for the [atomic weapons] program." Predisposed to discredit Oppenheimer, Teller took the lead in casting doubt on Oppie's loyalty.

Under questioning, Robb asked Teller if he thought Oppenheimer was disloyal. Teller answered: "I know Oppenheimer as an intellectually most alert and a very complicated person, and I think it would be presumptuous and wrong on my part if I would in any way analyze his motives. But I have always assumed . . . that he is loyal." Robb then queried if Teller thought Oppenheimer was a security risk. Teller replied: "In a great number of cases I have seen Dr. Oppenheimer act—I understood that Dr. Oppenheimer acted in a way which for me was exceedingly hard to understand. . . . To this extent, I feel that I would like to see the vital interests of this country in hands which I understand better and therefore trust more." These carefully phrased words of Teller, although not very conclusive, were the most damning of all the statements from witnesses—besides Oppie's—in the entire month of the PSB hearing. Working behind the scene, Strauss and Hoover worked hard to bolster the case against Oppenheimer.

Maj. Gen. Roscoe Wilson also questioned Oppenheimer's motives, although he testified under orders from the chief of staff of the air force. Wilson did not discuss any specific examples of when Oppie violated security regulations, but he pointed to a suspicious "pattern of activity" that included support for the One World international concept to control nuclear weapons, opposition to several methods of detecting Soviet testing of atomic bombs, as well as confrontation over the development of a nuclear-powered airplane (an idea that eventually proved unfeasible). Even though Wilson strongly supported nuclear weapons, he later said his testimony against Oppenheimer was "one of the great sorrows of my life." He recalled afterward that Oppenheimer has been "remarkably kind to me, and really a great mind, an incredible mind. . . . This really has been on my conscience."

William Borden, the person who had initiated the hearing process with his damaging letter, also appeared on the witness stand. At the beginning of Borden's testimony, his letter accusing Oppie was given to Oppenheimer's lawyers. For the first time, the defense team saw the document that was the foundation of the prosecution's charges. Garrison protested that the charge made in letter, that Oppie had been and possibly was still a Soviet agent, established an entirely new charge. Chairman Gray agreed that the hearing board had no evidence that Oppenheimer participated in espionage and dismissed Borden's main accusation.

On May 6, the Gray Board ended with a three-hour summation by Garrison. He argued that the case against Oppenheimer lacked merit: "I would like to tell you what this case seems to me to look like in short compass. I wish we could dispose of it out of hand on the basis . . . that for more than a decade Dr. Oppenheimer has been trusted, and that he has not failed that trust. That in my judgment is the most persuasive evidence that you could possibly have."

Garrison provided legal and "commonsense" reasons to reject Oppie's security clearance revocation. He cited Oppenheimer's service to the country both during the war and afterward. He disputed the witnesses who attacked Oppenheimer's character and motives and suggested that the board members review the friendly witnesses and their testimony as they contemplated their decision. Garrison concluded at the end of three hours: "I am confident . . . that when you have done all of this, you will answer the blunt and ugly question whether he is fit to be trusted with restricted data, in the affirmative. I believe, members of the board, that in doing so you will most deeply serve the interests of the United States of America, which all of us love and want to protect and further."

After four weeks of testimony, after thirty-eight witnesses, after all the behind-the-scenes manipulations and outright skullduggery, after all that Strauss and Hoover had done to defrock Oppie, they had to wait for the judgment of the three members of the board. Many people nervously awaited the Gray Board's ruling — Strauss, Hoover, President Eisenhower. No one waited more nervously than Robert Oppenheimer.

CHAPTER SEVEN

The Fallout

Our civilizations perish; the carved stone, the written word,
the heroic act fade into a memory of memory and in the end are
gone. The day will come when our race is gone; this house, this
earth in which we live will one day be unfit for human
habitation, as the sun ages and alters.

J. Robert Oppenheimer, *Atom and Void*

AS the Atomic Energy Commission, the scientific community,
and those in government anxiously awaited the verdict of the
Gray Board, much rode on the outcome. The AEC and the FBI
had invested vast resources and energy in defrocking Oppenheimer. Their motivations wedded what they thought was best for
the country with personal vindictiveness. Those who feared that
the Soviet Union presented a clear and present danger to the
United States sought to remove any liberal influences from the
government, especially from the AEC and the nation's atomic
facilities. Those who supported Oppie — and who thought the
Personnel Security Board hearing a sham — thundered about
the wrong direction the country had taken. For both groups,
Oppenheimer's security hearing was a pivotal event during the
Red Scare of the 1950s. The future of the nation's nuclear enterprises had reached a turning point.

THE GRAY BOARD DECIDES

The Gray Board's sessions, although not directly connected
with the infamous McCarthy hearings, still made up one of the
last show trials of that era. If the charges had been filed a year
later, Oppenheimer might have dodged such a hearing and kept
his security clearance; however, history combines certain peo-

ple at certain times to create certain events and consequences. All these pieces have to come together in a timely manner, and when they do, a pivotal moment sometimes changes the world for decades to come. Such a key moment came at Los Alamos with the creation of the Atomic Age during World War II. Another such moment happened with the rush to judgment of J. Robert Oppenheimer at the end of May 1954.

The Gray Board reconvened after a short break, and for ten days the members reread sections of the hearing transcript, weighed the witnesses' testimonies, and grappled with whether they could trust Oppenheimer with the nation's top nuclear secrets. Two of the hearing officers, Gray and Morgan, strongly felt that they could not trust Oppenheimer with such sensitive material. To everyone's surprise, Evans returned to the deliberations having changed his mind. He no longer believed in Oppie's guilt. In the end, the Gray Board voted two to one to recommend to the AEC that Oppenheimer's security clearance be revoked. Strauss had continued to work on the board during the interim, fearful that Evans would gain Morgan's support and vote in Oppie's favor.

In the majority report that explained their decision, Gray and Morgan cited Oppenheimer's prewar support for left-wing and liberal causes and his friendship with Communists. However, they concluded that they found "no evidence of disloyalty." To the contrary, they found "much responsible and positive evidence of the loyalty and love of country" on Oppenheimer's part. The majority opinion of Gray and Morgan centered on the last charge, that Oppenheimer had delayed the hydrogen bomb program. Here, their reasoning grew twisted. Although they agreed that Oppie did not directly obstruct the development of the H-bomb, they concluded that his lack of support and enthusiasm had harmed the program. So, even though Gray and Morgan thought that Oppenheimer was a loyal citizen with a "high degree of discretion reflecting an unusual ability to keep to himself vital secrets," they ruled that giving him back his security clearance would not be "consistent with security interests of the United States."

Evans did not agree with the majority decision and submitted a minority report. Explaining his reasoning, he stated that "most of the derogatory material [about Oppie's past] was in the hands of the Committee when Dr. Oppenheimer was cleared in 1947." "They apparently were aware of his associations and his left-wing policies: yet they cleared him," Evans continued. "They took a chance because of his special talents and he continued to do a good job. Now when the job is done, we are asked to investigate him for practically the same derogatory information. . . . To deny him clearance now for what he was cleared for in 1947, when we must know that he is less of a security risk now than he was then, seems hardly the procedure to be adopted for a free country." "To damn him now and ruin his career and his service, I cannot do it," Evans concluded:

The Gray Board's decision hit newspapers at the end of May, and even though most stories supported the decision, some reported it as an injustice. Public opinion ran mixed. Strauss countered the negative reporting with a bold but questionable move. He decided to release the entire transcript of the hearing, which totaled 992 pages, in the belief that when members of the public read Oppenheimer's admission of lying to security personnel during the war and cavorting with Communists, they would agree that he posed a security risk. At the beginning of the hearing, Gordon Gray had promised all of the witnesses that their testimony would remain confidential. This made little difference to Strauss. He had his staff at the AEC inform most of the witnesses, but not all, that the transcript, titled "In the Matter of J. Robert Oppenheimer," would soon become public knowledge. Teller had the most to lose in having his testimony splashed across the nation's newspapers.

THE AEC DECIDES

To ensure that the AEC commissioners approved the Gray Board's ruling, Gen. Kenneth Nichols, the general counsel for the agency, composed a letter reviewing the charges brought against Oppenheimer. Here again, the actions of the AEC became twisted, because Nichols and others were dismayed with the Gray Board's decision. They realized that to revoke Oppenheimer's clearance because of his opinion concerning the hydrogen bomb could backfire. It might chill future collaborations with scientists who would worry that their frank opinions — if counter to a future governmental policy—could come back years later to destroy their careers and lives. Conversely, Nichols and his colleagues also believed that Oppie was a Soviet agent. So, Nichols rewrote the charges against Oppie for the commissioners, leaving out his opposition to the H-bomb and instead accusing him of being "a Communist in every respect except for the fact that he did not carry a party card." In essence, Nichols ignored the Gray Board's opinion and offered the AEC commissioners an entirely new reason to revoke Oppenheimer's top-secret clearance — that he had lied to the Gray Board about his politics. Along this line of thinking, Oppie was disloyal at best and, at worst, a spy.

Although Oppenheimer's lawyer Lloyd Garrison asked to personally address the commissioners before they rendered their decision, his request was denied. As a result, Oppenheimer's defense team never had a chance to refute Nichols' letter. In fact, they never even saw it. In a case full of irregularities that would have been grounds for appeal if this were a trial and not a hearing, Nichols' letter switching the charges and then the denial of the defense's request to address the commissioners were the gravest injustices of all.

As Strauss had stacked the deck against Oppenheimer during the Gray Board hearings, he also sought to manipulate the AEC commissioners with his persuasive powers. If those failed to convince members to vote against Oppenheimer, Strauss dangled in front of at least one of them the suggestion of possible future financial benefits for not backing Oppenheimer. Several AEC members strongly supported the ruling against Oppie, while scientist Henry Smyth decided to vote against the revocation. Eugene Zuckert also leaned toward absolving Oppie of security concerns; however, his term on the AEC would end on June 30, and he had few prospects for future employment. As a consequence, Strauss and Zuckert signed a contract that set Zuckert up to be a personal adviser and consultant to the chairman after he left the commission. With the commissioners lined up to provide the desired outcome, the AEC met toward the end of June to render its ruling on the matter of J. Robert Oppenheimer.

The commissioners concurred with the Gray Board in a four-to-one vote and ruled against giving Oppenheimer back his security clearance. The majority of the commissioners agreed with the charge that Oppenheimer had "substantial defects in his character." Smyth—who worked in the Manhattan Project during the war—disagreed with the majority and, for the days leading up to the decision, wrote and rewrote his minority opinion. During this feverish activity, Smyth lamented to the aides helping him: "You know, I'm doing all this for a fellow I've never liked very much. Of course, I'm not doing it for him." In his report, Smyth argued: "The past fifteen years of his life have been investigated and reinvestigated. For much of that last eleven years he has been under actual surveillance, his movements watched, his conversations noted, his mail and telephone calls checked. This professional review of his actions has been supplemented by enthusiastic amateur help from powerful personal enemies." Of all the people involved with this case, of all those who had weighed the evidence and evaluated the man, Smyth's statement that Oppenheimer was a target of powerful enemies who had chased him for more than fifteen years without finding anything new that incriminated him rings the most true.

On June 29, 1954, the AEC formally revoked Oppenheimer's clearance to access top-secret information. Surprisingly, Oppie's clearance would have lapsed by itself on June 30, when his contract with the AEC ended. If the commissioners and Strauss had done nothing, Oppie would have lost his clearance anyway. That the AEC forced a hearing, and then released the transcript to the public, smacks of more than removing a suspected security risk. It publicly humiliated Oppenheimer, removed him from his position as a spokesman for the Atomic Age, and

warned others about the dangers of disagreeing with governmental policies.

A PUBLIC UPROAR

Beginning with the Gray Board's verdict in May and then when
the security board transcripts hit newspapers in June, the public
reacted to the closed-doors hearing. Even before the AEC had
decided at the end of June, personnel from the nation's nuclear
facilities rallied to support Oppenheimer. At Los Alamos, 282
atomic scientists signed a petition protesting the hearing. Another 1,100 scientists and university professors across the nation made similar petitions. One of the first responses to the
decision came from the Federation of Atomic Scientists (FAS),
which issued a statement blasting the Gray Board: "Many of us
who know Robert Oppenheimer can only respond by doubting the good judgment of the majority of the board. . . . There
can be little respect for their conclusions." Commenting from
Los Alamos, David Hill, the retiring chairman of the FAS,
warned, "A suspicion will persist, in light of the committee's
recommendation, that Dr. Oppenheimer is being penalized for
giving his honest opinion several years ago against the ad-
visability of a 'crash program' to build the H-bomb."

Reactions from the Hill crowded the front page of the *Santa
Fe New Mexican* on June 17. In addition to the almost three
hundred scientists who protested the Gray Board's vote for revocation, approximately two hundred more lab personnel (including five of the seven division heads at the laboratory) signed
a petition disagreeing with the board's decision. The petition —
which was sent to President Eisenhower, Rep. W. Sterling Cole
(chair of the Joint Congressional Committee on Atomic Energy), and the five AEC commissioners — informed Washington that scientists on the Hill were "deeply disturbed" by the
recommendations of the security board, adding, "It is inexcus-
able to employ the personnel security system as a means of
dispensing with the services of a loyal but unwanted consultant."

Dr. Hill released another statement criticizing the AEC that echoed the sentiments of Ward Evans of the Gray Board: "Political crimes of the sort committed against (Dr. J. Robert) Oppenheimer and our country must not be possible in the government of a free country," he asserted. Hill predicted that the consequences of such a policy, "if continued, will eliminate the men of independent mind from our defense establishment." One scientist told political columnist Joseph Alsop that the decision against Oppenheimer "would certainly be demoralizing" among Hill personnel. Lab director Norris Bradbury admitted as much later that fall when he speculated that this is "not going to make it easy to draw people into classified work." Several scientists talked to the *New Mexican* on the condition that they remain anonymous. According to one, "The general effect of the Oppenheimer hearing at Los Alamos . . . was a crystallization of the attitude: There-but-for-the-grace-of-God-go-I." Like Oppenheimer, other scientists on the Hill had been equally guilty of opposing the Super. The message was clear for the personnel at the lab: if you disagree with official policy, your work at the lab could be terminated and your career ruined.

Sympathetic letters poured into the Oppenheimer household at Princeton. Even before the hearing was over, former First Lady Eleanor Roosevelt sent this comment to Oppenheimer: "I have, of course, no question of your loyalty and I wanted to tell you this and to say that had I personally been a physicist I would have had grave question as to whether I wanted to develop the H-bomb." Gordon Dean, a respected lawyer who had served as the chairman of the AEC just prior to Strauss, wrote from his prestigious law office in New York City: "It goes without saying that nothing that has transpired has shaken for one moment my personal confidence in you nor lessened one whit my gratitude for your outstanding assistance to the Atomic Energy enterprises; and your photograph remains on my office wall in the same conspicuous place." Luia Browne, who lived in Oppenheimer's old house in Berkeley, sent this message: "I felt all through both hearings sick at heart for you; and also for our country. One wonders in something close to fear how much longer we are condemned to suffer through this illness."

Newspapers across the country for the most part supported the AEC. An editorialist for the *Newark Star-Ledger* wrote: "The board and the commission . . . learned that (Oppenheimer) was a fellow traveler: that he had Communist friends and attended meetings with them; that he was engaged to one woman Communist and married another woman Communist. . . . He first neglected to tell the government about a Communist friend trying to tap him for atomic secrets, then lied about it, then told the truth. . . . It is a mystery why Dr. Oppenheimer permitted his supporters to make a cause celebre out of the case." An editorial in the *Albany Knickerbocker News* speculated, "An examination of the lengthy reports convince us that had he not been a scientist, and so distinguished a scientist, he would have been unceremoniously tossed out of the atomic picture long ago." On the streets of Santa Fe, credit manager H. S. Ledbetter voiced his concern: "If all the stories are true about his Communist associations, there is bound to be something. A person naturally is affected by his associates no matter who they are." A range of opinions and editorials polarized the public on the matter of J. Robert Oppenheimer.

THE VERDICT'S AFTERMATH

Some of the main players in the matter of J. Robert Oppenheimer saw the hearing as a stepping stone to more important postings in government or business. The prosecuting attorney, Roger Robb, won an appointment as a federal judge. Lewis Strauss, who desired to enter the highest levels of government as a cabinet secretary, failed in this quest. He left the AEC in 1959 when President Eisenhower nominated him to serve as the secretary of commerce. After a contentious confirmation hearing in the Senate, Strauss was not approved. As an indication of the many enemies Strauss had made over the years, either through his heavy-handed manipulations concerning Oppenheimer or his other dealings in government, he was only the eighth cabinet nominee to be rejected by the Senate up to that time. Zuckert received a contract to serve as Strauss's per-

sonal consultant; however, he later regretted the role he had
played in the Oppenheimer decision. Zuckert admitted: "It was
the saddest thing I ever took part in. It cost me a lot of friendships, and I had to be on the same side as people I did not
respect."

Henry Smyth, the sole dissenter of the AEC commissioners,
was later appointed by President Kennedy as the U.S. ambas-
sador to the International Atomic Energy Agency in Vienna.
After serving in that important post for almost a decade, Smyth
returned to his tenured professorship at Princeton.

Edward Teller left a mixed legacy after the hearings, matching the mixed reactions he received. Once the transcripts and
his role in testifying against Oppie became public, many scientists shunned him. Later in that summer of 1954, when he
showed up to do some work at Los Alamos, several colleagues
refused to shake his extended hand. In later years, Teller attempted to rehabilitate his role in the proceedings by saying
that right before he testified, Robb had showed him Oppie's
testimony in which he had admitted to lying to security agents
during the war. Teller claimed that this revelation shocked him
into saying what he did against Oppenheimer. Despite his
claim, Teller had worked behind the scenes for years with the
FBI and the AEC to cast doubt on Oppenheimer's loyalty. Like
most people, including Oppenheimer, Teller seemed to selectively remember the past in a way that made himself look better.

Even though Teller lost favor with some atomic scientists, he
played an increasingly significant role in atomic policy. He
could not replace Oppie as a popular spokesperson, but with
Oppie disgraced, the government turned to him for advice,
which set the direction of the nation's nuclear weapons program for decades. Eventually this path led to the creation of the
Strategic Defense Initiative (the Star Wars program) in the
1980s. Teller was the type of scientist that the government and
defense establishment came to want — not One World and liberal like Oppenheimer, but hawkish and conservative. In this
respect, Oppenheimer's security revocation removed a moder-
ating voice from atomic policy consideration and set the stage

208 J. ROBERT OPPENHEIMER

for an aggressive nuclear program and arms race that continued for the rest of the century.

One of the best evaluations of the Gray Board's security revocation and the AEC decision comes from an oral history that Los Alamos National Laboratory conducted in 1980 with Dr. Emilio Segrè, a Nobel Prize–winning nuclear physicist who worked with Oppie at Los Alamos. When asked why the hearings occurred, Segrè answered: "They took place because there was a political situation in which a side of this political struggle wanted to damage, as much as possible, the others. Who were the parties in this political struggle is a complex thing . . . but I would say the Air Force, part of the Atomic Energy Commission, part of the armed services. . . . One part having won, wanted to consolidate their victory by destroying an important chief of the opposite party. Oppenheimer was there in the middle, pretty innocently, I feel." When asked what politics were involved, Segrè replied: "Politics of rearmament, politics of the hydrogen bomb, struggles between laboratories, and I think apart from a few people, the majority were acting in good faith. . . . They had very strong feelings, and as it happens in this kind of thing, they did a tremendous injustice, a really damnable thing, thinking that they were doing a great service to the country." For Segrè, Oppenheimer served as a symbol, a person at the wrong place at the wrong time, caught in a political battle over which he had little control.

PICKING UP THE PIECES

Oppenheimer probably knew from the beginning that the Gray Board and then the Atomic Energy Commissioners would move against him. Nonetheless, the revocation of his security clearance pained him, and he retreated to Olden Manor at Princeton. To recover from the stress of the hearings and then the turmoil — both private and public — of the verdict, the Oppenheimers went to the Virgin Islands and sailed through the blue waters of the Caribbean. For the rest of his life, Oppie and his family spent several months a year on St. John, sailing, walking on the beaches, gardening, and holding parties. They eventually built a rustic house overlooking Hawksnest Bay and spent Christmas, Easter, and at least a month each summer on the island.

Life had changed for Oppie and his family. Henry Smyth, the dissenter on the AEC, was later asked if the hearing had affected Oppie. He replied, "Oh yes, it killed him." Schatzi Davis, who had lived near the Oppenheimers in Los Alamos, visited them that fall. She expected to find the usual lively household, but instead she saw Oppie and Kitty looking sad and tired. By most accounts, Kitty drank even more than before. The couple's son, Peter, later observed: "My father's tragedy was not that he lost his clearance, but my mother's slow descent into the hell of alcoholism."

Robert and Kitty's friends on St. John voiced similar opinions about the couple as those who knew them in the crucible of Los Alamos. Inga Hiilivirta, a Finnish woman who met Oppie on St. John, commented: "Robert was a very humble man. . . . I adored him. I thought he was kind of saintly. His blue eyes were just marvelous. It looked like he could read what you were thinking." Another island friend, Doris Jadan, noted: "Kitty, of course, was something else. She was disturbed. But [she and Robert] were both very protective of each other. . . . The devil had struck through part of her and she knew it." In terms of Kitty's relationship with her husband, Doris continued: "She was the great trouble in his life and she knew it. . . . She loved Robert. There's no doubt about that. But she was a tangled person. . . . I think in fairness to her, she may have been as good a wife as he could have had." Kitty and Oppie now lived in a world without access to top-secret information but in which many of their family secrets and their tangled personalities lay open to all.

A RETURN TO THE INSTITUTE

Without his time-consuming consulting trips to Washington, Oppie had more time to devote to directing the Institute for Advanced Study. Some of those there felt that he became a better director after the security clearance revocation. What Oppie had accomplished at Berkeley before the war and at Los Alamos during the war—making these facilities into world-renowned centers—he continued at the institute. Granted, the IAS had earned its world renown before Oppenheimer arrived; however, he brought scientists, artists, mathematicians, humanists, and intellectuals to Princeton for research and fellowship. The institute not only grew as a center for physics, but as a place that invited interesting people from a variety of fields to join a celebration and exploration of intellectual curiosity.

Throughout his tenure as the director of IAS, Oppenheimer attracted illustrious scholars to the institute. Homer Thompson, an authority on the ruins of ancient Greece; Harold Cherniss, an expert on the Greek philosophers Plato and Aristotle; Arnold Toynbee, the eminent world historian; George Kennan, the U.S. diplomat who was a specialist in Soviet affairs; and T. S. Eliot, the poet who wrote *The Wasteland*, all spent time at the institute. Oppie brought these and other distinguished visiting scholars to IAS to augment the prominent mathematicians and scientists who held the regular faculty positions there.

Oppenheimer almost lost his position as the director of the institute right after the Gray Board decision. Lewis Strauss, not content to destroy Oppenheimer's governmental service, then went after his academic position. Strauss tried to rally the others on the institute's board of governors to force Oppie to resign, but little came from Strauss's accusations against Oppenheimer. Princeton was not Washington, D.C., the Institute for Advanced Study was not the AEC, and the director of the institute no longer had top-secret files in a safe at his office that would necessitate FBI surveillance.

With the changes in their life, Kitty and Oppie also began to travel more. In the late 1950s and the early 1960s, they went to France, Belgium, Brazil, Greece, Israel, Latin America, and even Japan. The trip to Japan held special meaning for both the Oppenheimers as well as the Japanese people. Concerning a speech Oppenheimer gave in Osaka, a local newspaper reported, "The slender, penetrating scientist and educator spoke on 'Tradition and Discovery' with a tone of deep concern but not without a vein of optimism as a man greatly responsible for the tapping of double-edged atomic energy." During a private audience with a group of Japanese scientists and professors, Oppenheimer noted that the day before President Roosevelt died, FDR had worked on a speech about atomic weapons. Oppie continued: "In the speech, [Roosevelt] spoke of the mastery of man over the forces of nature and then he said, 'What we need if we are to survive is a science of human relations.' I have always been bothered by that speech, because if we have to wait for the science of human relations, we may very well not be here."

At one point, Japanese journalists quizzed Oppenheimer about the atomic bombing of their country. Oppie replied: "I do not regret that I had something to do with the technical success of the atomic bomb. It isn't that I don't feel bad; it is that I don't feel worse tonight than I did last night."

One of the trips abroad created a crisis within the Oppenheimer family. Leaving to serve as a visiting professor in Paris for a semester in 1958, Oppie took Kitty and fourteen-year-old Toni with him. Kitty, however, had insisted that Peter, who was seventeen at the time, not accompany them. Perhaps due to Peter's birth soon after Oppie and Kitty's marriage, perhaps because, as one family friend observed, "Kitty was very, very impatient with him [Peter]," a rift grew between mother and son. Kitty forced Oppie to choose between them. As Oppenheimer's personal secretary, Verna Hobson, remembered: "There came a time when Robert had to choose between Peter — of whom he was very fond — and Kitty. She made it so it had to be one or the other, and because of the compact he had made with God or with himself, he chose Kitty." A key indication of Kitty's personality was that not only had she alienated her son, but she forced her husband to take her side as well.

A PUBLIC INTELLECTUAL

After the PSB hearing, Eisenhower attempted to reach out to Oppie when he sent a personal note to Strauss. The president asked Strauss whether Oppenheimer would be interested in working on the desalinization of water, adding, "I can think of no scientific success of all time that would equal this in its boon to mankind." If Oppie ever received this message, he ignored it and instead turned to the task of addressing the people of the United States and indeed the world as a public intellectual.

Although Oppie lost his security clearance, he conducted a delicate balance between challenging the governmental policies and continuing to serve as a conscience for atomic scientists. He never publicly complained about the AEC's revocation of his security clearance. He was loyal in that regard to the end of his life. An example of this was his appearance on "See It Now," the popular and influential TV show hosted by journalist Edward R. Murrow. On the January 4, 1955, show broadcast to a national audience, Murrow asked Oppenheimer what he did at the Institute for Advanced Study. Before answering, Oppie lit Murrow's and then his own cigarette. As they smoked, Oppie replied that he wrote about what he thought he knew, that he tried to understand physics, and that he attempted to figure out why things were the way they were.

Oppenheimer's only reference to the tortuous AEC attack on him from the year before was in reply to a question about secrecy. Oppie observed that the trouble with secrecy in the government was not that it inhibited science, but that it gave to a small part of the government the power to decide what was best for all. For Oppie, "the solution [was] to let almost anyone to say what they want." "We've got to have a free and uncorrupted communication," he said. "These dangers that we live with cannot be dealt with in any other way." Committed to candor, Oppie called for an open debate about nuclear policies. Since Trinity, Hiroshima, and Nagasaki, however, atomic secrets had changed what the American people could know. Over the years, Oppie walked the fine line between engaging the public in a debate about nuclear weapons policy and not revealing any top-secret information about atomic bombs.

Oppie gave numerous lectures as he traveled around the nation and the world discussing science and the modern world. Thousands of people flocked to hear him, and even though Oppenheimer's lectures were often dense and obscure, many felt enlightened just hearing him talk. His celebrity status and charisma rubbed off onto those who heard him. For example, in the spring of 1958, Oppie talked to the International Press Institute in Washington, D.C. As reported in a story carried by the *Washington Post*, Oppenheimer began his speech by saying: "As knowledge grows, in some ways things get simpler. They do not get simpler because one discovers a few fundamental principles which the man in the street can understand, and from which he can derive everything else. But we do find an enormous amount of order; the world is not random, and whatever order it has, it seems in large part 'fit' . . . for human intelligence. We can understand [that] an enormous variety yields to some kind of arrangement, simplicity, generalization."

At times, Oppenheimer spoke in more pessimistic terms. At a conference in Berlin in 1960 for the Congress of Cultural Freedom, he observed: "Traditionally, the national governments have accepted as their first and highest duty the defense and security of their peoples. In today's world they are not very good at it. . . . We have come to doubt the adequacy of our institutions to the world we live in; beyond that, we have come to doubt certain aspects of the health of our own culture." For Oppenheimer, the challenge of nuclear weapons and the inability of governments to make their citizens safe from those weapons not only led to a cynicism about national governments but also the breakdown of cultural institutions.

After listening to Oppenheimer talk, people often came away slightly confused but also strangely enlightened. Julian P. Boyd, who was the editor of *The Papers of Thomas Jefferson*, wrote to Oppenheimer to acknowledge this power that he had over people. Boyd commented, "There are many of us who ponder your words very carefully and pay serious attention to what you have to say, first of all because you are a poet and a humanist and then because you are a scientist." Many people found great value in Oppenheimer's ability to speculate with the touch of a poet on the obscure but now frightening ability of science to change, even destroy, the world.

As he began serving as a public intellectual, Oppenheimer also made the transition to a new form of media. Beginning with *See It Now*, he used TV programs to address the public. For example, in December of 1959, Oppenheimer taped an interview in Britain for BBC Television. He was asked to talk about what he predicted for the coming decade of the 1960s. He commented: "I hope that these ten years will see further alterations in the relation between states and their functions to exorcize the unprecedented dangers of modern warfare. . . . That we will begin to re-knit human culture, and by the insight and the wonder of the world of nature, as science has revealed it, into relevance and meaning for the intellectual life, the spiritual life of man."

Although Oppie would not live to see the end of the new decade, hopes for the peaceful use of nuclear energy and a ban on nuclear weapons never left him.

Along these lines, Oppenheimer had some support among Washington's power elite. Henry L. Stimson, the U.S. secretary of war during World War II, wrote when he resigned in September 1945: "Mankind will not be able to live with the riven atom without some government of the whole." Building upon this idea of an international government to control nuclear weapons, Oppie recalled two reports that he helped write in the early postwar period: "One of them . . . ended roughly: 'If this weapon does not persuade men of the need to put an end to war, nothing that comes out of a laboratory ever will.' The other said: 'If there is to be any international action for the control of atomic energy there must be an international community of knowledge and understanding.'" Like Don Quixote, Oppie continued to tilt at the windmill of the threat posed by nuclear weapons and to work for the end of war.

In 1962, Oppenheimer gave a series of lectures at McMaster University in Canada called the Whidden Lectures. Published in 1964 in a book called *The Flying Trapeze: Three Crises for Physi-*

cists, Oppenheimer wondered: "It seems as though having made something potentially pestiferous, like nuclear bombs, we ought to go ahead and find something potentially helpful in getting rid of them. . . . Instead it is much more likely that our thoughts will turn to things that are easier to do than that, that are more at hand than that." Today, his prediction rings true. Faced with the grim reality of nuclear proliferation and the prospect of atomic terrorism, world leaders often switch from these horrific possibilities to issues more immediate or easier to solve.

Oppenheimer never gave up on a One World solution to the dangers of nuclear proliferation and to the hope for world peace: "I think we believe that whenever we see an opportunity, we have the duty to work for the growth of that international community of knowledge and understanding . . . with our colleagues in other lands, with our colleagues in competing, antagonistic, possibly hostile lands," he said. As convoluted as that sentence reads, it is typical of Oppenheimer. He sounds tentative while at the same time demands action, an action that was not popular among those who distrusted the international community, especially the Soviet Union. Oppenheimer himself had such a distrust, but he continued to insist that the sharing of nuclear secrets with other nations could solve the threat of an atomic Armageddon. For this, he was chased, chastised, and finally censored in 1954.

The revocation of Oppenheimer's security clearance not only removed him personally from participating in the formulation of atomic policy, it also removed from that scene the One World concept of sharing nuclear secrets. Nuclear hawks like Edward Teller, who demanded a robust arms race with the Soviet Union, moved into positions of authority and, after 1954, directed the United States' nuclear affairs, at least until the Soviet Union fell in 1989.

THE MILITARY-INDUSTRIAL COMPLEX

The postwar period after 1945 did indeed usher in a new era in the relationship between the military, government, and business. Prior to World War II, the United States expanded its military in times of national emergency, only to drastically reduce it after each war was over. The Cold War changed this policy. To be prepared to fight a war — possibly a nuclear war against the USSR at a moment's notice — forced the United States to maintain a large military force. In supplying the military with increasingly sophisticated and advanced systems of weapons technology, which Oppenheimer had set in motion, U.S. corporations have spent trillions of dollars, funded by the Department of Defense and the U.S. Congress. These corporations — which are now known as Martin Marietta, Boeing, Raytheon, and TRW, among many others — have grown in both size and power.

Tellingly, in his last speech to the nation as he left office on January 17, 1961, President Eisenhower talked about the continuing Cold War with the Soviet Union: "We face a hostile ideology global in scope, atheistic in character, ruthless in purpose, and insidious in method. Unhappily the danger it poses promises to be of indefinite duration." Having acknowledged the threat from Communist Russia, Eisenhower then warned about the dangers at home from the military-industrial complex. Today, this is one of Eisenhower's most quoted ideas. The following long quote helps one to fully understand what the president had in mind as he said farewell to his career with the nation that he had served for fifty years, mostly as part of the military establishment that he now cautioned against:

> Until the latest of our world conflicts, the United States had no armaments industry. American makers of plowshares could, with time and as required, make swords as well. But now we can no longer risk emergency improvisation of national defense; we have been compelled to create a permanent armaments industry of vast proportions. Added to this, three and a half million men and women are directly engaged in the defense establishment. We annually spend on military security more than the net income of all United States corporations.
>
> This conjunction of an immense military establishment

and a large arms industry is new in the American experience. The total influence — economic, political, even spiritual — is felt in every city, every Statehouse, every office of the Federal government. We recognize the imperative need for this development. Yet we must not fail to comprehend its grave implications. . . .

In the councils of government, we must guard against the acquisition of unwarranted influence, whether sought or unsought, by the military-industrial complex. The potential for the disastrous rise of misplaced power exists and will persist. We must never let the weight of this combination endanger our liberties or democratic processes.

Acknowledging the grave threat posed by the Soviet Union, Eisenhower expressed his concern about the rising power of the corporations that the nation depended on to protect national security. The outgoing president and ex-general then called for an informed public to make sure that the military and industrial complex be kept in check so that liberty could also prosper. In a government built on checks and balances, who would counter the power of the defense-related corporations?

In his own way, Oppenheimer had sought to counter the growing might of the military-industrial complex of nuclear power. International in scope, his call for a One World government also tried to provide a check and a balance. Oppie was perhaps one of the first causalities of the military-industrial complex as his removal from the halls of power in 1954 set the stage for Teller and his colleagues to support an active program to expand nuclear weapons, even into space. The person who created this new age — the person who helped invent the atomic bombs and then tried to counter their effects — was effectively targeted and neutralized.

Teller's policies created a MAD (mutually assured destruction) world doctrine with large and expensive defense systems. MAD proposed that neither of the superpowers during the Cold War would launch a pre-emptive strike against the other since both sides had redundant weapons capabilities that would ensure their mutual destruction. From nuclear weapon–laden

bombers circling the globe, to thousands of nuclear-tipped missiles ready to launch at a moment's notice, to stealthy submarines prowling off the enemy's coasts, the United States and
the USSR were poised to strike at each other like scorpions in a
bottle. But if they did, both nations would cease to exist. The
legacy of this arms race remains contested. To be sure, the Soviet Union failed in its experiment in Communism by 1989;
however, both the United States and Russia still target each
other with nuclear weapons, and other countries continue to
secure nuclear weapons for their arsenals.

OPPENHEIMER REHABILITATED

The beginning of the sixties brought a new president into the
White House. With John F. Kennedy, a Democrat, in office,
some of those who despised Oppenheimer left their positions,
replaced by men who were more friendly to Oppie. In 1962, the
White House invited Oppie to a dinner that honored forty-
nine Nobel Prize winners. In his welcome to the guests, President Kennedy joked: "I think this is the most extraordinary
collection of talent, of human knowledge, that has ever been
gathered together at the White House, with the possible excep-
tion of when Thomas Jefferson dined alone." As Oppenheimer
was reintroduced to Washington, Glenn Seaborg, an old friend
who now headed the AEC, asked if Oppie wanted to remove
the black mark from his name with a new security hearing.
Oppenheimer replied, "Not on your life."

In April 1963, Oppenheimer heard to his surprise that Kennedy had decided to honor him with the Enrico Fermi Award.
Along with the tax-free $50,000 prize and a medal, the lifetime
achievement award was a way Kennedy could try to correct
some of the wrongs done to Oppenheimer a decade earlier.
Oppie was scheduled to receive the award at a White House
ceremony on December 2, but President Kennedy's tragic assassination on November 22 cast doubt on whether these plans
would continue. Despite the national mourning and turmoil in
the aftermath of that black day in November, President Lyndon

Johnson kept to the original schedule and granted the Fermi award to Oppenheimer in early December. To David Lilienthal, the first chairman of the AEC and Oppenheimer's friend, Oppie looked like a "figure of stone" at the ceremony—"gray, rigid, almost lifeless, tragic in his intensity." On the other hand, Kitty was exuberant. In accepting the award, Oppenheimer talked about the brotherly spirit of scientists working together to make a better world without resorting to war. He then turned to Johnson and thanked him by saying, "I think it is just possible, Mr. President, that it has taken some charity and some courage for you to make this award today. That would seem to me a good augury for all our futures." After the ceremony, Oppie and Kitty went upstairs to see Mrs. Kennedy, who was still in the White House. She told Oppenheimer that her husband had truly wanted to give him the award. As a senator, Kennedy had cast the deciding vote against Lewis Strauss during his confirmation hearings for the position of secretary of commerce at the end of Eisenhower's administration. Kennedy had changed his vote to no after he heard how Strauss had conducted the security hearing against Oppenheimer.

A further sign of Oppenheimer's rehabilitation politically and publically occurred in 1964 when he visited Los Alamos for the last time. Norris Bradbury, Oppie's successor and still the director of the national laboratory, introduced him as "Mr. Los Alamos." The loud and long standing ovation from the overflowing audience touched Oppie. He gave his lecture as a tribute to Niels Bohr, who had passed away two years prior to the visit. Despite Oppenheimer's clash with the nuclear establishment a decade earlier, most of those at the lab who continued his work in the field of atoms and advanced physics acknowledged their debt to Robert Oppenheimer.

Ironically, a new initiative to create a nuclear-free world is gaining momentum. In January 2008, former Secretaries of State George P. Schultz and Henry A. Kissinger, former Secretary of Defense William J. Perry, and former chair of the Senate Armed Services Committee Sam Nunn released "Towards a Nuclear-Free World." They cited Mikhail Gorbachev, the last

Serving as the chairman of the General Advisory Committee for the Atomic Energy Committee, Oppenheimer often traveled with other scientists as well as military officers and governmental officials to oversee the vast national nuclear complex. In April 1947, the committee visited Los Alamos, as seen here. *Left to right,* James B. Conant; Oppenheimer; Gen. James McCormack, Jr.; Hartley Rowe; John Manley; I. I. Rabi; and Roger Werner. *(Courtesy of J. Robert Oppenheimer Memorial Committee)*

At the Oppenheimers' home in Princeton, New Jersey, soon after they arrived in 1947, Oppie reads to Peter and Toni with their dog Buddy at their feet. Oppenheimer took over as director of the Institute for Advanced Study from Albert Einstein in the spring of 1947. *(Courtesy of J. Robert Oppenheimer Memorial Committee)*

Edward Teller, a colleague of Oppie's during the Manhattan Project, became one of his chief accusers during the Personnel Security Board hearings in 1954. *(Courtesy of the Los Alamos Historical Museum Photo Archives)*

Oppie visited brother Frank and his family in southwestern Colorado in 1960. After Frank lost his position as a physics professor at the University of Minnesota because of his prewar Communist Party activities, he bought a ranch in the Pagosa Springs area. Dorothy McKibben is on the left, and Frank's wife, Jackie, is next to Oppie. *(Courtesy of the Los Alamos Historical Museum Photo Archives)*

Visiting Japan in September of 1960, Oppie and Kitty were escorted by Mr. and Mrs. Kiyokata Kusaka. *(Courtesy of J. Robert Oppenheimer Memorial Committee)*

As a sign of Oppenheimer's rehabilitation, President Johnson awarded him the Enrico Fermi Award in December 1963 during a White House ceremony. *(Courtesy of J. Robert Oppenheimer Memorial Committee)*

president of the Soviet Union, who warned, "It is becoming clear that nuclear weapons are no longer a means of achieving security; in fact, with every passing year, they make our security more precarious." To counter this threat and attain the goal of a "world without nuclear weapons," they call for nations to manage the risks of the nuclear fuel cycle to prevent fissionable material from falling into the wrong hands. Although not exactly the Acheson-Lilienthal Report of 1946, their plan echoes the One World or None sentiment Oppie espoused in the early Atomic Age. In particular, they call for "an international consensus on ways to deter or when required to respond to secret attempts by countries to break out of [nuclear] agreements." Shunned by the U.S. government in the late 1940s, perhaps Oppie's dream of controlling the proliferation of nuclear weapons by international cooperation will finally get a full hearing.

A QUICK DECLINE

In the spring of 1965, Oppenheimer informed the trustees at the Institute for Advanced Study that he wanted to retire at the end of the school year in 1966. He told them that he was close to retirement age anyway, that Kitty was ill, and that his relations with some of the faculty were "intolerable." To retire in comfort, Oppenheimer wanted to live on the campus of the institute, and the trustees agreed that he could build a house near Olden Manor. Lewis Strauss, still on the institute's Board of Directors, tried to sabotage this plan, saying it would be a mistake to allow Oppenheimer to live on campus, and had the board reverse its decision. Oppie worked his charm with the board and by spring 1966 received permission to start construction.

Oppenheimer would never live in his new house. By the end of 1965, his persistent smoker's cough had worsened. During his family's winter vacation to St. John, he complained of a "terrible sore throat." A medical checkup in February produced the news that after forty years of heavy smoking, Oppie had throat cancer. He underwent surgery in March, which did little to help, and then submitted to radiation treatment, which his work at Los Alamos and on the General Advisory Committee had helped to develop. Despite the aggressive treatments, he held only "a faint hope" that the cancer could be stopped. In the meantime, his family and friends noticed how his already slight build shrank even more. The cancer in his throat began to restrict his ability to swallow food, and the radiation treatments further reduced his desire for food. At the Princeton commencement in June, he had to use a cane and a leg brace to accept an honorary degree.

In July, doctors examined Oppenheimer and declared that the radiation treatments had knocked out the cancer. To recover from the debilitating treatments, he and Kitty retreated to St. John. Their friends on the island were shocked to see the ghost that appeared before them. In late August, doctors examined Oppie again and confirmed their original opinion that he was cured. However, he still had a nagging sore throat. A month later, the doctors reversed their prognosis.

By November, Oppenheimer's health worsened, as he guardedly wrote to one of his New York doctors who had moved away: "By the first days of October, the malignancy was very manifest and it spread to the left palate, the left Eustachian tube and the corner of the tongue. Dr. Farr was not hopeful enough of surgery to be willing to perform it, and the best bet seemed to be to get after the tumor again; this time with a betatron. . . . The doctors say that the malignancy is clearing up and visibly yielding to the radiation; but it is an appropriate time for me to keep an open mind." This letter about the alarming spread of the throat cancer to other parts of his mouth and head, and the faint hope provided by radiation treatment, is a classic example of Oppie's studied diffidence.

By January, Oppenheimer knew that the radiation would not stop the progress of the tumors. As the cancerous tumors spread beyond his throat, they attacked his hearing and speech. He admitted in one letter: "I am in some pain . . . my hearing and my speech are very poor." Those senses continued to deteriorate so that the near the end, he only mumbled. On February

16, 1967, Louis Fischer, a journalist friend, stopped by Olden Manor to visit Robert. Later, Fischer wrote of this last meeting with his friend: "He looked extremely thin, his hair was sparse and white, and his lips were dry and cracked. . . . His fingernails were blue."

Two days after Fischer's visit, Oppenheimer died in his sleep. Kitty cremated his remains and took them in an urn to Hawksnest Bay on St. John. With Toni, Peter, and other family and friends, Kitty dropped the urn off the coast of the island. Oppie had told Kitty that he wanted his final resting place to be in the bay off of their vacation home.

The troubled life of Robert Oppenheimer did not end with his death. His daughter, Toni, had a gift with languages. She lived in New York City for a while in the 1960s and 1970s. She obtained a temporary job translating for the United Nations, but to get hired for a permanent position, she had to receive security clearance. The FBI reopened its files on her father, and the security clearance never materialized. Toni also married and divorced twice. Eventually, she returned to St. John to live in the house on Hawksnest Bay. There, in January 1977, possibly despondent over her inability to get security clearance for the United Nations position, she hanged herself. In a suicide note, she gave the house to the people of St. John. There is a community center at the spot, above the stretch of shore now called Oppenheimer Beach.

Oppenheimer's son, Peter, has lived in northern New Mexico for several decades. He is a carpenter and has two adult children. He is reclusive and adverse to talking about his parents. At times, he has supported Concerned Citizens for Nuclear Safety, a local nuclear watch group. He still owns Perro Caliente in the high mountains above Pecos, New Mexico.

Several years after Oppenheimer's death, Kitty began living with Robert Serber, the colleague who had given the first lectures at Los Alamos that became *The Los Alamos Primer*. In 1972, she bought a fifty-two-foot sailboat and set off to sail across the Pacific with Serber. Off the coast of Columbia, she grew ill, and Serber returned her to Panama where she went into a hospital. There she died of an embolism on October 27, 1972. Kitty's ashes were scattered in Hawksnest Bay at the same place where she had dropped Oppie's urn.

THE ATOMIC WEST

Even though he died in 1967, Oppenheimer's impact on the United States continues to this day, and not just due to his contributions to the creation of nuclear weapons. He helped reshape the economic and political borders within the United States. The American West was transformed by the Atomic Age, changed from a frontier region not as developed as the rest of the country to a section at the forefront of advanced technology. From the plutonium processing plants in Hanford, Washington, to scientific laboratories in California and New Mexico; from atomic facilities in Texas, Idaho, and Colorado to the nuclear weapons testing grounds in Nevada, the atom brought a rapid and drastic revolution to the West. Billions of dollars washed over the region like a drought-ending thunderstorm, and tens of thousands of people immigrated to the West to support the research, development, assembly, and storage of nuclear weapons. Assuredly, the West had progressed in relation to the rest of the country during the early part of the twentieth century; however, the placing of key nuclear facilities in the region put the West on the leading edge of not just nuclear enterprises, but computers, lasers, nuclear medicine, and many other advanced technology industries.

As a result of its atomic facilities, the American West served on the front line of the Cold War in the second half of the twentieth century. Laboratories at Los Alamos and Sandia in New Mexico and the Lawrence Livermore lab in California developed and assembled nuclear weapons systems. Western military bases stored and could deliver such weapons. And the nuclear weapons testing grounds in Nevada all bolstered the image of the West as a bastion of national security. The American public associated the West with nuclear weapons as they saw photos and newsreels of mushroom clouds rising above

desert floors and of windblown military bases launching nuclear missiles and strategic bombers into the dawn sky.

Throughout the history of the United States, the West has
captured the American public's imagination. Since colonial
times, the West has beckoned with a promise of fulfilling the
American dream. After the U.S. Census Bureau declared the
frontier closed in 1890, the country looked to new frontiers.
The frontier of science, plopped down on a high desert plateau
in New Mexico in 1943, preserved the tradition of the western
part of the United States as a place of invention and vitality,
of path-breaking innovations and pace-setting projects. The
Atomic West, by creating a new age, furthered the legacy of the
frontier that had rejuvenated the nation time and time again
throughout its history.

The person who chose the location of Los Alamos, the one
who first placed a nuclear facility in the West, was of course J.
Robert Oppenheimer. Without his original decision, the history of the region — both in terms of the generously funded
federal operations in the West and the West of popular imagination — would be vastly different.

Some of the people involved in the creation of atomic bombs
and the destruction of Hiroshima and Nagasaki have expressed
regret about their participation in the Manhattan Project. Oppenheimer never expressed such feelings. In a 1966 letter to
David Bohm, an old friend who asked him whether he had any
regrets or guilt, Oppie replied, "What I have never done is to
express regret for doing what I did and could at Los Alamos; in
fact, on varied and recurrent occasions, I have reaffirmed my
sense that, with all the black and white, that was something I
did not regret."

Looking toward the future as he was wont to do, Oppenheimer spoke at the opening of the Niels Bohr Library of the
American Institute of Physics in 1962. "The times that we have
lived through are truly heroic times," he said. "They are certainly times of great change, and . . . the achievements in physics in this century seem to me to stand with the high points of

the whole of history of human knowledge. . . . We are so engulfed by the changes, the massiveness, the ferocity, the brashness, the virtuosity, the confusion of the current scene in physics, that we do not understand it very well, and it may not be possible for us to understand it." Then he called on historians — if humans did survive — to render a final judgment on the scientists' accomplishments: "The enterprises which are now under way . . . should make it possible, if there are serious students of the human predicament in the future, to know very much more about what has befallen us than we who are acting and living in it. And they will see both good and bad things, and they will see them in wiser and deeper perspective than we who act in it."

By chasing J. Robert Oppenheimer, one sees both good and bad, and through that, a deep recognition of his contributions to the course of human history. Having helped change the American West, the rest of the country, and even the world, Oppie also offered humankind a different path for its atomic future. Not having taken that path, the world continues to wrestle with the legacy of atomic energy.

Bibliographic Essay

The root of all historical research is archives. At archives, historians like me find the basic documents, the DNA of the past. We use personal letters, governmental reports, official exchanges, memoirs, oral histories, and unpublished accounts of the life and times of someone like Oppenheimer. From these primary sources, historians then analyze and assemble a narrative about the past that is their interpretation of what happened. So historians are dependent on archives to provide the basic information about their subjects.

The Library of Congress's Manuscript Division in Washington, D.C., holds the main collection of Oppenheimer's own papers. In the almost three hundred boxes of material, a wealth of information about all of the phases of Oppie's life can be found. Oppenheimer kept many of the documents that detailed his life, from newspaper articles to the speeches he gave to the letters he received, including some hate mail. At the Manuscript Division of the Library of Congress, there are also collections of private papers from other people who helped launch the Atomic Age.

The American Institute of Physics has a wonderful archive and library with excellent primary sources and oral histories about Oppie and his work in the field of nuclear physics. Atomic historian Spencer Weart and the AIP archival assistants Heather Lindsay and Julie Gass helped me ferret out a wide range of documents and personal accounts about Oppenheimer. Sharing lunch and conversations about atomic matters with the staff of the AIP also proved enlightening.

The National Archives at College Park, Maryland, holds

many of the official governmental records, papers, and photographs of both the Manhattan Project and the Atomic Energy Commission. Much valuable documentation about Oppenheimer's involvement in these agencies came from the National Archives. Also connected with the National Archives are the libraries of President Truman in Kansas City, Missouri, and President Eisenhower in Abilene, Kansas, where additional information about Oppenheimer's relationship with the federal government and these presidents was found.

The Los Alamos Historical Archives, directed by Hedy Dunn, the head of the Los Alamos Historical Society and Museum, and archivist Rebecca Collinsworth have a variety of documents on Oppie, his two years at the birthplace of the Atomic Age, and his continued influence on the town and the people who work at the Los Alamos National Laboratory. The Los Alamos Historical Society continues to preserve the history of the Manhattan Project in the books that it publishes, the conferences and speakers that it holds on the Hill, and the exhibits that it mounts at its museum. Along those lines, the Bradbury Science Museum at Los Alamos, formerly directed by John Rhoades (now retired), also helps preserve this history in its exhibits and educational activities. The Los Alamos National Laboratory has extensive holdings about the scientific work conducted at the lab, photographs of key personnel, and oral histories of people who worked with Oppenheimer.

Also in New Mexico, the Center for Southwest Research at the University of New Mexico houses the Ralph C. Smith Collection, which holds some fascinating history about Los Alamos and the Atomic Age.

Oppenheimer's own writings also help tell his story. Alice Kimball Smith and Charles Weiner collected Oppie's letters and speeches in their *Robert Oppenheimer: Letters and Recollections* (Cambridge, Mass.: Harvard University Press, 1980). Oppenheimer's *The Open Mind* (New York: Simon and Schuster, 1955), a series of eight lectures that he gave in the 1940s and 1950s, discusses atomic weapons and scientists' place in society. In 1964, Oppie published his Whidden Lectures as *The Flying*

Trapeze: Three Crises for Physicists (London: Oxford University Press, 1964) with chapters on "Space and Time," "Atom and Void," and "War and the Nations." Many of these writings are collected in *Atom and Void* (Princeton, N.J.: Princeton University Press, 1989).

Oppie was also featured in many national magazines, particularly on the cover of *Time* on November 8, 1948, and *Life* on October 10, 1949. Oppenheimer's own article that called for more openness in atomic matters was published as "Atomic Weapons and American Policy" in *Foreign Affairs* 31, no. 4. Oppie also wrote "The Atom Bomb as a Force for Peace" for the *New York Times Magazine* on June 9, 1946.

Oppenheimer's own words are unwittingly found in two other collections of documents. The first is "In the Matter of J. Robert Oppenheimer: Transcript of Hearing Before the Personnel Security Board." Almost one thousand pages long, this verbatim transcript of the Gray Board and its security hearing on Oppenheimer is full of anecdotes, character references, and most importantly, Oppenheimer's own retelling of the fateful events in his life. Along similar lines, "J. Robert Oppenheimer FBI Security File" is a gathering of the FBI interviews, intelligence reports, and transcripts of his phone conversations, which comprise thousands of pages of documents contained on three rolls of microfilm. Being able to read long-lost phone conversations between Oppie and Kitty or between them and other people is an unintended consequence of the FBI surveillance of the Oppenheimers.

In terms of secondary sources, a proliferation of biographies has appeared about Oppenheimer over the last few years. Martin Sherwin and Kai Bird won a Pulitzer Prize for their *American Prometheus: The Triumph and Tragedy of J. Robert Oppenheimer* (New York: Alfred A. Knopf, 2005), an extensive history of Oppenheimer's life and contested times. This definitive history is a result of Sherwin's several decades of chasing Oppie. Priscilla McMillan—another historian, who worked for years on her book—released *The Ruin of J. Robert Oppenheimer and the Birth of the Modern Arms Race* (New York: Viking, 2005), which is a lively and engaging overview of Oppie's life that brings new insights into the complicated events that resulted in the removal of his top-secret clearance in 1954.

Gregg Herken, in his *Brotherhood of the Bomb: The Tangled Lives and Loyalties of Robert Oppenheimer, Ernest Lawrence, and Edward Teller* (New York: Henry Holt, 2002), explores how Oppenheimer worked in a network of scientists such as Lawrence and Teller to first create a center for theoretical physics at the University of California at Berkeley and then to invent an atomic bomb at the laboratory in Los Alamos. A colleague of Oppie, Jeremy Bernstein, wrote *Oppenheimer: Portrait of an Enigma* (Chicago: Ivan R. Dee, 2004), which attempts to make sense of the elusive man. Historian of science David C. Cassidy put Oppenheimer's life in the context of the twentieth century in *J. Robert Oppenheimer and the American Century* (New York: Pi Press, 2005). Charles Thorpe offers *Oppenheimer: The Tragic Intellect* (Chicago: University of Chicago Press, 2006), an insightful and analytical biography.

Jennet Conant's *109 East Palace: Robert Oppenheimer and the Secret City of Los Alamos* (New York: Simon and Schuster, 2005) offers a lively narrative of the city that created the bomb and the many people involved with the endeavor. In *J. Robert Oppenheimer: Shatterer of Worlds* (New York: Fromm International, 1985), journalist Peter Goodchild gives readers an informative and concise biography.

The Atomic Heritage Foundation, led by Cindy Kelly, has accomplished miracles in the last few years in preserving historic buildings and holding conferences that bring together experts in the field. One such conference celebrating the centennial of Oppenheimer's birthday in 2004 was organized at Los Alamos by the foundation. A volume of the presentations at the conference, *Oppenheimer and the Manhattan Project: Insights into J. Robert Oppenheimer "The Father of the Atomic Bomb"* (New York: World Scientific, 2006), edited by Kelly, surveys Oppie's life from the viewpoint of scholars as well as those people who knew him. A book of reminiscences, *Oppenheimer* (New York: Charles Scribner's Sons, 1969), published the year after Oppenheimer died, contains a rich series of stories about the man from people like I. I. Rabi, Robert Serber, and Glenn Seaborg—his close friends and colleagues. A key person in Oppenheimer's rise to the upper levels of science and government was Gen. Leslie R. Groves. Robert S. Norris completed a biography of the general in charge of the Manhattan Project in *Racing for the Bomb: General Leslie R. Groves, The Manhattan Project's Indispensable Man* (Hanover, N.H.: Steerforth Press, 2002). The general's autobiography, *Now It Can Be Told* (New York: Harper Row, 1962), provides rich details about the man who chose and thus knighted Oppenheimer as director of the civilian laboratory of the Manhattan Project.

The preeminent atomic historian, Richard Rhodes, wrote the enthralling *The Making of the Atomic Bomb* (New York: Simon and Schuster, 1986), which won a Pulitzer Prize, and then extended the story about nuclear weapons with *Dark Sun: The Making of the Hydrogen Bomb* (New York: Simon and Schuster, 1995). Both of Rhodes's books provide essential background and key history about Oppenheimer's life and career. Ferenc Szasz produced three wonderfully useful accounts about Los Alamos that include Oppenheimer. Szasz's *The Day the Sun Rose Twice: The Story of the Trinity Site Explosion July 16th, 1945* (Albuquerque: University of New Mexico Press, 1985) examines not just the July 16 detonation of the world's first atomic bomb, but the experiments and the work conducted at Los Alamos to create the first nuclear weapons. His *British Scientists and the Manhattan Project: The Los Alamos Years* (New York: St. Martin's Press, 1992) covers the important component of scientists and personnel who came from Britain and joined the work at Los Alamos. Szasz also includes a chapter on Oppie in his *Larger than Life: New Mexico in the Twentieth Century* (Albuquerque: University of New Mexico Press, 2006).

Several scientific and technical books aid our understanding of the complex interactions of subatomic and atomic particles that led to the creation of a nuclear explosion. Lillian Hoddeson, Paul Henricksen, Roger Meade, and Catherine Westfall compiled *Critical Assembly: A Technical History of Los Alamos*

238   BIBLIOGRAPHIC ESSAY

during the Oppenheimer Years, 1943–1945 (Cambridge: Cambridge University Press, 1993), which is the best account of Oppenheimer's administration of the lab during the war. David Hawkins's *Project Y: The Los Alamos Story, Part I: Toward Trinity* (Los Angeles: Tomash Publishers, 1983) and Edith Truslow and Ralph Carlisle Smith's *Project Y: The Los Alamos Story, Part II: Beyond Trinity* (Los Angeles: Tomash Publishers, 1983) also explain the scientific and engineering discoveries behind the atomic bomb. James Kunetka wrote an account of the laboratory in *City of Fire: Los Alamos and the Atomic Age, 1943–1945* (Albuquerque: University of New Mexico Press, 1979). The original lectures on atomic weapons given at Los Alamos in 1943 are printed in Robert Serber and Richard Rhodes's *The Los Alamos Primer: The First Lectures on How to Build an Atomic Bomb* (Berkeley: University of California Press, 1992). Released within a month after the end of the war, Henry Smyth's *Atomic Energy for Military Purposes: A General Account of the Scientific Research and Technical Development that Went into the Making of the Atomic Bombs* (Princeton, N.J.: Princeton University Press, 1946) is surprisingly revealing about some of the processes created to make the weapons.

The story about radiation is detailed in several books. Barton Hacker's *The Dragon's Tail: Radiation Safety in the Manhattan Project, 1942–1946* (Berkeley: University of California Press, 1987) and *Elements of Controversy: The Atomic Energy Commission and Radiation Safety in Nuclear Weapons Testing, 1947–1974* (Berkeley: University of California Press, 1994) are valuable tools in understanding the effects of radiation on the human body and how the nuclear weapons industry has contributed to that issue. At the beginning of the Atomic Age, nuclear physicists and the medical doctors who worked with them sought to determine the dangers of various levels of exposure to radiation. Eileen Welsome's *The Plutonium Files: America's Secret Medical Experiments in the Cold War* (New York: Dell Publishing, 1999) tells the chilling tale of the various experiments that exposed uninformed patients to different types of radiation to determine how the human body would react.

Histories about people (including the Oppenheimers) at Los Alamos during World War II abound. Marjorie Bell Chambers's unpublished Ph.D. dissertation "Technically Sweet Los Alamos: The Development of a Federally Sponsored Scientific Community" (University of New Mexico, 1974) led the way for social histories of the town. My own book, *Inventing Los Alamos: The Growth of an Atomic Community* (Norman: University of Oklahoma Press, 2004), details the social and cultural history of the town during World War II and then in the early postwar period as the community served on the front lines of the Cold War. Edith Truslow and Kasha Thayer wrote *Manhattan District History: Non-Scientific Aspects of Los Alamos, Project Y, 1942 through 1946* (Los Alamos: Los Alamos Historical Society, 1973) about the town that supported the lab. Several fascinating collections of memoirs of wartime Los Alamos that mention Oppie are in Lawrence Badash, Joseph Hirshfelder, and Herbert Broida's *Reminiscences of Los Alamos, 1943–1945* (Dordrecht, Holland: Reidel Publishing, 1980); Bernice Brode's *Tales of Los Alamos: Life on the Mesa, 1943–1945* (Los Alamos: Los Alamos Historical Society, 1997); Eleanor Jette's *Inside Box 1663* (Los Alamos: Los Alamos Historical Society, 1977); and Jane S. Wilson and Charlotte Serber's *Standing By and Making Do: Women of Wartime Los Alamos* (Los Alamos: Los Alamos Historical Society, 1988). Peggy Pond Church's *The House at Otowi Bridge: The Story of Edith Warner and Los Alamos* (Albuquerque: University of New Mexico Press, 1959) evokes the woman who first met Oppie when he wandered around the mountains of New Mexico in the 1930s and then served the scientists of the Hill when they arrived. Hal K. Rothman also wrote about Los Alamos in his environmental history of the Pajarito Plateau *On Rims and Ridges* (Lincoln: University of Nebraska Press, 1992). Laura Fermi, the wife of the famous physicist, wrote a memoir, *Atoms in the Family: My Life with Enrico Fermi* (Chicago: University of Chicago Press, 1954), which discusses their times in Los Alamos and Fermi's work on atomic weapons.

All of these books focus on the social history of Los Alamos and at times, Oppie and Kitty's contribution to the town. In addition, Mary Palevsky's *Atomic Fragments: A Daughter's Questions* (Berkeley: University of California Press, 2000) explores the moral dilemmas of working on this weapon of mass destruction. Edward Teller told his own story of his involvement in atomic affairs in *Memoirs: A Twentieth Century Journey in Science and Politics* (Cambridge, Mass.: Perseus Publishing, 2001).

The destruction of the Japanese cities of Hiroshima and Nagasaki is graphically told in many books. John Hersey's *Hiroshima* (New York: A. A. Knopf, 1985), first published in the *New Yorker* in 1946, offers many eyewitness accounts from the victims of the atomic bombing. Shogo Nagaoka, under the auspices of the Peace Memorial Museum in Hiroshima, wrote *Hiroshima Under Atomic Bomb Attack* (Hiroshima: Peace Memorial Museum, n.d.), which also gives explicit accounts of the effects of the atomic bomb on humans. Along similar lines, the Hiroshima International Council for the Medical Care of the Radiation Exposed and the Peace Memorial Museum compiled and published *Effects of A-Bomb Radiation on the Human Body* (Tokyo: Bunkodo, 1995), which provides additional insight into how radiation harmed humans in Hiroshima and Nagasaki. The official report by the U.S. government, the U.S. Strategic Bombing Survey's *The Effects of the Atomic Bombs on Hiroshima and Nagasaki* (Santa Fe, N.M.: William Gannon, 1973), also shows in graphic detail the effect of nuclear weapons on urban areas.

To provide a broader perspective and a wider context of the American West, several historians have added to our understanding about how Oppenheimer and atomic enterprises transformed the region. Richard W. Etulain's edited volume, *Contemporary New Mexico, 1945–1990* (Albuquerque: University of New Mexico Press, 1994), looks at how the state changed during the Cold War. Michael Malone and Richard W. Etulain's *The Twentieth Century West* (Lincoln: University of Nebraska Press, 1989) places this change in the context of a century of rapid transformation in the West. Richard Bernard and Bradley Rice's *Sunbelt Cities: Politics and Growth Since World War II*

(Austin: University of Texas Press, 1983) examines the postwar westward tilt that Oppie started. Gerald Nash — through his books about the American West, like *The American West in the Twentieth Century: A Short History of an Urban Oasis* (Albuquerque: University of New Mexico Press, 1977) and *The American West Transformed: The Impact of the Second World War* (Bloomington: Indiana University Press, 1985) — was one of the first historians to call attention to the revolution of the region due to the war. Kevin Fernlund edited *The Cold War American West, 1945–1989*, which covers many key topics about how the West reacted to the postwar period.

Another topic covered by historians concerns the public's reaction to atomic weapons in the early postwar years. Spencer Weart's *Nuclear Fear: A History of Images* (Cambridge, Mass.: Harvard University Press, 1985) insightfully explores the many manifestations of the public's unease about nuclear enterprises after 1945. Paul Boyer's *By the Bomb's Early Light: American Thought and Culture at the Dawn of the Atomic Age* (New York: Pantheon, 1988) is a wonderful overview of how atomic weapons impacted America from 1945 to 1955.

Attempts to control atomic weapons took center stage in the early postwar period. Alice Kimball Smith wrote *A Peril and a Hope: The Scientists Movement, 1945–1947* (Chicago: University of Chicago Press, 1965) about the nuclear scientists' work to influence the national government's atomic policies in the early Atomic Age. In a similar vein, Lawrence Wittner's *One World or None: A History of the World Nuclear Disarmament Movement through 1953* (Palo Alto, Calif.: Stanford University Press, 1993) informs us of the attempt to create a world organization to control nuclear weapons and proliferations. The story of the agency that eventually controlled atomic energy in the United States, the Atomic Energy Commission, is told in several volumes. George Mazuzan and J. Samuel Walker in *Controlling the Atom: The Beginnings of Nuclear Regulation, 1946–1962* (Berkeley: University of California Press, 1984) retell the early battles over who would administer atomic energy. Richard Hewlett and Oscar Anderson also wrote about the AEC in *The New World, 1939–*

1947: A History of the Atomic Energy Commission (University Park: Pennsylvania State University Press, 1962). Martin Sherwin examined the political and diplomatic impact of the atomic bomb in *A World Destroyed: The Atomic Bomb and the Grand Alliance* (New York: Vintage Books Random House, 1977).

Where do historians find all of these secondary sources to provide them with the information for their books? Of course, local libraries — in this case, the Zuhl and Branson Libraries at New Mexico State University — have many of the aforementioned titles. However, some of the hard-to-find and out-of-print books come from other places. John Randall of John Randall Books in Albuquerque donated some out-of-print books to my research. I am grateful for his generosity. Coas, an incredible used bookstore in Las Cruces operated by the Beckett family, always has gems of unusual books. There I found the original transcript of the Oppenheimer security hearing. Numerous friends and colleagues over the years have contributed their own thoughts and, at times, books to the cause. I could not have written *J. Robert Oppenheimer, the Cold War, and the Atomic West* without these people, primary documents, and books about this enigmatic man. I am indebted to them all.

Index